WINCHESTER DIVIDED

The Civil War Diaries of Julia Chase and Laura Lee

Edited by
Michael G. Mahon

STACKPOLE
BOOKS

Published by
STACKPOLE BOOKS
5067 Ritter Road
Mechanicsburg, PA 17055
www.stackpolebooks.com

Printed in the United States of America

10 9 8 7 6 5 4 3 2 1

FIRST EDITION

Library of Congress Cataloging-in-Publication Data

Chase, Julia, b. 1831
    Winchester divided : the Civil War diaries of Julia Chase and Laura Lee / [edited by] Michael G. Mahon.
        p. cm.
    Includes bibliographical references and index.
    ISBN 0-8117-1394-6
    1. Chase, Julia, b. 1831—Diaries. 2. Lee, Laura, b. ca. 1823—Diaries. 3. Women—Virginia—Winchester—Diaries. 4. Winchester (Va.)—History, Military—19th century. 5. Winchester (Va.)—Social conditions—19th century. 6. United States—History—Civil War, 1861-1865—Personal narratives, Confederate. 7. Virginia—History—Civil War, 1861-1865—Personal narratives. 8. United States—History—Civil War, 1861-1865—Social aspects. 9. Winchester (Va.)—Biography.
    I. Lee, Laura, b. ca. 1823. II. Mahon, Michael G. III. Title.

F234.W8 C48 2002
975.5'991041'092—dc21   2002020505

To the memory of
my grandmother Julia M. Froehner
and
my grandfather John H. Beyer

CONTENTS

ACKNOWLEDGMENTS

While working on this project, a number of individuals and institutions provided valuable assistance for which I am grateful. Their efforts only helped make this book better and for that I would like to extend my sincerest thanks.

I would first like to thank the College of William and Mary in Williamsburg, Virginia, and Margaret Cook, Curator of Manuscripts and Rare Books, for granting permission to edit the Laura Lee Diary. I also want to thank the Winchester-Frederick County Historical Society and Mary Ellen Hassler, Director of the Archives Committee, for extending the same permission in regards to the Julia Chase Diary.

I also owe a special debt of gratitude to Rebecca Ebert of The Handley Library in Winchester, Virginia. She took a special interest in this project from the start and responded to my numerous questions and requests for materials with her customary skill and professionalism. As always, she was a pleasure to work with and I appreciate all of her efforts on my behalf.

At Stackpole Books, I would like to thank William C. Davis, who saw the merit in merging the two diaries together and was instrumental in making this book a reality. I also want to thank Leigh Ann Berry, who has worked with me throughout this entire project, and whose ideas, comments and editorial skills have served to make this a better book. Another individual I owe thanks to is Ryan Masteller, whose efforts in putting together all the different aspects of this book during the latter stages of its production are noted and greatly appreciated.

I also would like to thank three other individuals. Virginia Mauler, of the Picture Collection Department, at the Library of Virginia, who provided assistance in obtaining several pictures. George Skoch, who once again allowed me to use his renowned skill as a topographer to draw the maps. And I would especially like to thank Ben Ritter, local historian of Winchester, Virginia, who read the entire manuscript and corrected several errors, and graciously provided a number of photographs from his vast collection for use in this book.

INTRODUCTION

During the four years of the American Civil War, the Shenandoah Valley of Virginia was of vital importance to the Confederacy, from both an economic and military standpoint. Economically, the region was readily acknowledged as the most agriculturally productive section of the state, and the Valley's farmers provided the Confederacy with vast quantities of all kinds of subsistence during the first eighteen months of the war. Militarily, the Valley was the scene of continuous fighting, including two of the most brilliant campaigns of the entire war. Furthermore, it acted like a shield, protecting the eastern plain of Virginia and Richmond from invasion, as any Federal army marching up the Valley would be moving farther and farther away from its objective as it advanced.

In the Valley itself, the city of Winchester also played a crucial role. Founded in 1743, the city over the next century had developed into the leading economic and transportation center of the region. Located about twenty-five miles south of Harpers Ferry, the city by 1850 had become the focal point of a major road network that connected it with the other leading towns throughout the Lower Valley. Realizing the importance of the railroad, the town's civic leaders also raised funds to build a connecting line to link up with the Baltimore and Ohio Railroad, which only added to its economic growth. Goods and agricultural products from as far away as southwest Virginia and Tennessee made their way to the city's thriving depots and warehouses for shipment elsewhere.

When the Civil War erupted in April 1861, Winchester's importance intensified in scope. Immediately after the firing on Fort Sumter, the city became a military command post and major supply depot for the Confederacy, with industrial and agricultural supplies of every description being collected from the region for military use. In addition, it also became one of the primary training grounds in the Lower Valley for the thousands of volunteers who had enlisted at the first call to arms. And to their credit, the vast majority of Winchester's residents did whatever they could to support their fledgling nation.

But not all of the Valley's citizens embraced the Confederate cause. From the start of the war, a small but significant number of residents throughout the Lower Valley and in Winchester opposed the idea of an independent Southern Confederacy and remained steadfastly loyal to the Union throughout the conflict, despite the obvious consequences.

Thus Winchester was actually a city of divided loyalties, and this book is based upon that division. While working on a previous study of the Shenandoah Valley, I came across the diaries of two women, Julia Chase and Laura Lee, who resided in Winchester during the war. Julia Chase was an avid supporter of the Union, while Laura Lee was an equally strong advocate of the Confederacy. Both diaries are rich in intimate feelings and emotions as well as personal opinions on how they felt about the war as it unfolded. Merging the two diaries together illustrates the two women's different perspectives on many of the same events of the conflict.

Only a limited amount of personal information exists on the two women. Julia Chase was born in Maine in 1831, the daughter of Charles (1794–1864) and Nancy (1798–1879) Chase. The family later moved to Winchester, where her father served as the U.S. Postmaster. She was thirty years old at the start of the war and lived with her parents in their home at the northeast corner of Loudoun Street and Fairfax Lane.

Laura Lee was thirty-eight years old when the conflict started. Her parents were Daniel (1777–1833) and Elizabeth (1783–1853) Lee. Daniel was a lawyer and former member of the Virginia House of Delegates (1802–04), and later served as county clerk of Frederick County (1812–31). When the conflict started, Laura resided in the home of Mary Greenhow Lee, the wife of her deceased brother Hugh Lee, at 132 North Cameron Street. At the time, the Lee household also consisted of Laura's sister Antoinette Lee, as well as Robert, Lewis, Laura, and Louis Burwell, the four children of Susan Lee Burwell, also deceased.

Though little documentary evidence can be found, much about Julia and Laura can be ascertained from the diaries themselves. First, it is clear that they were well educated. Both had an excellent command of the English language and spelling, and they wrote in a clear, concise, and descriptive style that few women of the time exhibited. It is equally clear that they were very religious. As the events of the war unfolded, each prayed for her side's success and believed the final outcome was ultimately in God's hands, accepting the results as His will and voicing little complaint. Both were very adept at analyzing the abilities and shortcomings of their military leaders and the current military situation the country faced.

For example, during the early years of the war, Julia repeatedly wondered why the Federal forces always seemed to move in slow motion, while the Confederate soldiers conversely always reacted quickly and were able to take advantage of many military situations. Finally, and maybe most importantly, the diaries show that the lives of both women were controlled in many ways by hope, fear, and rumor—hope that their side would be victorious; fear that they rarely knew what was about to happen to them; and in rumors favorable to their side, which was how they endured and continued to face the future.

Neither diary covers the entire length of the conflict. The Julia Chase diary covers the period from July 2, 1861, to September 21, 1864, with a gap between February 8 and May 1, 1863. The Laura Lee diary begins on March 11, 1862, and continues until April 5, 1865. It is regrettable that neither is complete, and one can only wonder what Julia or Laura would have said about the events in the time periods omitted. The entries' timing gives a balance to the book, as the opening months of the conflict are seen through the eyes of one participant, and the closing months through the eyes of the other.

Finally, as editor, I have kept my intrusions to a minimum. Rather than correct the numerous spelling, punctuation, and grammatical mistakes in the diaries and clutter the text with an inordinate number of [*sic*]s after each infraction, I have elected to let the errors remain, and have interceded only when necessary to help the reader understand the meaning of a particular entry. After all, in the end, this is their book and should be spoken in their words, not mine.

CHAPTER ONE

July 1861–February 1862

"The war will I think commence in earnest"

It did not take long for war to come to the Shenandoah Valley. On April 18, 1861, less than a week after the firing on Fort Sumter, Virginia military forces seized the Federal arsenal at Harpers Ferry, capturing thousands of small arms and other valuable military supplies. But in the months following, fighting was limited to minor cavalry skirmishes along the border, and for the most part, the war became one of preparation, as both Harpers Ferry and Winchester turned into training grounds for the thousands of recruits pouring into the region.

Yet in spite of the lack of military activity, Julia quickly discovered that the war continued to have an ever-increasing impact on the daily lives of Winchester's residents. The war consumed everything, and the simple everyday task of feeding one's family became troublesome, as food shortages were commonplace and the few supplies that could be found demanded a high price. Realizing what the future held, Julia made a telling comment in August when, after voicing her disgust over the current state of affairs, she said: "Our winter, I fear, will be rather a hard one. I hope we shall not have a severe one in regards to the weather."

As a Unionist, Julia also had to contend with the fact that she now was considered the enemy by those who a short time before had been her friends and neighbors. She and her fellow supporters lived in a constant state of uncertainty and had little recourse as the Confederates began to arrest a number of individuals throughout the Lower Valley. An astute lady, Julia realized as well that this was only the beginning and that the worst was yet to come.

Julia Chase—July 2, 1861. Some 5 or 6 regiments, who have been encamped here, for 2 weeks past . . . left this evening for Martinsburg. The

1

Federal forces, to the number of 15,000 it is said, are crossing the river at Williamsport. . . . Our Southern troops are very boastful of their fighting powers—and if their actions are as great as their words—I fear the Federal troops chances will be rather against them.

Julia Chase—July 4, 1861. But few rejoicings in this state, or any other of the Southern States, in regard to this day, which has been observed for so long a time—when Independence was declared by our forefathers. Into what a sad condition our beloved country has fallen—God have mercy on us, and defend us from our enemies. There are a great many sick soldiers in town. A week ago, 2000 was reported on the sick list—numbers have died; but among the Mississippians it seems more fatal than any other. . . . My father thinks that the 2 armies will hardly get into it before a year, and that this war is to be a war of 5 years—God in his mercy forbid—that all his predictions in regard to this War shall be fulfilled—he thinks he shall not live to see the end of it—which I pray may not be of such long continu-ance. This will be the worst of wars probably that has ever taken place in the world—and oh what hard fighting there will be. One party trying to suppress rebellion—the other, as they think and say, defending their rights, — if the Southers cause is a just and right one—God will certainly defend them, and give them success—but, if not, how can we expect it.

Julia Chase—July 5, 1861. No news of importance—only that our Southern troops will not engage in battle until reinforced—the farmers from the neighboring counties have been drafted—& were called off in the midst of harvesting.

Julia Chase—July 6, 1861. The Militia have been drilled this morn— & we learn that those who came in yesterday are not pleased at all, finding so many men lounging about town—& they obliged to leave their fields of wheat, thinking probably their wheat was of more consequence to them than the fighting.[1] It is thought by many that Winchester will be laid in ashes—& precautions have been taken—and the town fortified in places, in case the F. [Federal] troops should attempt to enter. I hope that our fears may not be realized in regard to our town & homes. . . . I wonder if the people of this country really know what they are doing.

Julia Chase—July 7, 1861. Today the troops all returned from near Martinsburg—no engagement took place between them and the Federal troops. The warmest day I think of the season—and I fear many of the sol-diers will be added to the sick list. . . . How little like Sunday, is today— how long are these things to be? I fear, if any length of time, we will hardly know how to spend our Sabbaths as formerly.

Julia Chase—July 8, 1861. Nothing of importance today—the soldiers having rather a holiday—another of the Georgia soldiers, a friend of those who are sick here, dined with us. The captain of their regiment, who called in this afternoon—says that there will be at least 1500 added to the sick list from the march of yesterday—thinks there was no necessity of their leaving at such a time, in the heat of the day. One poor fellow after getting into town, was lying flat on the pavement as if he could go no further.

Julia Chase—July 10, 1861. Our troops in commotion, there is a rumor that the Yankees are approaching this place, and it is said that the Army here have orders to leave at 1 o'clock P.M. Again, it is said, that they were not going out of W[inchester] but remain here behind their barracks. The town is being fortified in every direction. No one is allowed to leave town without a pass from Gen. Johnston[2]—& one poor woman from the country who had come to town & left 3 children at home, was not allowed to leave, but had to remain all night. I don't think she will be in a hurry to come back again.

Julia Chase—July 11, 1861. We have had fine rains this week—very much needed for the corn—very heavy claps of thunder and vivid lightning. I went down to town this morning but found it very unpleasant walking, especially by myself, so many soldiers on the street, one has to push right through all. Mr. W.—— who has been sick here a week, and we thought improving the last day or two, does not feel so well this afternoon—some fever, he thinks—and I guess little alarm, but then so many are sick, and numbers have died—that I suppose it is natural they should feel so.

Julia Chase—July 12, 1861. Mother and self went to church this afternoon and still had to push through the crowd—it seems rather worse in the morning than after dinner. Showery today—with thunder—and since dinner quite cool. The frequent changes in the weather goes hard with the soldiers. But very few out to church today—and the gentlemen very scarce—except some soldiers who were present. Many families have left town this week—afraid to remain, I suppose. Winchester will now be the battle ground.[3]

Julia Chase—July 14, 1861. Troops still arriving, and our troops who have been here for weeks, are marching towards Bunker Hill, a distance of 12 miles. It is said the Federal troops are at that point, consequently we may expect a battle before many days. There was a skirmish among the picket guards of the 2 armies; a young man of this place by the name of Steele was wounded. Report also is that Gov. Wise[4] has been routed in Western

Virginia with the loss of 1700 men, but before another day, probably we shall hear a different account altogether.

Julia Chase—July 15, 1861. All is commotion—troops moving in all directions—not going to meet the Federal forces—but are to remain by their fortifications. Many persons alarmed and speak of leaving town on the morrow—we shall remain here until it is absolutely necessary for us to go.

Julia Chase—July 16, 1861. Don't know how this day will end—It was thought last evening that before 24 hours, hard fighting will take place—but we hear that the Federal troops are not advancing, and things this morning seem quiet—after dinner soon 2 regiments passed by—and our town was all astir. We hear that others are to come—some estimate the force here to be 40,000 & others about 25,000. Our lives are still preserved and we remain at home in safety. Father came up and said he had just told Mary she & the children had better be leaving in the morning. I ran up stairs and told mother. Thought I would finish packing my trunk, but in the midst of it, Capt. R. came in and thought there was no necessity for it, that he did not think for a moment Winchester would be endangered, and that probably there would be no fighting until August. . . .

Julia Chase—July 19, 1861. Our troops are ordered out, it is thought in the direction of Strasburg. Gen. McClellan's[5] forces are supposed to be drawing near that point, cutting off thereby all communication between the army here and at Richmond. . . . The troops of the Confederate army are now passing by—they number I believe 4,500 men—they will have a warm march in the heat of the day. Their artillery consists of 10 large cannons. The wagons containing baggage extend from Taylor Hotel to our house. 110 wagons more have passed in rear of the troops besides others up Piccadilly Street. . . . We have just heard that the army are moving to Manassas Junction & that they have been fighting for 24 hours, that Gen. McClellan's troops are advancing in very large numbers. It is now near 4 P.M. and the Confederate troops are still on the move—having commenced leaving about 2 o'clock. . . . All the army have left, excepting the sick, who will move on as soon as able. We are without any sugar in our town. The merchants have advanced on all their goods, and if this state of things continues, I know not what will become of us.

Julia Chase—July 20 [21], 1861[6]. The Militia are still coming in, and great many complain bitterly of their being called out, when so many Volunteers in this state. News came this afternoon that Beauregard[7] had driven the Federal forces back 3 times in the battle at Manassas Junction, with the loss ———— on the Confederate side, they having fired behind concealed batteries, and the loss of ———— of the Yankees, but we place little dependence upon anything we hear—the accounts are very contradictory.

Julia Chase—July 22, 1861. Nothing stirring today. No stages running from Strasburg, and no news by telegraph—not in running order I believe. We have news this afternoon that our 1st Regiment have been cut to pieces. Capt. Clark of the Rifle Company & Major Moore are killed, and Capt. Avis of the Continentals, badly wounded. A Mr. Nolan brought the intelligence—we shall probably have further accounts in a few hours. Some hearts will be sad tonight—and though these our townsmen differ from us, yet we feel sad if such should prove true.

Julia Chase—July 23, 1861. The news of Capt. Clark & Major Moore being killed is not correct—both were wounded but this has been a sad day to many hearts in this vicinity. 4 of the dead belonging to Martinsburg passed through town this afternoon. . . . 5 belonging to this town came on immediately after—when the bodies passed along—the stores on Main street were closed. . . . Sadness seems to pervade every countenance. We hear that the 7th & 8th Georgia Regiment were cut in a terrible manner. . . . probably many killed or badly wounded, and to think this is but the beginning of the War. Oh, it is horrible to think of—and the scenes connected with the accounts we have had of the fighting has been in my mind nearly all day.

Julia Chase—July 27, 1861. Our skies are very dark. The Federalists were completely routed at this battle at Manassas—& unless God interposes, I fear that this Government will not be able to maintain itself—but it may be He intends that our Government, under which these Americans have lived so happily for many years, shall be destroyed—if so, we can but submit, feeling that He knows what is best for this people. The next attack will probably be on Washington and then there will be hard fighting on both sides. The Militia are coming, in great numbers, for what purpose I can't tell. I suppose to protect our town. I should not want to rely upon them, if danger comes,—for the greater part are without arms, tho' they will be supplied with such, before long.

Julia Chase—July 29, 1861. We had the pleasure of hearing from brother G—also Cousin Treby, it was quite a treat—but we have no way of answering their letters, there being no mails this side of Strasburg.

Julia Chase—July 30, 1861. Mr. Crum dined with us today—he is a strong Union man. His son, if not sons, have offices in the Confederate Army.

Julia Chase—July 31, 1861. Father not very well today. We are having excessively warm weather this week and this is certainly the hottest of the season.

Julia Chase—August 1, 1861. A fine rain this morning, just what we wanted for the corn. Dr. Boyd called. He says the Troops from the South are pouring in at Manassas in great numbers. We shall probably have another battle soon.

Julia Chase—August 3, 1861. We hear tonight that Mr. Smith has been put in jail. Being from Washington he was suspicioned, will probably have to remain there but a few days. One or two others were put there also— rather mortifying, I confess—but what we must expect in times like these. The weather still continues very warm.

Julia Chase—August 5, 1861. Mr. Hartley spent the afternoon and took tea—he takes sides with the secessionists and I hope the conversation between he and father may not be repeated to F[ather's] disadvantage, tho' Mother and I have our fears. Rain very much needed, our gardens are suffering for want of it, the weather continuing still very warm. We have no news from the army.

Julia Chase—August 8, 1861. Another very warm day and no prospect of rain. We hear that the Federal troops are again at Martinsburg, numbering about 4000. Some 800 cavalry from Staunton came in today.

Julia Chase—August 13, 1861. We have had fine rains for some past days, just such as needed. The weather has [been] considerably cooler. We had the pleasure of hearing from our friends in the West today. We hear that Mr. Bowles has been arrested at his home—also Mr. Faulkner at Washington.

Julia Chase—August 14, 1861. The Winchester papers seem to be filled with accounts of the Confederates gaining victory in all quarters— here in the State as well as in Missouri. If the Federal army do not better than they have been doing, it would be better for them to give up at once I think. Find many persons anxious for peace, all would desire it, I imagine, could it be an honorable one, but I suppose the Northern army must gain some battle before there could be thought for a moment, a cessation of hostilities. Hope they will not prove cowards—what a disgrace it would be to them.

Julia Chase—August 15, 1861. The weather still cool but quite pleasant. We hear all communication between Richmond & this point has been cut off. We shall expect very soon to hear of the Army advancing upon

Washington. . . . Calicoes are selling a shilling per yard. White sugar 25cts. Lb. Coffee is 25 to 30¢. Our winter, I fear, will be rather a hard one. I hope we shall not have a severe one as regards the weather.

Julia Chase—August 19, 1861. The cars left this morning for Charlestown, the first time in weeks. No Federal Troops there at Harper's Ferry. Very pleasant today. No news from the army. The town is being fortified in a N. Westerly direction, some 1,000 men were to work today.

Julia Chase—August 21, 1861. We hear discouraging news in regard to the Federal army. How long must it be before their arms are crowned with success? We hope that certainly if their cause is the just one, they may indeed not fight in vain, but that God will strengthen and assist them. . . . Mother, Charlie M. and self walked to the cemetery this afternoon. We found 33 of the graves in close connection were the soldiers who had died here this summer—also 4 of our town soldiers who were killed at the battle at Bull's Run.

Julia Chase—August 22, 1861. A fine shower early this morning—appearance of more—somewhat cooler. A Gentleman sold a sack of salt this week for $8.00—it is getting to be quite a serious thing having no salt on hand. We have no idea what the coming winter is to be to us—great many persons are buying what winter clothing they will need, at this time, fearing if they delay purchasing, they will be unable when they need them to get anything—heard last week that writing paper was selling at the Junction, 25cts. a sheet—and spool cotton in Charleston, S.C., 25cts. per spool.

Julia Chase—August 23, 1861. Father applied for a pass to Martinsburg but Gen. Carson would not give him one, gave his reasons for doing so, tho' I imagine that some others would have no difficulty procuring it.

Julia Chase—August 25, 1861. Dr. Boyd[8] preached today. I think if he would dispense with Politics in the pulpit, it would be better for the community. Heard that a Mr. Pendleton, step brother of Dr. B, also one or two other Union men from Martinsburg had been brought to town this day—perhaps they are retaliating—for Mr. Chas J. Faulkner who it is said has been imprisoned in Washington. These are dreadful times. A Mr. Kneaster of M[artinsburg], who is a Union man, had his things taken from his store and are being sold about town.

Julia Chase—August 26, 1861. It is said that there are 4,000 sick soldiers at the Junction, and today there is a paper in circulation to see who will accommodate some of those sick ones. Some persons think that if the Federal Troops enter Martinsburg again, it will be to burn the town, but I hope such may not take place. . . . We have heard for several days past that a portion of Johnston's army will quarter here this winter. That, I suppose, depends altogether whether the fighting continues all the winter. I hope tho' we will have no more soldiers that what are here.

Julia Chase—August 29, 1861. This is quite a rainy day. . . . Dr. Boyd called in today and had quite a spirited conversation with father; of course they did not agree in every thing—and while he spoke of the evil of the Federal troops had done with private property near Martinsburg, even to the destruction of female apparel, he did not say a word in regard to the firing of 72 shots by McDonald's cavalry[9] on the Confederate side into a passing engine car from Cumberland. I wonder which was worse. There is evil no doubt & enough too among the soldiers of both armies but let us have both sides of the picture. A Mr. Samuel Pancoast,[10] with whom Father years ago had dealing with in business matters, was brought to town by some of the soldiery, being a Union man he was suspected. He seems to take things fair & easy & is now & has been since his arrival at the Virginia House. Probably will get off without any trouble.

Julia Chase—August 30, 1861. 2 others of our citizens have lost sons who were in the army, Mr. Bowles and Mr. Glaize. I take it before this war closes that there will be but few families who will not escape with the loss of friends.

Julia Chase—August 31, 1861. Coffee today is selling at 35cts a pound and we have commenced using Rye with our coffee that we have on hand.

Julia Chase—September 2, 1861. Weather quite warm again. One of the engines that was thrown in the river at Martinsburg, when the Confederate army was at Harper's Ferry, has been brought into town today by 32 horses, to be taken to Richmond. It was quite a sight as it passed by—looking very much like an iron monster. . . . No salt to be had in town. What will the people do. Some of the Secessionists storm about it. Mr. Ridenour of Charlestown sent up to see if any could be procured, there being none at that place.

Julia Chase—September 5, 1861. Young Peter Miller died this morning, after an illness of some weeks. He returned from the Junction with some others who were sick about a week ago. How many of our young men who have left this town will return again, I wonder. With the exception of these our sick in town are improving. . . . Mr. Rea selling coffee at 38cts. today. He will make money if there is any way to do it.

Julia Chase—September 8, 1861. A good number of the militia returned to their homes today. There has been a great deal of dissatisfaction since they were called out, and it is said that while we have 5000 of them here, there should be but one fifth of that number.

Julia Chase—September 10, 1861. The Militia have gone to Duffield's Depot to tear up the track of the Western Road . . . between Strasburg & this place. Grab & catch what you can seems to be the order of the day these times. Matches that we have been paying 62½ cts. per gross now command $6, and scarce at that. An agent from Richmond is here trying to get some. Coffee is selling at 50¢ lb. Soap is 16 to 18cts.

Julia Chase—September 11, 1861. Some of the Militia & a portion of McDonald's left town today. It is said that those of the militia who left a day or two ago . . . have been taken prisoners, and that the Federal troops are going to surround us on all sides, but that has been rumored so often, we place but little confidence in it.

Julia Chase—September 18, 1861. The Charlestown Militia came up this afternoon to report themselves, we hear. No news of any importance from the army, only that they are moving on in large bodies towards Alexandria & troops are pouring in from the South. . . . The papers speak of Mr. Ross Winans & other members of the Legislature of that state [Maryland] again being arrested & to be taken on to Fort McHenry, also that Mr. Chas. J. Faulkner has been removed from Washington City to . . . New York. We infer that he is looked upon as a traitor to his country, by their dealings towards him. I had never expected to have heard this of him. He was a great friend of father's.

Julia Chase—September 21, 1861. Heavy rains this afternoon & the weather changed quite cool. It has been very warm throughout the week. . . . Calico is selling in Richmond 30cts a yard. Coffee 40cts lb. I fear the poor as well as others will suffer much this winter. No coal to speak of, and wood selling $4.50.

Julia Chase—September 25, 1861. It is rumored that McDonald's Cavalry have been surrounded & McDonald taken prisoner—that there has been fighting between the 2 parties there is no doubt . . . but the story is not credited by some of the Secessionists. . . . We are deprived of gas—for how long a time don't know, tho' we expect to have coal for that purpose shortly. This war causes trouble in everything and way, in this part of Virginia, we are put to a great deal of inconvenience & expense to procure things. Several cases of Diphtheria & Scarlet fever. A son of Mr. Eggleston died of Diphtheria on Sabbath last.

Julia Chase—September 26, 1861. A daughter of Mr. John Nulton died of scarlet fever yesterday. Her throat, it was said, was swollen to the chin. . . .

The secessionists are down on Col. McDonald for running away from his men. They were surrounded whilst he took french leave. He is not popular at all with the people, and should not I think have had command at all. By the papers I see that Col. Mason has been appointed Confederate Minister to England. Wonder if he won't get caught before reaching that country.

Julia Chase—October 7, 1861. The last few days have been as warm as any during the summer. The Militia have returned again. One of the pickets, on Sat. night . . . shot a man. He lived until the next morning. Whether a spy or not, cannot say.

Julia Chase—October 11, 1861. Mr. Johnson, a broker of Baltimore, by whom father sent George money, was arrested last week and taken to Fort Lafayette. He was about leaving for Europe to make negotiations between that country & the Southern Confederacy, but his plans are all frustrated. . . . The militia of this county say they are going to their homes tomorrow unless they are paid, having been here 3 months and have not received the first cent. We hear also that the Federals have entered Staunton, also that Gen. Wise & Lee have been driven off by some of the Federal cavalry, but we place but little dependence on much of the news we receive. . . . Tea is selling $2.00 per lb.

Julia Chase—October 15, 1861. It is rumored this afternoon that there has been a skirmish between the U.S. forces at Harpers Ferry and the Confederates, that the militia ran, and 2 of Col. Ashby's[11] men were brought to Charlestown wounded. We shall probably hear today whether it is correct or not. Had an opportunity of sending a letter off today by Mr. Pancoast, who is en route for Washington. He has been in that city & seen the President & others. Mr. P's object in going was to see if supplies could not be sent to the families of Hampshire, who are suffering want of much, they being loyal to the U. States. The President told him he had rather 10 secession families should have things rather than one Union family should suffer & supplies might be sent provided the army here in this state did not get them.

Julia Chase—October 24, 1861. We hear of nothing but disgrace and disaster attending the U.S. Troops in their fight at Leesburg, or rather, at Big Run, 1½ miles from that town. Some 600 were taken prisoners, also a large stand of arms, and Col. Baker of Oregon killed, besides some 3 or 400 of the soldiers drowned in crossing the river. . . . The Country's cause tho' a noble one, so far has been very badly managed and the Union people are mortified enough and hang their heads very low. It is to be hoped that a change for the better will take place very soon and the troops and the commanding officers retrieve their character for fighting. . . . I fear this war will never end and we can look ahead & see the desolation & ruin which it will cause all over the country.

Julia Chase—October 26, 1861. Sad hearts today in the Miller family. Mrs. Bet Cross died this morning, after an illness of but a few days. She left a babe about 1 month old. Before her death she gave it to her mother to take charge of, her husband being in the South she was not permitted to see him. . . . Her death will be greatly felt. It seems to me that our whole town will be in mourning for friends before many years have passed.

Julia Chase—October 27, 1861. We have news this morning which is cheering to the secessionists, as well as the Union people. Col. McDonald, who was in command of some 600 men, and who is very unpopular with every body, has we learn been taken with 60 of his men, their horses & all their baggage. Some of his men who escaped came into town this morning & gave the news, and we really hope it is true.

Julia Chase—October 28, 1861. How little dependence is to be placed on anything we hear. One of McDonald's men staid here last night, said he saw McD. in his carriage and the carriage surrounded by Federal troops, that they had Col. McD. safe surely, when lo & behold he came some time last night and is here in town—so much for persons who say they see such and such things.

Julia Chase—October 31, 1861. Heard that Jackson's Brigade[12] was coming here to protect the people of Winchester from the Yankees.

Julia Chase—November 5, 1861. None of the soldiers have arrived yet tho' Gen. Jackson is in town. We learn that some of the citizens of Winchester sent a petition on to Gen. Johntson to have some of the army quartered here this winter, so I suppose after all that W[inchester] has done for the soldiers, they will hardly refuse them. It was rumored that the U.S. Troops were again at Harper's Ferry, and some of our ladies were terribly alarmed—poor creatures, they are to be pitied.

Julia Chase—November 7, 1861. We have news Sunday of the resignation of Gen. Scott,[13] his age and increasing infirmities are the reasons assigned.

Julia Chase—November 9, 1861. Our town is all astir in consequence of the arrival of Jackson's Brigade. The citizens of Winchester feel perfectly safe now, I suppose. Jackson's orders are, however, that the soldiers are not to be in town (for which I am very glad). Some of the Continentals resisted the militia who were commanded not to let them remain, but by persuasion they left without further trouble.

Julia Chase—November 12, 1861. Father thinks he will be deprived of his walks out of town, as the roads are guarded and persons obliged to get passes, and those who do not care to ask for them feel, I suppose as they were limited indeed. It would have been a good thing had the soldiers not come back again. There are many I know who do not want to see them. We heard last night that a Mr. Vance, who lived near Col. Blue's, was shot by some of McDonald's men.

Julia Chase—November 15, 1861. Mr. Pancoast . . . has been arrested a second time by the Southern Soldiers, because he is a Union man. The first time they could prove nothing against him and now the charge is: He had a few pigeons that he bought and his enemies wish to make out they are carrier doves and are for the purpose of sending messages to the injury of the Southern Confederacy. . . . Mr. P understands he is to be sent to Richmond, and showed us a letter from his wife in which she said that his property was to be confiscated and she was not even allowed the use of her corn to feed her stock. Rather a hard case, as Mr. P. says he has not done or said anything treasonable. . . . These are terrible times and the worst I fear not yet come.

Julia Chase—November 17, 1861. Two soldiers called here tonight to see if they could obtain their supper. . . . We had nothing very inviting to set before them but they seemed thankful for it. They told us they expected to remain here this winter, as their lieutenant had told them orders had been given for 1000 shanties to be put up for the use of the soldiers. Was sorry to hear it, as we have to pay such high prices for everything. Wood sells at the rate of $6.00 a cord, pepper at 80cts a lb., butter 40cts, eggs 20 & 25.

Julia Chase—November 18, 1861. The troops are moving their quarters from near Kernstown and are going in the neighborhood of Mr. Carter's, that they may obtain wood and water. Heard that they cut down all the fences nearly, so they make destruction wherever they go. It will be quite lively in our part of the town now, as they will have to pass and re-pass our house in going to the camp. . . . Mr. Pancoast has been moved from his boarding house to the guardhouse. He will not relish that so well. The soldiers are moving a regiment a day to their new quarters, not having wagons enough to transport their baggage for all to go at once. Good News: Col. Mason and Mr. Slidell, who had been appointed Ministers[14] to Europe by the Confederate Congress, have been taken prisoners . . . and are safely lodged in Fort Monroe, so Mr. Mason had the pleasure of returning to Virginia again, tho' in rather a different way than he would prefer. In a speech before some of the troops here in the early part of the summer, he said he stood before them an original rebel & was proud to say it . . . .called the Northerners all sorts of bad names, and that there was no love or affinity between them and the South, that all the people thought of was making money and did not know what a home was. . . . These men who have caused so much mischief and harm will have their punishment sooner or later, wherever they be, North or South. Port Royal in South Carolina, we hear, has been taken by the U. States Troops, and it is said the South Carolinians, the very ones who of all others should fight well, did very badly—the officers even threw down their swords. So much for S. Carolina, the mischief maker & bringer on of this war. We also hear that the U.S. Troops have been successful again . . . in an engagement that has taken place in some of the S. Western States. We hope that these things will encourage those who are stationed in this part of the country, that they may fight nobly—no retreating or defeating for a long time to come, that they may be successful in the end.

Julia Chase—November 28, 1861. The Militia, some portion, left today for Bath. Tea is selling at $3.00 a lb., coffee 75cts., pepper $1.25 and everything else in proportion, tho' sugar is offered at 12½ cts. per lb., but not much at that.

Julia Chase—December 1, 1861. Dr. Stiles gave us a grand discourse this morning. Subject: Redemption & values of the Soul—but all the good and grand effects to me were lost by his bringing in politics. He said, in speaking of the beloved South, their homes and firesides being invaded by the ruthless invading arms of our Northern neighbors, and how our soldiers from all parts of the South had risen up as one man, and crushed down the enemy, driven all before them & seemed to glory in it. . . . In the afternoon at the Union prayer meeting, he made some remarks to this effect: that the great difference with the South now was, not that the South could not become reconciled with the North, or the North make peace with the South, but that the South had sinned, sinned greatly . . . and in all the prayers he heard while at the North not one was offered up for the South & his heart wept sore; & he rejoiced greatly when he trod his first step on Virginia soil, and while at a meeting in Richmond he heard prayer offered not only for the South but for the North & West. . . . Such meeting are of no pleasure or good to me but rather the reverse, & the impression to me I think left on the minds of the people is that the Northern people are the worst of persons, and for one who has lived among them and received so much money from them, in behalf of the Southern Aid Society, of which he was the corresponding secretary, it does not become him thus to speak I think—but perhaps I am all in the wrong & he right, tho' I hope such is not the case.

Julia Chase—December 3, 1861. Mr. Rea selling salt today at $30.00 a sack. People are getting their rights in good earnest, and bacon I think will sell at a good round price. Flour has advanced some & will in all probability as they are sending from New Orleans to Richmond for such.

Julia Chase—December 9, 1861. Dr. Stiles preaches his last sermon this morning . . . and leaves tonight or in the morning for the South. . . . Some 2 regiments, with 18 pieces of cannon have gone to Martinsburg to destroy all the locks of the canal, thereby preventing all communication between the Federal army and Washington, also cutting off their supplies. I really hope that their plans may be frustrated & they return here wiser men, not so confident of success and their boasting powers cooled down a little. God grant they may not be successful. Geo. Miller brought a sack of pepper & paid $130.00, what formerly cost from $10 to $12. Molasses selling $1.75 per gal. and pepper has been selling for over $2.00. If these are our rights we don't want such rights any longer, but restore us to our former peace & happiness. The weather for the past week has been charming, more like April than December, almost dispensing with fires.

Julia Chase—December 15, 1861. The troops stationed here, we learn, are ordered off for Harper's Ferry, Martinsburg and Romney. We also hear that other troops are coming here. . . . The war will I think commence in earnest, what out future will be none can tell. We shall expect to hear of a great fight before long. God forbid that these Southern soldiers should be successful again in the coming battle, but may the U.S. Troops have their arms strengthened and bold and fearless heart to do their duty & do it manfully—but how much happiness would it bring to every one, if this great trouble was ended, and all was peace & happiness again.

Julia Chase—December 18, 1861. Today we hear that the battle has commenced between the 2 armies at Martinsburg. . . . I have been hoping all along that the Union people in Winchester might be cheered with glad tidings of a victory on their side in this case, but as like other engagements have all proved successful to the Southern soldiery in this part of Virginia, we are almost afraid to hope it will be otherwise.

Julia Chase—December 23, 1861. Winter has set in with good earnest, now it is rain, hail and snow, and dreadful high winds—seems as if the house would blow down. Jackson's Brigade have got back again, without accomplishing their purpose, were pretty well peppered I guess, and we hear that in a skirmish at the Junction between Stewart's brag cavalry and some infantry were whipped by the U.S. troops. Good news indeed. May they continue on and gain noble victories for a long time to come.

Julia Chase—December 24, 1861. Very cold today. If such weather continues during the week we shall have very good ice. Some of the troops are moving off today, towards Romney we hear. May they come back quicker than they go, getting another whipping. Some 7 or 8000 more troops are expected here, so they will number nearly 20,000 & are to be quartered here all winter, so we understand. This weather is rather hard for them, and it won't be quite so nice as last June & July. Oh, if this war were only over and we were living as we once were. Mother sick in bed today.

Julia Chase—December 25, 1861. Christmas. The Dr. thinks Mother has strong symptoms of Typhoid. She is very restless.

Julia Chase—December 26, 1861. Mother had a bad night, tho' rather easier today, not so much fever. We hear that in a skirmish in Missouri, the Confederates have been whipped, 1500 taken prisoners, 2 tons of powder & a great many arms captured by the U.S. troops. More troops arrived today, Virginians & Tennesseans. We see a great many strange faces passing by—very lively on the street. Mother has not so much fever tho' suffers otherwise. . . . 15,000 troops are around and about us. Nothing but soldiers—soldiers.

Julia Chase—December 29, 1861. Mother was cupped today—rather better this afternoon. A beautiful Sabbath day.

Julia Chase—January 1, 1862. A lovely New Year's day, more spring than mid-winter. The troops are preparing for a march, it is thought towards Bath. Bridges have been built in that direction. Their object I suppose is to destroy them. Mr. Chas. J. Faulkner has been released from Fort Lafayette and now is in town. He is aid-de-camp to Gen. Jackson. Foreign news say that England has concluded to let the Emperor of France decide whether the taking of Mason & Slidell by our Government is legal or not. The secessionists were not expecting that & they are dreadfully put out about it. Mother is improving.

Julia Chase—January 5, 1862. Mr. Mason and Slidell have been released by the U.S. Government. . . . Some 4 deaths in the town among the soldiers this week. Jordon Springs Hotel has been taken as a hospital and 200 of the sick carried there. Mother improving slowly. Sat up a few moments this morning.

Julia Chase—January 7, 1862. Cold wintry weather indeed. Wood selling at $10 per cord. Tea $4 per lb. News today that the Federal soldiers have driven out those quartered at Hanging Rock & taken all their arms, cannon, etc. Some fighting I suppose, as the wounded and sick have been brought in town. . . . We hear some dreadful accounts of their doings. Oh, the horrors of War. Would that it was all over. Some 60 wounded have been brought in town.

Julia Chase—January 12, 1862. Our town has become a complete hospital. Nearly 1500 are said to be here sick. Some are being removed to Staunton, Lynchburg, and we have great deal of sickness among the children & others. Some 3 funerals today. Miss Sarah Spotts died last night—buried this afternoon. A child of Mrs. Elizabeth Gibson, also one of Mrs. Kinzel's was buried. Scarlet fever is prevailing to a considerable extent too. If there is as much sickness where the soldiers are as in this part of the country, the whole South must become or is a complete hospital.

Julia Chase—January 17, 1862. We have 1800 sick soldiers in town and deaths are occurring every day. 2 Georgians came for something to eat. Said while in Morgan Co. the week before, they were without fire for 4 days and were obliged to lay on the cold wet ground. The weather was very severe and they experienced in that campaign, if they had not before, all the hardships of a soldier's life. They had not eaten anything since morning of the day before they came here. We understand that some seven were frozen to death, 2 of which were Georgians. . . . More die from exposure and sickness than are killed on the battlefield.

Julia Chase—January 18, 1862. We have had but one pleasant day this week—snow, rain, or sleet all the time. 19 deaths have taken place since yesterday afternoon, up to noon today. We have had application nearly every day for soldiers to board here. . . . Mother has not left her room yet, but will I think next week, towards the close. Mr. York's house is to be used as a hospital, and it is said that rooms are to be pressed even if the parlors are to be used. I hope that all those persons who are well able, have plenty of rooms and servants, will not be exempted. . . . The Secretary of War, Mr. Cameron, has resigned. . . . He differed from the Cabinet, in regard to the emancipation of all the Negroes of the country. What a world of trouble this slavery business has caused. It enters into every thing.

Julia Chase—January 19, 1862. Intended going to church today, but was prevented by the rain. We have given up the Sabbath School until the lecture room is made vacant by the soldiers, who are there sick. Nearly all the lecture rooms are occupied by them. George M. sent to Richmond for a pound of saffron and paid $45.00. Who ever heard of such prices. It is extravagant prices we are paying for everything a well man needs & ruinous prices for what the sick require. When our money fails, we will be in a terrible condition surely. Oh this War! War! When will the end come. 15 funerals from the hospitals today.

Julia Chase—February 1, 1862. Snow, rain, and with no prospect of fair weather; we have scarcely had 6 pleasant days during the entire month of January. Gen. Jackson, who has been in command of the troops here, has resigned. Difference of opinion with him & the War Department. Loring's Brigade who were left at Romney are very much dissatisfied & unwilling to remain—difficulty of getting provisions to them. We learn they are coming back to Winchester. Sorry for it. The Union people hoped that if the Yankees intend coming back here they had done it while Gen. Jackson was in command, he being considered a pretty good general.

Julia Chase—February 4, 1862. Sarah Smith was buried this morning from Loudoun St. Church. She will be very much missed in her family. Her death followed soon after her mother's. Loring's Brigade, we hear, are ordered to Kentucky: Joy go with them. Salt is selling at the rate of 20cts. per pound. Joe Ginn & Mr. Dooley have been in the guardhouse since Monday. Mr. G. frets a good deal. They were going to run the blockade & get to Baltimore—one reason that they might not serve on the militia, as all persons from the age of 16 to 60 are to be drafted. Sorry times these.

Julia Chase—February 10, 1862. The U.S. troops have destroyed the Hotel, Win[chester] & Potomac R.R. Depot & other buildings at Harper's Ferry. The story is that Mr. Baylor from Charlestown, with some men were lying in ambush at Harper's Ferry and sent a Negro over in a boat to entice 2 of the U.S. soldiers over on the Virginia side. When near the shore, they fired upon them, killing them immediately, and in retaliation the U.S. troops sent boom shells & destroyed these buildings. If it be true, it was a very cowardly, mean act of the Virginians & they cannot say anything now about the Yankees being such dreadful persons. Oh! What a horrid state of things we are involved in. When will the end come?

Julia Chase—February 15, 1862. We have news of the Federal troops taking some of our militia up to the Bloomery. Young Dr. Robt. Baldwin, Richard Gray, are among the number taken. There is a good deal of laughing among some of our townsmen, at their running, but I fear they forgot one of their sayings, which is: That a Virginian never runs, never surrenders. Think we have had plenty of example to prove they are like a great many other people—run when danger comes. It seems that most of the officers, who should have done their duty by being at their posts, took good care to be out of the way, when they found the Federal forces were near them. Not much bravery in this part of Virginia I think among our soldiers. . . . We have no gas now. Not any molasses in town. Brown sugar selling at 20cts a lb. . . . It is said that Gen. Jackson will not serve any longer, though it is believed that his resignation will not be accepted. Don't know whether his men will serve under another general or not.

Julia Chase—February 19, 1862. Rain, rain, rain. This month is similar to the last. Will the sun ever shine. . . . We hear a great many conflicting rumors in regard to the battles at the South; one dispatch saying the Federal troops are successful, followed by another that the Southerners are gaining the day. It is believed, however, that the U.S. troops have taken Fort Donelson.[15] Mrs. Eliza Russell has lost her youngest child of Scarlet fever. This disease is said by the Drs. to be raging like wild fire.

Julia Chase—February 26, 1862. We heard last night that the Federal troops were all around us, but no news today of their whereabouts. It is also rumored that Tennessee has requested to be admitted into the Union, but we place no confidence in it, but what a blessed thing were it true. Good bye to secessionists & the Southern Confederacy then.

Julia Chase—February 27, 1862. Great excitement in town today. The cars came back about 11 o'clock, with the news that Charlestown was in possession of the U.S. troops. Col. Baylor's men had been taken by them. We did not hear if the Col. himself was taken. It seems, however, that only the cavalry are at C[harlestown]. Some say 500. The secessionists seem terribly uneasy, our good minister among the number.

CHAPTER TWO

March 1862–September 1862

"Thanks be to the Lord, we are free"

In the spring and summer of 1862, the war came to the Shenandoah Valley in a forceful way. In March, the Federals advanced up the Valley and occupied Winchester. Two weeks later, the two forces clashed at Kernstown, a short distance south of the city, where the Federal army defeated Jackson and forced him to retire farther up the Valley. Jackson counterattacked in late May, and in what has become known as the Confederate Valley campaign, defeated three different Federal armies in five separate engagements. The Confederate victories raised Southern morale at a time when it was most needed and made Jackson a national hero. In September, the region once again became the focal point of operations, with the Confederate Army of Northern Virginia recuperating in the countryside about Winchester following the battle of Antietam.

The brutal fighting and constant presence of the military forces of each side awakened both Julia and Laura to the harsh realities of war. And yet as horrified as they were by it, death had at the same time become just another aspect of their daily lives. They also came to realize that in light of the conflict, justice and civil liberties had lost all meaning. Julia confronted this reality in March, when the Confederates arrested her father and carried him away. Laura, too, came to realize this fact in the wake of the Federal occupation of the region, as the soldiers confiscated or destroyed whatever they wanted, leaving many citizens devoid of everything they owned, and not the least bit concerned about how they would survive. But as distraught as Julia and Laura were over the dire state the country had fallen into, each remained loyal to her cause and steadfast in her convictions.

Julia Chase—March 3, 1862. Quite a number of our people are leaving town, frightened almost to death of the Yankees, that they will come

19

and catch them. Dr. McGuire[1] has sent his family off and says he intends burning his house. Dr. Smith has left, Heist family, female portion, Charles Rouss about leaving. Mr. Philip Williams[2] & his wife remain to take care of the property. The Clarke people we hear are sending off their furniture as fast as possible and leaving. The Federal pickets are within 4 miles of Berryville. We understand there is a large force at Charlestown. . . . The town is under martial law. General Jackson has sent off all provisions that were here and I suppose will be ready to run when the Yankees are near. The banks have sent off all of their Specie, books, & c. Hope we are not going to have a continuance of the weather we have had the last 2 months. The Virginians have always said never surrender, that they never ran. Pretty good number are running now fast enough.

Julia Chase—March 7, 1862. Our town all in excitement this afternoon. Artillery flying by, people running, soldiers going in all directions. The Federal pickets have advanced as far as Stevenson's Depot and we heard that some little fighting was done. Jackson's Brigade have passed by on their way to Strasburg it was said. Scarcely had they got out of sight before some 50 wagons with baggage have changed their course and gone back to campground. The Yankees they say have been driven back and therefore they are coming to their old quarters, but if they had been whipped, Jackson had intended running off. . . . Cold with some wind today but no prospect of ice.

Julia Chase—March 9, 1862. Mr. Rielly buried this afternoon. There have been 4 deaths in that family within the past week, and a younger daughter is now lying at the point of death. . . . We have expected and rather hoped the Yankees would have made their appearance ere this, tho', if as we fear, it would have been by Winchester being laid in ashes by Gen. Jackson before their arrival. We are very glad they did not advance. . . . Good many wagons were burnt up yesterday, fearing I suppose they might eventually fall into the hands of the Union troops. How much better would it have been to have given them to so many families who are suffering for the want of wood. A gentleman in town gave $12 yesterday for a load of very inferior stuff. Warm weather would be very desirable. Very much like Spring today. Our pastor, Dr. B. prayed today for the first time, that a blessing & not a curse might rest upon those whom he calls his enemies that they, meaning the Federal forces, might have the disposition to return to their homes— willingly, I imagine, would they do so, were the South to lay down their arms and return to their homes. Our minister seems very uneasy about the

Yankees coming here; asked a gentleman what he intended to do. He told him trust in Providence & that he (Dr. B.) must do the same. The Union Hotel, which since the war broke out was changed to Ion, removing the U and N, have within a few days replaced the letters, giving it its original name. Oh, the Virginians, how bravely they talk when their army is near, but how different when there is any sign of the U.S. troops making their appearance. The women seem terribly alarmed at the thought of the Yankees coming here, as if they were monsters in human form.

Julia Chase—March 10, 1862. We are fallen upon fearful times; great many Union people have been put in the guard house, and a number today. Smith Gilkeson, Mr. Jas. Rea, Amos Wright & c. Some 4 or 5 Unionist were brought in town last night, one of which we hear was killed. We are expecting nothing else but Father will be arrested, as we learn the secessionists have 150 names down of the Union people.

Julia Chase—March 11, 1862. Our fears are more than realized. Father has been taken to the guard house, there about 2½ hours, and then hurried off to Strasburg. I saw him twice before he took his final leave, but oh, how indignant I felt towards the whole town. To take an old man lying sick on the sofa is outrageous, but we hope for the best, tho' we look upon it as a high handed piece of business. Mr. Geo. Aulick, Besore, Sydor, York, and others were carried off as prisoners also. The older men had the privilege of riding to Strasburg by paying their fare. The rest had to walk. Sad, sad day to us.

Laura Lee—March 11, 1862. Col. Baylor and Lt. Minor came out to breakfast this morning, not having heard any of the news of the day. They went out and the first person who came in was Marshall Jones, who called to say good-bye and get a lunch for Bob[3] who would not leave the company. We said the long roll had beat and they were to march at 12 o'clock. He supposed, of course, for Strasburg. Then Col. Baylor came in and said he did not think it probable they would march today, and it was evident he expected a fight before leaving. We heard next that there was a reinforcement of 4000 men just out of town. We doubted it, but still it added to the excitement of the hour. From 12 till half-past, we were busy putting into place of safety, silver, papers, swords, flags, military clothes, war letters, in short, everything contraband, except the servants, who could not conveniently be stored away. I do not think the Yankees with all their cunning will find our hiding place. Johnnie Mason dined with us, and he and the other gentlemen were in great uncertainty as to the next move, as ourselves expecting a fight, but still uncertain whether it would be this evening. They told us good-bye and we stood on the porch waiting for—we care not what. We heard the troops were in motion and—we suppose for Strasburg, but instead of that cavalry, artillery and Loring's infantry marched past here down the Berryville Road, and took position there. Jackson's brigade was posted on the Martinsburg Road, not two miles from town. The report was that there were 6000 of the enemy on one road, and 10,000 at Mrs. Carter's on the other, and both advancing rapidly. Our whole force was scarcely 5000. . . . This is our weakest time, and the Yankees know it and are trying to take advantage of it. Yet not withstanding the disadvantages, Jackson seems unable to resist the temptation to give the Yankees a thrashing. We were so restless and miserable that Mary and I determined to go to Mr. Mason's to have our few things, while having been left in the house, brought away. After we sent off all that was of any value, we walked to the top of the hill at the back of the house, from which we could see the whole of the surrounding country. It was a lovely evening. The stillness not broken by a sound, and it seemed impossible to realize that two hostile armies were lying below in sight of each other, and that every instant might bring us the sounds of strife. We heard, when we returned home, that the Yankees on the Berryville Road had marched . . . to join the main body on the Martinsburg Road, and finding this, Jackson had concentrated all his force at the fortification. . . . Just at dark, we were startled by loud churning and found that our men were marching back through the town. Johnnie Baldwin called for a moment to say that Bob could not leave the company to say good-bye. . . . In a few moments Col. Baylor came in to tea and said that the men had gone back to their wagons to get supplies, and it was still uncertain when they would go. I was again in despair, I had hoped the danger of a fight was over.

Julia Chase—March 12, 1862. Glorious news. The Union Army took possession of Winchester today and the glorious flag is waving over our town, but oh, if the troops could only have come a day or two sooner, then our people would have escaped the clutches of the Southern Army. We suppose the destination of the prisoners will be Richmond. God forbid they should reach that city while Jeff Davis reigns there. It does us some good to see some one outside of Dixie, and we hope the troops will show by their conduct to the Virginians that they are not all monsters and have not come for the purpose of cutting their throats & destroying their homes.

Laura Lee—March 12, 1862. After a wretched night, listening from daylight for the sound of the guns, we found at 7 o'clock that our men had been gone for several hours, except Ashby's cavalry, which lingered in the town until the enemy marched in, which they did at 8 o'clock, swarming in on every street, with flags flying and bands to every regiment playing "Yankee Doodle," "Hail Columbia," and "Dixie." This was the only demonstration they made of a triumphant entry. They marched in perfect silence through the streets, which, with the exception of Main Street, were entirely deserted by our citizens. In our street every door and window was closed and not a creature visible, except a few servants at the corners. It looked like a vast funeral, and it felt even <u>more so</u>. I suppose they were ashamed to make demonstrations of triumph when sneaking into a town they were afraid to fight for. . . . Think of us in the hands of such a set! At first we felt overwhelmed with feeling of degradation and humiliation, (but never a particle of fear) but soon indignation got the mastery, and now we feel nerved for all that may come. On Main Street some Union flags were thrown out, and a few handkerchiefs waved by people who have always been known here as disloyal, but it is proved to the Yankees that the Union feelings which they boasted prevailed here, and was kept down only by fear had no more real existence then the rest of their fabrications. . . . Mr. Charles Graves opened the Post Office and invited them to take possession, which they did at once. Randell Evens, who has a restaurant for our soldiers closed his house and they broke it open and marched in. They have taken every unoccupied house, the market house, courthouse, and lecture rooms. . . . The servants are crazy with delight at it all, thinking it an entertainment gotten up for their special benefit. Today some of the gentlemen went to see Hamilton, Shields and three of the generals to know what we have to expect. They say private property shall be respected and that any soldiers who insult a lady shall be shot. That sounds well, but I do not trust them. I believe it is only a first in the hope of making us Union people. I have known all the time that we shall be kept in a state of constant terror by the reports if we believe them. . . . Mr. Barton has been among them today, and has given them some very plain talking. He told them they were entirely mistaken in expecting to find Union feeling here, that there was almost none.

Laura Lee—March 13, 1862. We have had two brushes with the Yankees today, and have come off safely. We were scarcely dressed this morning, when we were told that two soldiers were at the door, inquiring for Mrs. Lee. Mary and I went down and found two rough looking creatures who said they had come for a secession flag which was here. Mary told them that there was none here, that we had had one but had sent it to a place of safety. They said they must search the house. We asked for their authority. They said they had the authority. We told them they could not come till they brought an officer to prove it. They went off looking very sheepish, and we found it was only a ruse to do what they had been doing in other places. Pretend they have power to search, and in doing so steal whatever they can carry off. The cavalry have taken possession of the yard and stables at Mr. Clarke's last night, and are using everything and burning his wood without the slightest restraint. . . . Some of the gentlemen of the town are trying the policy of being very polite and conciliatory, but Dr. Robert Baldwin[4] is an honorable exception to this. He will not speak to them or even look at them and says not one shall ever enter his house. . . . Several persons have taken the Yankees as borders. Mrs. Magill, Mrs. Dandridge, Mrs. Severs, Mrs. Barton, and Ludwell Baldwin are now our scouts. They go out among the soldiers and hear them talk and then come and tell us. The creatures are swarming in every part of the town and we cannot lift our eyes without seeing them passing and every instant wagons of supplies are passing and re-passing. I hate all the sights and sounds that reach me. I feel as if it would have been preferable to have left everything, only to have escaped the horrible depression which is over everything, but it is needless to repine. We could not have left the girls, and we could not have taken them. We can only hope and pray for deliverance. . . . We had another attack this evening about the flag. A dashing young officer rode up to the door, with a soldier in attendance. The former dismounted and rang the bell. Mary opened the window on the steps. We never open the door without looking to see who is there, for we are determined that not one of these creatures shall enter the house, if we can keep them out. The young man came to the window and asked if she was Mrs. Lee. He then said he had heard that some men had been here in the morning to search for a flag, and that he had come as a gentleman to beg that she would give it up, as if the men were determined to search, the officer would have no power to restrain them. Mary said she had already told them that the flag was not here, and that if her word was not sufficient, she would seek the protection from such an insult from the commanding officer. The young man was very mad and bit his lip to control himself. He asked if the Confederate officers had always been able to control their soldiers. She told him the men never need restraint. She asked him to tell her who had informed about our flag. He said there were many good union people here. Her only reply was a scornful smile, a slight bow, and closing the window. He looked very indignant to be kept at the door like a servant and then summarily dismissed. To do him justice, he behaved very well, was perfectly respectful and polite, and was evidently a gentleman. Also very handsome and elegantly equipped. Yet he made nothing out of the Secesh, as they call us. . . . Although the town is filled with soldiers in the day, at night, it is perfectly quiet. All are obliged to be at their camps. These men have a dogged, sullen, look. They do not laugh or jest as our men do. . . . They say they have not been paid for four months, as a consequence, they steal everything they can lay their hands on. . . . Mr. Peyton Clarke was complaining to some of them of the depredations they had committed at his father's and one of them told him it made no difference. They were playing thunder all over the country.

Laura Lee—March 14, 1862. There was another demand for the flag today. A soldier came to the window and asked if we had not one, and when Mary answered indignantly that she had answered that question to Gen. Shields,[5] he seemed satisfied, and said that . . . he had not come to demand it, but he wished to buy one to send home as a trophy. We are glad to hear that they are very much disappointed in their reception here. They say they were never treated with such scorn, as by the Winchester ladies. They are beginning to carry off numbers of servants, some to the camps, and some to work on the railroad at Harper's Ferry. Foraying parties go all around the country and carry off everything moveable. When our army was here they were never allowed to burn a rail, and if they did it, they were compelled to split another to replace them, but now we see wagon loads of rails and some times whole panels of plank fencing going through the town. They have stolen every article out of Mr. Layette Washington's house, and all his servants. He has actually no personal property but the clothes he has on. They burn and destroy all of value, in mere wanton mischief.

Julia Chase—March 17, 1862. A petition has been gotten up, in behalf of the prisoners, but we don't expect it will avail much. 2 of our citizens, Dr. Robert Baldwin & Mr. Swartzwelder, refused to sign their names, tho' I doubt not could we but look into the heart of many of the secessionists who did sign, that they really rejoice that these Union men were taken.

Laura Lee—March 17, 1862. We did not go to church yesterday, fearing the churches would be over run with Yankees. Gen. William Challian, from New York went to Mr. Williams to say that he wished to occupy the church. Mr. W. is very conciliatory . . . made no objection to his having it, but told him that he did not think a number of the congregation would attend. He expressed great surprise, and asked where was the choir! Mr. W. said they were particularly Southern and he was <u>certain</u> they would not go.

Laura Lee—March 20, 1862. Another day of anxieties. Hugh[6] has been gone for two days. He staid at home all last week because he could not get a pass, but on Tuesday he went out saying he would try to get some work in town. He has not been back, and today we heard he had passed through town with a regiment.

Laura Lee—March 22, 1862. This has been a most exciting day. By breakfast time the troops began to march down the Berryville Road, leaving here. By dinner time 8 regiments, 2 large batteries and 4 large bodies of cavalry had passed, and to our great distress, we found that Evan[7] had gone off with them. It was a great shock. I thought if there was one who would be faithful, it would be Evan, but there are few who can withstand the temptation to be free. They do not look forward to the hardships and difficulties of a free Negroes life. Great numbers have gone today. . . . It is only young men and boys who they entice off. It is particularly annoying to us now to lose Evan. . . . Our kitchen cabinet consists now of Sarah and Betty. It is true there is very little work to do, for we can scarcely get anything to cook. Even if the market people were not afraid to come to town, they have nothing to bring. Everything is stolen. We live principally on bacon, beans, rice, dried apples, and often dry bread. The railroad is not allowed to bring anything but army stores and groceries are as scarce and high as ever.

Laura Lee—March 24, 1862. Ah! This day of horrors. We were roused this morning by Mrs. Barton rushing into our room in a frantic state, telling us to wake up and nerve ourselves to hear the worst. That Jackson had been defeated[8] and driven back with fearful loss, that the town was filled with wounded and dying, the jail and churches with prisoners, and that she was just sending out for Logan Marshall's dead body. We were so stunned at first that we could not remember how excitable Mrs. Barton is, and how apt to believe the worst. We dressed as rapidly as possible and went down the street to try and find what was the real truth. The streets were thronged with men and women on the same errand as ourselves. Everyone was denied permission to the prisoners, and we could hear nothing of Bob or our friends. We were told that the prisoners were suffering for food, and hurried home to prepare it. Before we reached here we met some one who told us that Bob and Ronnie Barton & Willie Barton & Robert Bell were among the prisoners. It seems strange to say that the relief was inexpressible. It was so horrible to feel that our precious boy might be dead or horribly wounded. We found that Ronnie had written a note to relieve our fears. . . . At 12 [noon] we went to the jail, carrying clothes for the boys. They allowed them to come into the passage to see us. Bob and all of them were bright and cheerful, and insisted that we should not be uneasy, that they were very well treated and would do well. . . . At 2 p.m. the prisoners were marched by, 160 in all. . . . After Bob was really gone, we had time to realize the horrors which surrounded us. Wagons and ambulances filled with the wounded had been coming in all night and all the morning, and were still coming without cessation. The ladies were hurrying to the hospitals to feed the poor creatures, friends and enemies alike. . . . Logan Marshall is not dead at all, but safe with our army. I am perfectly exhausted, and feel half dead, but still have life enough to be intensely thankful it is no more.

Laura Lee—March 26, 1862. Mr. Noonan died this morning. Two other of our men have died and many of the Yankees. There are many more who must die. They are very patient and uncomplaining & grateful for kindness. Before they came here, we thought nothing would induce us to enter the hospitals, but we never thought of having our own troops and their wounded and dying together. We could not stay away. We are having ones now moved into the wing, and are getting them fixed comfortable. We have furnished them with fresh clothing. Many persons have applied for permission to take the wounded & nurse at home and the Provost has permitted that it may be done. . . . Our loss on Sunday is now definitely ascertained to be 160 prisoners, 85 killed, 86 wounded, here, 56 slightly wounded, who went up the Valley with our army.

Laura Lee—March 28, 1862. Our boys are in Baltimore & are receiving the greatest kindness and attention from the people. They are supplied with clothes and everything they can need. If they are only allowed to remain in Baltimore, we shall be so thankful. . . . That villain of villains—Seward,[9] is to be here tonight and is to stay at Mr. Seivers, that [is what] people get for allowing the Yankees to get a foothold in their houses. They agreed to take Gen. Banks [10] and staff as a protection to their property. And last Sunday evening, when Gen. Shields had his arm broken in the fight, Gen. Banks took him to Mr. Seivers and established him there and since then Banks has gone up the Valley and Shields is in command here. And there are swarms of soldiers in and around the house all the time. This evening Shields sent to Mr. Seivers to order a room to be prepared for Mr. Seward. I would not submit to such degradation if I were to be beggared by refusing.

Laura Lee—March 31, 1862. Yesterday, Sunday, was a terrible day of rain and sleet, but we twice went to the Union and in the afternoon to the

York hospital to look for some of Col. Baylor's friends. . . . Heard the surgeons say the army has been more demoralized by the kindness which have
been shown the wounded than by the battle. . . . They say they are sorry
they allowed the women to enter the hospitals. Many die daily. The wounds
from minie balls are horrible and almost always fatal. No news from our
army. When are these horrors to end?

Laura Lee—April 1, 1862. Gen. Shields and staff have gone to join
their main body at Strasburg. All the wounded except four who cannot be
moved have been taken to private houses, and today Miss Dix[11] arrived
with a corps of nurses from Washington, so we are relieved from the necessity of attending at the hospitals. It is a blessed release. We have to do most
of the housework, as Betty is our only dependence in that line. What is to
become of us if things continue as they are for any length of time, we do
not know. . . . Many people are worse off than us. The farmers are ruined,
everything destroyed except the land.

Laura Lee—April 3, 1862. Nothing new today. Nothing but these
dreadful creatures and the sense of depression and desolation which we must
have while we are in their power. I think I had better stop writing as the
prospect of our cause seems to be fading away. They are furnishing their
hospitals with everything to make them permanent, and say they are to be
the hospitals for Bank's division during the summer. How <u>can</u> we live
through it?

Laura Lee—April 5, 1862. Nothing today but these odious wagons
passing and re-passing all the time. Many troops have come here, some to
stay, some to go up to Woodstock where their main body is. Capt. Haskell
of Wheeling called to see Miss Lee. We declined to see him. He sent back
word that he had a message for us from Mr. Deshand. But as he did not
leave the message, we conclude he is indignant at being refused admittance.
I hope he is, the traitor!

Julia Chase—April 6, 1862. A second petition has been sent off, but
we fear it will meet with no better success than the first. Mr. Baum
preached in the Lutheran Church today, under rather embarrassing circumstances I think, so many of the congregation entertaining very bitter feeling
towards him. A gentleman of our town, one of his former members,
refused to give his hand, saying he was his enemy and therefore could not
shake hands. We have no news from father and have no idea of his whereabouts. Oh, if he was only at home with us.

Laura Lee—April 9, 1862. Another day of snow and sleet. Prayer
meeting at Mr. Barton's. Heard that Richmond had been illuminated on

Monday night, in honor of our victories. What could they have been! Oh, for a sight of some Southern troops. I have not the nerve to read these dreadful Northern papers. I glance at a few lines, and then throw down the paper in despair.

Julia Chase—April 10, 1862. Mrs. Gibbons sent a letter to Gen. Shields today in regard to the prisoners, and requested an answer. I send one off this morning. Hope really something may be done for our friends.

Laura Lee—April 11, 1862. There is another report that Mr. Buxton is a Yankee spy, and that he has been arrested by Gen. Jackson's orders. We feel anxious as he had many letters, but still we hope that he delivered them safely as he did the first set he took from here. . . . Our letters sent through the Provost Marshall are opened to be read. He says no one is to dare to send letters in any other way. But of course that is mere folly. Hundreds are sent and received every day.

Julia Chase—April 13, 1862. Was at church today, the first time since father left us—thought great deal of him while there. In company of Mrs. Hunt & Mr. Tuttle . . . visited the hospital at the academy. Found the sick doing pretty well . . . from there, the ladies expressed a wish to visit Mr. Mason's house. The 7th Va. Regiment are camped on the grounds, and the entire fence has been pulled down, and the ice house was being demolished while we were there. Heard this morning that father with the older prisoners had been sent to Richmond, but this afternoon learn that all are in Harrisonburg.

Julia Chase—April 14, 1862. The secessionists seem in great glee today. We hear that the Merrimac,[12] their iron clad vessel, has captured 3 of the Federal vessels, tho' the paper does not speak of them being very important. It is rumored also that an engagement has been going on at Yorktown[13] & Gen. McClellan has been repulsed 3 times, but Mr. Hunt, who came from Woodstock this morning, says they had no such reports at camp. . . . Some of our women in this part of the town are clapping their hands, saying that Jackson is on the road & will soon be here. Should such be the case a general stampede would take place here. God forbid our enemies should have power over us but may we be defended from them. Mr. Jas. Burgess called this morning, said he saw father the week before in Harrisonburg, he was well as usual, comfortably provided for, and doing very well; but tho' we are very glad to hear that, yet it does not bring him back.

Laura Lee—April 14, 1862. We have just heard the splendid news of our victory in the South (Pittsburg Landing).[14] Col. Baylor . . . writes in the most excited and delightful spirits. They say they will soon be back to release us. Oh, joyful sound! The sauciness of the servants is very hard to bear. The streets are filled with runaways who have flocked to the town from all around the country and who lounge about in everybody's way. The Yankees walking and talking with them in the most familiar way.

Laura Lee—April 15, 1862. A dismal rainy day. Nothing stirring about here. Heard more particulars of the battle in Tenn. Heard it is not so great a victory as we heard yesterday. At least we seem to have lost on the second day much that we gained the first.

Julia Chase—April 16, 1862. We have sad news today, if true, that father has after all been carried to Richmond and is now in that city. How I would like to have in my power those bad men who have done this wicked thing. God grant the news not be true; all hope is gone should F. be there.

Laura Lee—April 16, 1862. These dreadful Northern papers! According to them we are almost subjugated. Dr. Robert Baldwin was arrested today on the charge of refusing to prescribe for the Federal soldiers. He told the Provost he had refused and would continue to as so till the end. They kept him all the afternoon and then released him. . . . Dr. McGuire's house was searched today. It was reported that the Dr. had returned here, and they searched everywhere for him, but of course without success. I know where a wounded Confederate is <u>and the Yankees do not</u>. He is nearly well now and will try to slip him through the lines.

Laura Lee—April 17, 1862. The Germans are in camp, near town, but are allowed to come in but a few at a time. . . . The Commander here has issued a proclamation posted through town that if the citizens, male & female, did not treat the soldiers with more courtesy, he would not be answerable for the consequences. There is a whisper tonight of a great victory at Yorktown. The Lord grant it may be so, but I fear to believe it yet. Only thing makes us think it may be so, there have been no Baltimore papers today, and they are often suppressed when there is bad news for the soldiers to hear. . . . Hundreds of Negroes are in town, quartered in supply houses and warehouses, until they can be sent off. They have threatened to take Mr. Sheppard's house for the same purpose, turning the family out.

Julia Chase—April 20, 1862. A rainy Easter, quite cool. We heard last evening from Mr. Sherer's son, who left Harrisonburg 4 days ago, that the Union prisoners were at Harrisonburg, and father was rather low-spirited. If it were possible for me to go there I should certainly do it. The news in regard to the prisoners seems very conflicting, we hardly know what to believe. Gen. Banks' army has advanced to New Market, but we hear that

Jackson is beyond Staunton, the report of Freeman [Frémont] being there with a large force must be of course without any foundation. Would that the Federal forces only were there. . . . Received a letter from Gen. Shields in regard to father. He writes that he had consulted with Gen. Banks for immediate action, nothing should be omitted on their part for his release. God grant him success and return father and all others to their families.

Julia Chase—April 22, 1862. Have made all my arrangements & expect to start to Jackson's army at noon today. Later, disappointment, disappointment, the gentleman from whom we had engaged the horse and buggy is not willing for us to take it up the Valley, and will not even consent to be paid for them should we be so unfortunate to be captured. Geo. M. is trying to purchase a horse but that seems an impossibility. I had hoped I might have been fortunate enough to have started on my journey, but everything seems against me, but perhaps all may be for the best. . . . I can hardly feel reconciled to give up the attempt to see father. Had the prisoners fallen into any other hands than Jackson's there would be hope of their release, but he is a stubborn chap and we heard that he or his men say that some of the secessionists here ought to be sent to Fort Warren for remaining here while the Federal army is in possession of Winchester. God have mercy on them all. . . . Oh, what a day of reckoning will there be to many in our midst, for all the actions of the last few months.

Laura Lee—April 22, 1862. Last night we heard that our army had gone back to Harrisonburg, the Yankees following. Though the report is that our army has crossed the mountains to go to Gordonsville, evacuating the Valley. If this is true, we may as well resign ourselves to our fate. I think I shall stop writing.

Julia Chase—April 23, 1862. Was introduced to the Lieutenant Governor of Western Virginia and other gentlemen this morning by Capt. Haskell of Wheeling, and was told by one of them that they were going to send a special messenger to Gen. Banks today, asking that the secessionists here might be arrested & held as hostages until our prisoners return. Some such measures, had they been adopted by Gen. Banks when the army first came, would I think have induced Jackson to have given up those he carried off. The Secesh. are bolder every day, and they talk as saucy as you please. One of the gentlemen told me that the ladies in Charlestown conduct themselves shamefully, actually stop, when they pass the Provost Guard & spit in their faces. When those who consider themselves ladies conduct themselves in that manner all pretensions to ladylike actions are forever gone & . . . will long be remembered for their disgraceful conduct and ridiculous behavior.

Laura Lee—April 23, 1862. Feel encouraged to go on writing by what we have heard this evening! We certainly have had a victory at Yorktown, that Richmond had again been illuminated, that Jackson had not left the Valley, but was still this side of Staunton, and that only two regiments had been sent across the mountains to protect against flank movement. And best but not least, that the double-dyed villain Dave Strother,[15] the "Porte Crayon" had been captured near our camp with all his drawings, shoots [photographs], instruments, etc. There is no one whose capture could give such universal satisfaction throughout this part of the country.

Julia Chase—April 24, 1862. Glorious news! Glorious news! Father with all the prisoners from Frederick County have been at last released by Gen. Jackson, and arrived safely this afternoon, a very joyful and unexpected surprise. But oh, to look at these men and hear father tell of the treatment they received, of being days without fire, and hardships experienced, treated more like they were galley slaves instead of citizens of a Christian community, is rather more than flesh can bear, and we feel that there is a God above who will not and cannot permit such things to pass unnoticed. How the Southern Confederacy can ever expect their cause to prosper with such wicked actions is impossible. Father looked, when he got out of the stage, as if he had been sick for months, and says another tramp like the last few days would have killed the greater part of the prisoners. We fear the result these outrageous doings will have upon his health. God in mercy grant he may not sink under them.

Laura Lee—April 24, 1862. The Yankees are more outrageous and insulting than ever. A Doctor who had known Dr. Baldwin in Philadelphia called at his house yesterday to renew the acquaintance. When he found that the Dr. received his visit very coolly at the front door, and had no intention of asking him in, he flew into a violent rage and talked in the most abusive and threatening manner. Some of the soldiers beat and kicked Harry McDonald,[16] a boy 14 years of age before his mother's face because when they asked him if he was a "secesh," he answered "yes" and she had no redress except to abuse them, which she did with her whole heart and soul.

Julia Chase—April 28, 1862. Forts Jackson and Phillip[17] have surrendered and New Orleans is ours. This will be quite a blow to the South. Great deal of property and cotton has been destroyed. Gen. Jackson has left the Valley and has gone over the mountains, it is to be hoped never to return again unless as a prisoner, tho' the secessionists say & believe he will soon be back again.

Laura Lee—April 29, 1862. Sad and terrible news tonight. The papers are full of the taking of New Orleans, describing the circumstances in such a way, that it is improbable to doubt it. . . . We can hear nothing certain of our army. A large packet of letters which came from them on Sunday was captured and burnt by the Provost Marshall.

Julia Chase—May 1, 1862. The Confederate army are evacuating Corinth,[18] it is supposed retreating towards Memphis. The next thing we will probably hear they have retreated to the Gulf of Mexico.

Laura Lee—May 1, 1862. A cold rainy day, dark and dreary. The report about Yorktown proves to be false. That about New Orleans is confirmed. It is wonderful and terrible. Reports about Jackson's army contradictory. . . . All are anxious and distressed. We are almost in a state of starvation here. No fresh meat for a fortnight and almost impossible to get eggs and butter, and what we do get at fabulous prices. We can scarcely get wood enough to cook with. The country people as well as the merchants are charging an immense discount on Virginia money. Lincoln said he would make us suffer for the war, it is one of the true things the wretch has said on the subject. But if we can only hear that our cause is prospering our troubles a hundred times increase would be perfectly borne.

Julia Chase—May 3, 1862. We have the news of the capture of Baton Rouge[19] & the Confederate arsenal. . . . We have great many calling in to see father. His cough still continues and [he] is quite weak. Mr. Gibbons is sick in bed. Fort Macon, at Beaufort, N.C., has surrendered to Gen. Burnside. . . . Gen. Jackson is said to have fallen back to Gordonsville, and has been reinforced largely. Dispatch from Washington this afternoon that Yorktown has been evacuated by the Southern army & McClellan is following them up.

Laura Lee—May 5, 1862. Yesterday we were horrified to find a dispatch had come from Washington saying that Yorktown was taken. Today we find that it was one of Gen. Johnston's strategic retreats. The Yankees yesterday were very jubilant over it. . . . It is very current among us that our army is coming in our current direction. I will not venture to believe it for fear of disappointment. Indeed it is true, for this whole region is perfectly desolated. Nine-tenths of the servants are gone, at least as great a portion of the horses stolen, & all of the cattle, sheep etc.[20]

Julia Chase—May 7, 1862. Hear fighting took place yesterday between the Confederates & Franklin's Division at Williamsburg. 2 redoubts have been taken. . . . We soon hope to hear of Richmond being in possession of our troops, with the Stars & Stripes proudly floating over the city. . . . We are having quite pleasant warm weather now, the streets very dusty. . . . Father's health is improving, his appetite increasing & color better.

Laura Lee—May 9, 1862. The [*Baltimore*] *Sun* of today contained McClellan's report of a fight which he claimed to be a great victory for himself, but which private accounts represent to be perfectly the reverse. Passengers from Baltimore report that he is withdrawing a large part of his force from the peninsula and concentrating them at Fredericksburg, to march on Richmond in that direction. . . . It is one of our greatest troubles that we have only Northern accounts and are kept in a state of constant alarm and anxiety. We can hear nothing certain of affairs up the Valley, but the soldiers here report that all of Banks' army will be back here tomorrow. . . . Mrs. Barnes has just returned from Washington, and says that the people there are in high spirits and say that the rebellion is <u>almost</u> crushed out.

Julia Chase—May 11, 1862. Good news again. Norfolk is taken. The Merrimac, however, sunk by the Confederates & large amount of property destroyed.[21] What the feelings of the South can be is more than I can imagine. Where they expect to go, God only knows. May they see the error & willingly lay down their arms.

Laura Lee—May 11, 1862. Nothing but alarming and distressing reports that Norfolk is given up, the Merrimac destroyed & tonight Richmond is in the hands of our enemies. We are told that it is all a part of the program for concentrating our armies, but it is very dreadful to hear the Yankees shouting and exulting over their victories. There is a new Commandant here, a Col. from Maine and his regiment. The new provost is odious and audacious. He went to Mr. Clarke's today and told Sue that the house should certainly be taken for a hospital. That he was not placed here to protect rebel women and children.

Laura Lee—May 14, 1862. A constant rain today. No news in the papers from Richmond, but strong hints of foreign recognition and intervention. We received a short letter from Bob. He is well and speaks of receiving the kindest care and attention from many friends. I sent him a supply of clothes today by some prisoners who left here for Fort Delaware. . . . The Maine regiment that is occupying the town now, is much the most obnoxious of any of the Yankees we have had. The Lieut. Col. is a perfect brute and insults and browbeats every one who is unfortunate enough to be brought into contact with him. No one can leave the town without a pass, and a pass can only be obtained by the person's swearing that he or she is a loyal subject of the U.S. and will continue to remain so. Of course, no decent person will take such an oath, and much annoyance and discomfort is caused.

Julia Chase—May 16, 1862. The secessionists seem to be in great glee the last few days. Jackson, they say, will be very shortly in Winchester, and it may be so. We hear so much that is disparaging to Gen. Banks, we fear that Gen. Jackson will be here sure enough. . . . Some of the Unionists feel rather uneasy & will until Jackson's army is dispersed & routed out of this portion of Va. The Secesh ladies have all adopted Sun bonnets, some with long curtains called Jeff Davis bonnets. They put on many airs & frowns and sneers, and try in every way to put down the Union people. They are certainly very bold & impudent.

Laura Lee—May 16, 1862. Our sovereign master Provost says that these secesh women shall not wear calico sunbonnets on the street, as they are intended as a disrespect to the soldiers. Neither shall they wear white-muslin aprons with bodies!!! Calico and gingham sunbonnets are worn by all the ladies here and styled secession bonnets. They were adopted for their cheapness and for their defense against staring soldiers, but they resent it and say they are intended as an insult by imitating them. We do not care how we dress while they are here!

Julia Chase—May 18, 1862. Sick all day, feel as if I was taking the fever. Some of the Maine boys have been brought in sick to the Court House Hospital. Shall go down as soon as I feel well enough. Taking quinine since 5 P.M.

Julia Chase—May 19, 1862. Feel much better today, the morning quite cool & little cloudy, so we propose going to Shawnee Springs. Was at the springs, partook of the cool water, and proceeded as far as Miss Mary Hollingsworth's, went in and rested ourselves and viewed the country, water, & c. On our return home, when near Mrs. Barton's house, saw a guard at Mrs. Col. Tuley's door. Some of the secession young ladies in the neighborhood were talking quite loud and Miss Burrell remarked "the idea of a whole regiment coming to arrest a poor sick man." We saw some 7 or 8 soldiers at the house. It seems that a son of Mrs. T's, Jackson by name, was there and has been arrested as a spy & taken to the Provost Marshall. If anything proven he will be taken to jail.

Laura Lee—May 19, 1862. We had quite an exciting time this morning in this neighborhood, caused by a large number of soldiers surrounding

Mrs. Tuley's house, to arrest her son W. Jackson. It is true he has been confined to his bed three months with typhoid fever, but because he had been
in the army last summer, they have placed a guard in his room. The wonder is that they had not discovered him before. It is evident that they are
leaving this place. All day long wagons have been passing heavily loaded
with baggage and stores. The sutlers have all been ordered off and the huck-
sters and pie shops are closed. . . . Wrote to Bob today. Probably the last letters we shall be able to send in that direction.

   Julia Chase—May 23, 1862. There seems to be considerable excitement on the street since supper. We have news that the Federal cavalry on
the Front Royal Road have been routed & a portion cut to pieces & Ashby
is within 6 miles of town. God have mercy on us. Col. Beall of the 10th
Maine, says he will make a stand here but his men number so few he can't
do much. I have told father about it, and as we hear the cars are about or
will start at midnight he has gone up to see; he thinks that he would be the
first one taken, should Col. Ashby dash in town with his men, as he had
charge of the P. [Post] office. We shall sit up tonight.

   12 Midnight.—Mr. & Mrs. Cooper have come up to see what is the
matter. Mr. D. has been flying about to gather any information. We feel
very uneasy and wonder if Gen. Banks is going to retreat. His force is so
small in comparison to Gen. Jackson's that he will be cut to pieces, should
he make a fight. Why don't reinforcements come on. Father has come in.
The cars will probably not go off tonight. Some of the sutlers are moving
their goods & we are very fearful that we shall see terrible sights before
long. God have mercy on us. ½ 1 o'clock. All have retired but myself. Shall
sit up until daylight.

   Laura Lee—May 23, 1862. There is a great commotion in town
tonight. Wagons and horsemen passing constantly, and from the talking of
the soldiers as they pass, we infer that something very exciting has occurred.

   Julia Chase—May 24, 1862. The Union people are rather uneasy &
the secessionists are in their glory that Jackson's army is coming back. We
can't understand why it is the Secretary of War don't allow Banks to be
reinforced. We have no confidence, however, in Gen. B. and only wish a
more able Gen. had been put in command of the forces in the Valley. Have
been down to Mary's. George M. don't know what to do. Father heard the
commissary say, he had orders to have everything packed & sent off by
noon. Father will leave about that time. We are fearful that Gen. B. will
make a poor [fight] out of it, tho' we hear that reinforcements will be sent
on, but we would like to see them here.

1 o'clock. F[ather], Geo. M. & Abe have left for Martinsburg, but we hope to see them back before long. A few troops arrived this afternoon but not enough to answer the purpose. There is a good deal of commotion about town, every one is on the move. The Secesh are perfectly delighted and the children out in great numbers. The ladies have kept themselves very secluded until within about a week or two past, since they knew Jackson would be here. There is communication every day between the Army of Jackson & the citizens in town. Our troops and officers are not half strict enough. Some 50 letters & papers have been taken from Miss Belle Boyd, who has been making herself very officious since the Federal troops have been here. She acts as a spy I imagine. I should think there must be some complicity between a Federal officer & the Army, as he was in the company with this Miss Boyd. He ought with her to have been arrested. Another company have arrived in the cars tonight, but the wagons & soldiers are passing by in great numbers. How I wish we were all out of this place.

Laura Lee—May 24, 1862. Sure enough, we were roused this morning by Mrs. Barton's coming over to tell us that Ewell had attacked some regiments at Front Royal yesterday, destroying them and capturing $200,000 worth of stores which were packed in cars ready for transportation. All night fugitives were coming in, men and horses, both nearly dead with fatigue. The Provost announced that if any women dared to show exultation, she would be shot. About ten o'clock this morning we were made aware by the trains of wagons coming in that Banks' whole army was coming down here. The wagons passed through the town on the Martinsburg Road. Many dead and wounded have been brought in, the latter placed in hospitals here, which makes us fear that Banks intends to make a stand here. We hear that our friends are around us in every direction. . . . There is the greatest panic among the servants, the Yankees have assured them that Jackson is murdering all the Negroes as he advances, even cutting the throats of the babies in their cradles. An officer told Emily[22] that such is the case. Numbers of them believe it, and are terrified beyond belief. They have spread abroad a report too, that they intend to burn the town. Crowds have gone from here today, not only runaways, but many who have always been free. There has been a great stampede too among the Union men, who have been very saucy and insulting since their friends have been here. The wagons have been passing through town all day. . . . This afternoon, late, we were coming home from a news gathering walk, and we saw Banks and his staff ride in. His army is just outside of the town, and there is every prospect that another battle will be fought tomorrow on the same ground where the one was fought just two months ago. We have had a most exciting and fatiguing day, and I feel worn out. We go to bed with the prospect of being roused at daylight by the sound of a battle.

Julia Chase—May 25, 1862. Sabbath afternoon. Oh, what an awful day this has been. God grant I may never see the like again. The Confederate Army are in full possession of Winchester again. Gen. Banks has retreated in great disorder—why did he not act differently. Me thinks the women could have managed affairs better. The past night has been one of such great excitement. We all retired to our beds, but there has been so much moving of cavalry & wagons, & c. that there has not been much sleep. We fear that Banks thought more of getting the Negroes off than to save the poor soldiers, or save the country. We only hope he may be discharged immediately and a more efficient officer be put in command. About 6 o'clock this morn. the stampede commenced, of troops & individuals who had been boarding in town, or keeping stores. Nearly every darkie in town has left, completely crazy. The town has been fired in several places, & all the warehouses nearly are destroyed. We hear the magazine was to be fired, and we dreaded the consequence, being so near. All left the house except Mother, Mrs. New and self. We sent for Mary and the children, tho' before the fire broke out or ever we suspected such a thing. Mother and Mary came up, but on beholding the fire, and fearing our house may burn also, M. [Mother] goes back home again. Mother will not leave the house until the last moment, so I return after going with Mary. We started off with the 3 children & our most valuable things, silver, money, & c. Fortunately, Mr. Wolfe overtakes us & goes with us. In passing by some of the federal troops, when I asked them were they retreating, the answer given was, No, but get in the first house you can, as the Confederates are close upon us. We aimed for Mary's house, but all was locked and we knew not where to go. Darted up the alley at the hotel, but find on coming to Braddock St. the Confederates running pell mell with their horrid yells (which we shall never forget). The guns and shell firing in every direction. Oh, the horror of these moments. We rushed into the alley again and come down to Mr. Williams house, when again we behold the troops wild with excitement, firing in every direction up and down the street. We expected every moment to be shot down, but kind Providence was around us. We reached Mr. Knott's house, which was unfortunately a strong Secesh, tho' they cheerfully opened the doors when they found who was coming. We staid there but a few moments & after the soldiers had passed by started for Mr. Wolfe's and then did not know what had become of Mother. Mr. Wolfe, after returning from the fire, offered to go after her. She came, but was not willing to stay, so I accompanied her home & found the danger over in regard to the powder. While I was absent, some soldiers were brought in by Milton Baker's son & searched the house for Mr. Dennison. Oh, how frightened Mother was. Then, again, old Richcreek sent others here saying our house was full of Yankees. Fortunately, one of the soldiers acted the gentleman, and was not willing to go all over the house, but I insisted upon his going, Mr. Gibbons, who was there, accompanying me. Tho' there was no one here, the idea of having your house searched was awful. We are afraid to hear a step, or the bell ring, & keep the door & gate fastened all the time & shall while the army is here. What a glorious capture Jackson has had, taken some 1100 prisoners, captured a great many valuable stores. The troops are completely starved out, and we have had more calls for something to eat this afternoon than all the time the Federal army was here. The citizens in town have become demons almost. Lewis Brent has we learn shot down one or two of the Federal soldiers & one was shot at Mr. Reed's door, it is thought by Richcreek. Should the Federal army ever return again, they will be dealt with severely. Mrs. New left us this morn. To go up the hill out of danger, but she was exposed to the whole fight in this part of the town, and it is a miracle she was not shot down in cold blood. She passed through scenes she will never again wish to see. She came across a gentleman from Connecticut, who took charge of her & they were even obliged to lie close to the ground to escape being shot, tho' they fared much better than could even be expected. She has lost all her clothing & 80 dollars in money. We have offered her a home as long as we have a shelter, until we hear from her husband. The gentleman who came across her has thought it best to deliver himself up & will probably be taken prisoner.

Julia Chase—May 26, 1862. A cavalry Captain was on the porch this morning, who had been in all probability sent by the Sherrards, as the Breeden boy was with him, & inquired after Father. We gave him no satisfaction, but we have no fears for him now, as we trust & hope he is safe. He asked, good many questions of Mrs. New about Mr. & Mrs. Dennison. Said he, Mr. D. had been taken & the people wanted to hang him—which will be done, if it is true that he has been captured, the citizens being so much enraged about him. Would he had never stepped in town or made his appearance at this house. Every person will of course think we countenance his doings, which was far from the truth, as we think him a strong Aboli-tionist & he has not conducted himself with much prudence. The prison-ers at the Depot, we learn are half starved. The fact is the whole of Jackson's Army are completely starved out & can't of course supply the prisoners very bountifully. The sick & wounded at the Courthouse have been taken prisoners together with the female nurses. . . . We do really hope this army will not be permitted to remain long here & think Gen. Banks ought to be strung up. This war will never cease until the Abolitionists are made away with. Mrs. New and self were at the courthouse, took some oranges to the sick. We expect every moment to see some one coming to arrest her, so we think it advisable for her to seclude herself a little. Some who are living near us are determined to do all they can towards it.

Julia Chase—May 27, 1862. Mr. Joe Meredith (who came up with his family on Sat., not knowing the condition of things here) was arrested today. . . . He was taken to the Provost Marshall's office, who fortunately is a gentleman, said he must hear the charges brought against him, before arresting him & sent for these 2 very officious young ladies. Their charges were that they had heard Mr. Meredith was a Union man, strong Aboli-tionist & Black Republican, but would not give their author, so Mr. M. has been released on his parole. It seems to me the women & girls have been perfectly demonical, and I think if an example should be made of a few of them, it would have a salutary effect. . . . God have mercy upon this town. The people are terribly enraged against the Yankees, as they are all called, and trying in every possible way to taunt them. We are hoping and expect-ing any moment to hear of the Union army coming to our rescue.

Laura Lee—May 27–31, 1862. My last line was written last Saturday night, May 24th, and now Tuesday afternoon, May 27, I can scarcely com-pose my thoughts sufficiently to attempt a collected account of what has occurred in the integral. Thanks be to the Lord, we are free!!!!!!!!!!!!!!!!! On Sunday morning at daylight we were waked by the sound of cannonading. There had been a constant commotion all night of cavalry and small parties of infantry passing up and down the street, but nothing to indicate that the enemy intended leaving here. The firing indicated that the battle was much nearer the town than that fought on the 21st of March. We did not yet get up at once, but laid still listening to the guns and feeling very wretched about our friends. About half past 5 the reports were so incessant and so near, we dressed and went downstairs. . . . We went out on the front pave-ment, most of the people were at their front doors looking and listening anxiously. Even as soon as this, the wounded were being carried by to the hospital. Some in ambulances, some on crossed guns, and some assisted by other soldiers. It was horrible. Some were dreadfully mangled with blood streaming, but we could only pity and pray for them. This convinced us how near the fight must be. Some of those who carried the wounded looked very savage and sullen, but did not trouble us. . . . Later we ran out on the porch and found two large batteries passing by—briskly but not hastily. A very pleasant looking youth as he rode by called out, "Ladies they are too many for us, are you glad we are going?" We called out eagerly, "yes," but were afraid to say more, as some of the men looked very scary, through they said nothing. The youth bowed and said, "Thank You, Good-bye." I suppose he thanked us for not wishing them all killed, but indeed I felt no anger or hatred, but only delight that they were gone. . . . Our army was pouring through the town in pursuit on every street, Gen. Jackson heading them, when he found the enemy were running so fast, he ordered all on in the pursuit, even the artillery were allowed to unhitch their horses and mount and follow. By this time a rumor reached us that Marshall Barton was killed. David (his brother) rode up and said all were safe but Marshall who he told his mother was badly wounded, that they must send to him at once, but he whispered to Luke that he was already dead. He told us too that Bob McKim was killed. We were greatly shocked and saddened to hear of both. . . . Sometime after breakfast Marshall's body was brought home. He was shot near Mr. Hollingworth's and was carried there. He lived half an hour, and Mrs. H. said his last words were "Mother, Mother." Mrs. Barton[23] has borne it nobly. She says she gave her sons to her country, and she must not murmur at the sacrifice. She stayed downstairs all day Sunday, feeding the starving soldiers as they came back from the pursuit. The same was the case all over the town. I suppose there was scarcely a house in the place, where there were not scores fed. . . . All afternoon our friends were calling in or stopping at the door, and many were the joyous greetings. . . . That Sunday was a wonderful day, one to be remembered to the end of our lives. Not only for the joy and delight of seeing our friends back again, but for our wonderful deliverance from so many dangers. . . . On Wednesday the whole army marched on towards the borders, some to Martinsburg, some to Harper's Ferry, where the enemy was crossing. Already it was beginning to be rumored that our men might have to leave this end of the Valley to avoid being cut off. . . . On Friday a new excitement began. Shields appeared with quite a large force at Front Royal, and Fremont with another considerable force was moving across to Strasburg to unite with him, and thus entrap Jackson and prevent his retreat. It was a very nice plan, but old Jackson has been too quick for him. They have been sending off the captured stores all the week. . . . The whole army was ordered back through here to Strasburg, and by 9 o'clock began to pass through, and now, Saturday night, we are left quite alone. All the sick and wounded who it was possible to move were taken, all the prisoners (3000) were marched off with the army, and the numbers of fugitive citizens who returned so joyfully to their homes but a few days ago, have had to fly again. We felt almost despairing at being left again in the hands of our enemies. . . . We can scarcely bear to think that our little gleam of liberty is ended. The soldiers all seemed so sorry and grieved to leave us.

Julia Chase—May 31, 1862. The army, thanks to Providence, evacuates this place once more, and may they never come back only as prisoners, but we fear Jackson will give them the slip again, & should he escape, they deserve it. His force is thought to be about 30,000 men. It is not to be wondered that Gen. Banks was obliged to retreat. Some 51 cannon have passed by and the streets are completely crowded with troops, wagons, & c., the greater part of the day they have been passing by. . . . Gen. Jackson has had so much on his hands that the Union people have not been molested, tho' they have been in fear all the time.

Julia Chase—June 1, 1862. An awful stillness reigns. The town is as quiet as if every body were dead. We hear that the Federal army is within 2 miles of town. Cannonading has been going on all the morning and this will be another awful Sabbath. There are now so many rumors, we know not what to believe. Some say that Gen. Shields has been whipped, others that Shields whipped Jackson. We are very impatient to see the Federal Army marching into town. Some Confederate cavalry who have passed by say there is no army within sight of Martinsburg, so we know not what to believe.

Julia Chase—June 3, 1862. No Union troops yet, and tho' we hear of a large force coming in today, we shan't believe it until we see them. . . . We have had dreadful thunder storms of rain & hail since Sunday, with a prospect of more. The streams & rivers will be so swollen that troops can't move very far at this rate. . . . Great many of the Union people left town, fearing they might get into Jackson's clutches, but Gen. J. has learned we think a nice lesson from the Federal Army in regard to the treatment of prisoners, and in all probability, will hereafter treat them with more leniency. They have done better than we dared to expect.

Laura Lee—June 3, 1862. We were roused at 5 o'clock this morning by the clatter of cavalry and running to the window saw a company of Yankees dash past to the Union [Hotel] where we heard great cheering for a few moments, and then they rode down the Martinsburg Road. We cannot learn anything for certain. One report is that they were separated from their main body and are escaping through here. We are in a most singular condition. There are, evidently, a good many more Yankees in town today than have been before since our army left, but still no body of troops has marched in, & those here take no authority, and do not interfere in any way. There are reports this morning that Jackson has defeated Fremont & is ready for Shields, and also that we have had a victory at Richmond, but I never believe of victories until I see them. Just now at 1 o'clock, another company of cavalry dashed through town, down the Berryville Road without stopping an instant. What can it mean?

Julia Chase—June 4, 1862. Rain. Rain. With no prospect of clear weather we will probably have a flood. The citizens in town have been stealing at a great rate, sugar, cheese, crackers, & many other things the sutlers & commissary left behind, the women being worse than the men. . . . The Federal cavalry have at last made their appearance and the infantry will soon be here. The storm has probably impeded their progress. Gen. Seigel[24] commands the troops here, tho' an inferior officer to Gen. Banks, for which I am sorry. Gen. B. is an Abolitionist and ought not to be allowed to remain in the army. . . . Tho' there are so many Generals in the Valley now, yet we have our fears in regard to Gen. Jackson, and think he may again give them the slip. If such should be the case, he ought to make his escape, tho' we shall expect to see him again in our town. The troops will not show much mercy to our town now, as the conduct exhibited by the citizens the Sunday of the retreat will call down vengeance & retaliation upon them. A number of the stores have been searched, and all houses that have goods or arms will be searched also.

Laura Lee—June 4, 1862. There is no longer any doubt as to our position. The Yanks have got us again. They came in today with a large force, some of them say 10,000, others say 40,000, but of course the last is false. They are behaving outrageously, breaking into houses, stealing, threatening people with vengeance for the late defeat. We do not yet know who is in command. While we were at tea, some soldiers came to demand the flag which had been waved on Saturday from this porch. One of them was very abusive, cursed us, and said he <u>would</u> have it and coming back in the morning to search for it. The flag is secured, of course.

Julia Chase—June 5, 1862. More rain falling. The bridge at Harper's Ferry has been washed away, so that we don't know when Father and other Union citizens will get back. Mr. Gibbons returned yesterday with the Army, said our folks were in Frederick City, tho' he did not see them. A dispatch was received this afternoon from Gen. McClellan, that Gen. Pope is, with 40,000 men, in full pursuit after Beauregard, who has been driven out of Corinth. A heavy battle came off on Sat. & Sunday near Richmond between the 2 armies. Loss on both sides very heavy, some 3000 killed and wounded on the Federal side. We can easily account for the way in which Gen. Jackson was reinforced. Gen. McDowell, who was at Fredericksburg with a large force to prevent the Confederate army from coming up into the Valley, has been found to be a traitor and is in prison in Washington City. A rope around his neck would be the best thing for all traitors, and should be made an example of by the U.S. Government. By the time the war ends, it will be found who are loyal and those who are not. So many of our citizens have passed themselves off as unionists to the Federal army who held possession of our town some 2 months since, that they distrust every one and they are almost unwilling to believe that any Union persons are here. We hear very often now, that this town ought to be burned & we are almost afraid it will. A gentleman told me, that if the Maine Regiment had entered Winchester first this week, but few, if any, houses would have escaped the flames. We are feeling the horrors of war now in good earnest, and God only knows what further scenes are to be witnessed by us. May his protecting Arm be around and over us. . . . Rev. Norval Wilson was arrested on suspicion of having fired upon the Federal soldiers when retreating from town but was released. Dr. Conrad has also been arrested, on what charges I can't say. Mr. Hibbard also is in jail, for having great many goods belonging to the soldiers in his home.

Laura Lee—June 5, 1862. We are having a dreadful time. Before we were up this morning, parties of soldiers were demanding breakfast, cursing and swearing at us for refusing to give it. Directly after breakfast a large party came, ringing for us at the bell, and when Mary refused to open the door, the officer. . . said he would come through the window then, which he did, followed by several men, and more went in at the gate & came in through the kitchen. The officer said they had come to search for our flag, but would not molest us. He conducted the search himself & was as little disagreeable as the circumstances admitted. They found a gun Ron McKim had left here, an old sword, and a Yankee knapsack, <u>but no flag</u>. The officer gave us a certificate that the house had been properly searched, and it has proved very useful. For twice since large parties have come to search, and when we showed the certificate, they have desisted. The last party was headed by the deputy Provost Marshall himself.

Julia Chase—June 7, 1862. A number of Union citizens returned this afternoon. They have heard awful reports, that not a house was left standing in our town. We hear that some 3 or 400 Confederates have been found and taken prisoners, being concealed in houses.

Laura Lee—June 7, 1862. We have had a comparatively quiet day. We have a guard who sits out front during the day and sleeps in the vestibule at night, and his presence protects us from the rudeness of passing Yankees. . . . We hear that their army is suffering very much already from their scarce supply of provisions. The bridges are destroyed, and the river is so high that there is great difficulty in getting anything over. We fear this may be a source of great trouble to us, as they will not hesitate to seize food wherever found. The insolence of the soldiers is almost beyond belief, and their officers encourage the men in it by their own example. They say they intend to take the starch out of the "secesh" here.

Julia Chase—June 8, 1862. Father, with Geo. & Abe M. returned this afternoon. They had been as far as Baltimore. Our friends are returning a few at a time. . . . The colored people are returning, many of them also— great many families are without help at all.

Julia Chase—June 10, 1862. Gen. Shield's advance guard of 2000 were attacked by Gen. Jackson and repulsed with heavy loss, some 8 guns were captured. Jackson seems to have quite a number of feathers in his cap. He has done pretty well the last 3 or 4 weeks. It is to be hoped he will find his match before long.

Laura Lee—June 11, 1862. The Baltimore papers give accounts of 2 serious skirmishes on last Friday,[25] near Harrisonburg, in both of which they admit we were successful. There was fighting at Front Royal day before yesterday (Monday) but we cannot learn the result. These wretches are behaving more outrageous than can be imagined. They have taken possession of the lower part of Mr. Logan's handsome house today, by Gen. Hatch's orders. They went to Dr. McGuire's and said they must have part of that house, and have ordered Susan Jones to leave her father's house in an hour, as it is to be taken for a hospital. . . . Nearly all of the troops left here today, whether for Strasburg or Front Royal we cannot find out. There is some decided movement on foot, all the prisoners, and sick and wounded who can be moved are being carried off tomorrow. Fremont's reports admit a decided defeat last Monday.

Laura Lee—June 14, 1862. Gen. Jackson sent in a flag of truce yesterday with a communication to Gen. Banks, that if there was any more house burning or destruction of private property in Winchester, he would retaliate and take vengeance in some way which we do not know of. But the thrust was evidently effective, as an order was read at dress parade in the evening, that death would be the penalty to any soldier that set fire to a building.

Laura Lee—June 18, 1862. Still sick and suffering greatly. Large numbers of wounded (800 it is said) have been brought here today. They are reported to be Fremont's wounded last Sunday. . . . The report we have heard for ten days past, but hoped was untrue, of Turner Ashby's death, is confirmed today by extracts from Richmond papers. Another noble sacrifice to the cause of freedom! On the Saturday when the army passed through town, he dashed by here at the head of his regiment, and waved his hat when we cheered him. We little thought it was for the last time. He had seemed to bear a charmed life, had escaped so many dangers, that we hoped he would be spared to see the end.

Julia Chase—June 21, 1862. Chaplain Dennison and lady left this morning for Washington City. We hope he may never return again. He was very unpopular indeed & he is a strong abolitionist, and is too officious for his own good. . . . Our town is quiet, the troops having encamped out of town. We hear that Fremont has fallen back to Strasburg. The secessionists are quite jubilant today & expect Jackson in tomorrow. We hope they may be disappointed.

Laura Lee—June 21, 1862. I feel much better today, must get out of this bed to be ready for what is to come. Fremont has fallen back to Newtown and Jackson pursuing him. There is something very stirring on hand. All the soldiers who were here, except a small guard, were sent up the Valley this morning. Large numbers of sick and wounded have been sent off during the day, and the ambulances are constantly passing full. . . . They evidently intend to fight, from their sending men up from here today, and as tomorrow is Sunday, the fight day, it is scarcely possible that it will pass without a battle.

Julia Chase—June 23, 1862. Everything quiet, tho' there has been some considerable fighting in the neighborhood of Richmond & near Charleston. Our troops, the Southern papers say, at that point were repulsed with considerable loss. We feel very anxious in regard to the result at Richmond.

Laura Lee—June 23, 1862. Contrary to our anticipation, yesterday passed quietly. . . . Fremont has certainly fallen back to Middletown today, but where Jackson is, nobody knows. The Yankees say he has a hole in the mountains, where he goes sometimes with his troops, and that he has gone there now.

Julia Chase—June 27, 1862. Some 33 Confederate prisoners passed through, en route for the North. There has been heavy fighting before Richmond,[26] and thousands of lives will be sacrificed before the fall of that city. The Confederates will fight desperately, as so much depends upon the result of this struggle.

Laura Lee—June 28, 1862. Our boys are released on parole from Fort Delaware, and are to go to stay at Mr. Shields at Ceciltown, Md. for the present. We are, of course, delighted. Mrs. Barton is going there on Monday. Jane is so delicate that Mr. S. has not been able to tell her of Marshall's death. . . . We have had a decided victory at Charleston. The Yankees say there has been fighting at Richmond both yesterday and today, but we can hear nothing of the result.

Julia Chase—June 30, 1862. The papers of today speak of McClellan changing his base, or strategy, we are unable to say. The Confederates cut off communication between the White House & Washington, so there is no certainty about the result of the fight. Many think that Gen. Mc. has been outgeneraled, out-flanked & whipped. The Secessionists are very sanguine and think they will certainly hold Richmond, which we hope and pray they may be compelled to give up. God grant us final success at that point. It was rumored this morning that Richmond was ours, but the news was too joyful to be credited. May the approaching 4th be heralded by the glad tidings that the glorious old flag is waving over that proud city.

Laura Lee—July 3, 1862. Details in the Baltimore papers proving that McClellan has been defeated with terrible loss, but claiming at the same time that our loss has been equally heavy, and that the position they have now, is exactly what they wished and intended to have taken, before we attacked them. They say it is only another and more certain route to Richmond. It has only been a <u>rout from</u> Richmond so far. Our knowledge of facts at this time is gained only by inference, from what the papers <u>do</u> say, and <u>do not</u> say. They described the fighting as perfectly terrific, having continued for four days & say that the battles we have had before bear no comparison with it.

Laura Lee—July 4, 1862. We have continued <u>Northern</u> accounts of the terrific fighting near Richmond. It lasted four days, with dreadful loss, they say, on both sides. . . . They announce on the authority of the

Richmond Dispatch, that Jackson is killed. That is too great a calamity to be believed while there is any doubt of it remaining.

Laura Lee—July 9, 1862. They are moving everything from here in the greatest haste. Banks' army has gone from Middletown across to Front Royal, on the way to Washington. The soldiers here say that Jackson is very near here, but that he shall never retake this town, as they intend to destroy it before they leave it. They have been planting more guns on the heights this evening, and they are pointed on the town. There is great excitement and expectations on all hands of something startling.

Laura Lee—July 14, 1862. There has been no movement among the enemy here today, except that they have been firing over the town at intervals. They say to get their guns at the right range. More servants going off. I suppose at least three-fourths of the servants in this region are gone.

Julia Chase—July 16, 1862. Our town is again in a state of excitement, at least among the union people. We have rumors that the Confederates are coming to Winchester in a large force and fears are apprehended for the safety of the town, that it will in all probability be shelled by our troops to prevent Jackson from getting here. Some are wishing he may remain at or near Richmond, others that he may make his appearance in our midst. A number of the Unionists have left town and all the sutlers have gone. We think, however, that this was only a secessionist story gotten up for the occasion. Our hope in Gen. McClellan has nearly all gone. We really thought and expected Richmond would have been ours ere this. The prospect now is that owing to the defeat of McClellan, the Southern Confederacy will be recognized by England & France. God forbid that such should be the case. May Gen. Pope be found a general able to cope with the Southerners and a glorious victory be ours before long. Our Armies seem to be at a stand still; nothing going forward but all backward. If a change does not come soon & for the better our cause is almost hopeless.

Laura Lee—July 16, 1862. We were soon aroused early this morning by a great excitement, the pickets were driven in last night, and in the night the Provost Marshall withdrew most of the soldiers from the town to the fortifications. . . . We suppose it is only scouting parties of cavalry who are near here. The long line of hills at the west of the town is bristling with guns pointed on us. We hope it is only a menace, but there is no telling what madness may inspire them.

Laura Lee—July 17, 1862. The guards have all been withdrawn, and the town virtually abandoned, and our men consider it as such and themselves rescued, and they are going off. Some got off safely today, and more are going tonight. . . . A company of our cavalry came into the town tonight to try to frighten off the Yankees, by making them think there is a large force. We will be on the alert all night.

Julia Chase—July 18, 1862. There has been a raid in Kentucky, and Murfreesboro (Tenn.) has been retaken by the Southerners. 2 of our Generals captured in bed—they deserve it; to be found napping when danger so near. If our officers are not more vigilant and energetic, and that very soon, it would be useless to continue on this war. The Unionists are very much discouraged & mortified, to think that with all the means Government has at her command our glorious cause should progress so slowly, or rather not progress at all. The President has called out 300,000 more troops. It would have been better to have called out a million at the outset, and probability the cry would not so often be repeated, outnumbered by a superior force, as has been the complaint with our armies. May we have heard the last of such things, and we only hope and pray a new impulse may be given to our entire army, officers and men. . . . No news from the army, all remains quiet, only we hear of more rebel raids on different towns in the S. west, also in Indiana.

Laura Lee—July 21, 1862. Today is the anniversary of the Battle of Manassas, one of the first of many, many sad anniversaries which this generation will carry on their minds and hearts through life. The Yankees were a little premature in their announcement of having taken Gordonsville. The papers say today that it is still held by Gen. Ewell.[27] No special news from abroad. Our Yanks keep very closely at the fortifications. But few stay in the town.

Laura Lee—July 22, 1862. All quiet here. Morgan's[28] raid in Kentucky has caused the greatest excitement and panic among the Yankees. Pope's orders make us feel rather uneasy.

Julia Chase—July 25, 1862. Was at Church today—a good many empty seats. The Secesh do not entertain very kind feeling to the Unionists; let them disguise the facts as they may—actions speak louder than words.

Laura Lee—July 25, 1862. An order was received here yesterday from Pope,[29] that no supplies of any kind were to be permitted to enter the city of Winchester for the use of the citizens, and consequently, all the freight which came up on the cars yesterday was returned to Baltimore today. Also an order came that every man in Winchester who refuses to take an oath of allegiance will be sent beyond the lines. We cannot believe that this last tyrannical order will be carried out, but the Provost Marshall is coming back into town today, it is said, to apply the test.

Julia Chase—July 26, 1862. 3 Confederate soldiers were captured & brought to town today, bushwackers it is thought. One or two confederates were found hidden in some of our citizens houses this week and sent to Harper's Ferry. The secessionists do not relish the order Gen. Pope has issued, that all who are not willing to take the oath of allegiance to the United States, must pass beyond our lines, southward. We hear that there are 500 who will not take it, but then if they leave they think it will be but for a short time, and Jackson & army will be back again and all will be right with them and they can return. Should the Southern army . . . come back again it would be folly to issue such orders. The Union army are also to subsist off the secessionists while passing through the country, making the South pay for the war.

Julia Chase—July 27, 1862. Gen. Piatt,[30] the commander of our forces here, has been superceded by Gen. Kelly. The change seems to give general satisfaction. There seems to be changes completely going on among our officers. Would there be a master spirit arises and make a complete change in our entire army, at least push things forward more rapidly. New troops arrived today, also on Sat. infantry & cavalry. Our cavalry so far have not done well. These troops are represented by Vermont & Illinois. . . . May they perform their duty faithfully and become brave soldiers. The country people have so much difficulty in procuring passes in and out of town, that there is nothing brought into our place. They have been kept busy here for a day or two and then permitted to pass out, and no distinction is made between loyal & disloyal men. . . . We hear every day of persons going in and out of town with plenty of letters concealed about their persons. A stop ought to be put to it. The weather has been quite warm for two or three days past.

Laura Lee—July 30, 1862. Our new Gen. instead of being more lenient is even more rigorous than Piatt. He has arrested many persons today, and says the oath is to be administered to everybody tomorrow. The gentlemen are quaking. We are fully repaid for our exertions in the garden by having an abundance of fine vegetables.

Laura Lee—August 2, 1862. It is wonderful what a spirit is shown by all the classes, even down to the lowest and poorest. The men are unanimous in refusing [to take the oath], even though the alternative is banishment. . . . Some marketing has been allowed to come into town today. We are having some trees in the garden cut down for firewood. Some people have been without wood for days, but all make light of these privations. It is wonderful how much less of everything is necessary for comfort than we used to think. William is looked for typhoid fever. He came home several days ago to be nursed. There is a great deal of it, one or more cases in every house on the street. Anna Brown is extremely ill with it.

Laura Lee—August 6, 1862. The rules with regard to letters are very rigid. They say all persons detected in carrying letters will be regarded as spies and traitors, and treated accordingly, but their threats are disregarded, and the market people, who are always escorted around by a guard, constantly have letters about them. This afternoon we were arranging with a women to bring in letters from Newtown while her guard stood at a little distance, looking on, but of course, not hearing. The country people are eager to do anything which will outwit the Yankees. We heard that there were four hundred letters at Newtown for people here.

Laura Lee—August 7, 1862. Nothing heard today of any interest. The Union Hotel is given up to the runaways, it has been closed as a hospital for some weeks. . . . The papers today are jubilant over McClellan's having resumed the offensive, and recaptured Malvern Hill. The conscription in the North is causing great excitement.

Julia Chase—August 8, 1862. We have had very warm weather the past week, the hottest of the season. It must be very trying on the troops. The President has called for 300,000 more men by drafting, independent of the same number of volunteers. Large bounties are being offered to those who are now enlisting. We expect nothing more than brother George will have to go in the army now. Mr. Peyton Clark lost a child yesterday and Mr. Oliver Brown's oldest daughter died night before last. There is a good deal of sickness in town & county. . . . Gen. McClellan has resumed the offensive, after 5 weeks of inactivity. God grant he . . . may be successful for the future. The guerillas are committing great depredations in the S. West and are every day or so robbing the Union men in our midst. Mr. Jas. Ginn had 8 horses stolen, a night or two ago. A number of our townsmen, who are in Jackson's army, are near Winchester. Why our pickets are not sent out to capture them is more than I can say.

Laura Lee—August 9, 1862. We went to Anna Brown's funeral this morning, a most sad and touching service. We begin to feel anxious and a little depressed. We hear nothing from Jackson, he is <u>lost</u> again. It is true that always means that some great move is on hand. The most malignant spirit pervades the Lincoln government. If their plans could be carried out, they would be quite willing to exterminate us. The paper this evening says the rejoicings of yesterday were premature. McClellan has retired again from Malvern Hill. It was merely a reconnaissance, they say.

Julia Chase—August 15, 1862. We are having delightful weather now, after the excessively warm days of last week. A battle took place at Culpeper between Jackson & the advance of Pope's army commanded by Gen. Banks. . . . Rumors are that Burnside has come up in his rear, to cut off his retreat, but we only fear he, Jackson, will slip them as usual.

Laura Lee—August 18, 1862. McClellan is landing his forces at Aquia Creek, to cooperate with Pope, and there must be another battle before many days. I am so constantly anxious and wretched, now that Bob is back in the army. . . . Those wretches at the fortifications amuse themselves by occasionally sending a shell over the town, to remind us of our helplessness, and their power over us. The shells go shrieking through the air, alarming the timid people. This morning they fired one of the largest guns just at daylight, arousing the whole town. The shell struck a house, almost in the center of town, and it was a merciful Providence which preserved the lives of the family.

Laura Lee—August 20, 1862. Still this weary, dreary monotony, "Bluecoats" rambling through the streets, and occasionally the relief guard passing, and small parties of cavalry going out to relieve the pickets. The street blockade is not removed, and as the soldiers rob the gardens all the time, unless there is a change, we may come to the starving point. . . . The Yankees claim that they still hold Baton Rouge, and that the battle there was a great victory for them. We have no means of learning the truth. We can send letters out very easily, but it is very difficult to get them into town. Jackson has been <u>lost</u> for some days.

Laura Lee—August 22, 1862. The oath of allegiance business is stirring again, and to our great indignation, most of the prominent men here have agreed to compromise by taking a parole, which will exempt them from the regular oath, but still a great concession to the Yankees. It is shameful!!

Julia Chase—August 24, 1862. The guerillas have commenced their depredations on the railroad. This afternoon they fired into the cars, captured all aboard, but released the men with the exception of 3 soldiers, wounded rather badly one of the express men & took the safe, $3000 in it belonging to the government. . . . 2 companies of cavalry started out in pursuit of them, but the bushwhackers had the advantage by several hours.

Julia Chase—August 25, 1862. Several arrests have . . . been made. Mr. Philip Williams, ——— Nott, Klipstein, & Sherer were taken out to camp. Peyton Clark was arrested last week but was paroled not to leave his house.

Laura Lee—August 25, 1862. Yesterday we heard reports of fighting since Thursday in Orange and Rappahannock, that Pope was retreating and Jackson pursuing. The attack on the cars was a successful thing. A large amount of specie . . . was captured. . . . Today there is great excitement at the reports of the advance of our army, is said to be at Warrenton, Paris, Front Royal, Middleburg. One thing is certain, all day parties of soldiers, fugitives from the direction of Pope's army, have been straggling into town, and this evening heavy cannonading has been heard here. The Baltimore papers admit only "skirmishing" last week. This miserable compromise oath has been administered today to ten or twelve of our most prominent but most timid citizens. Many of the men bravely refuse to give any oath, parole, or promise to the Yankees.

Julia Chase—August 27, 1862. Great many arrests have been made today, in fact, all of the secessionists, and are considered as prisoners paroled.

Laura Lee—August 27, 1862. The papers say that we have captured some of their wagons, and among them the baggage of Gen. Pope and staff, which had all the papers belonging to that division among it. They say this is a great disaster, as by this means, we have become possessed of all their plans, orders and arrangements for the campaign.

Julia Chase—August 28, 1862. Last night a number had orders to be ready to leave this morning for Washington or Fort Delaware. . . . Mr. Nott, Kenton Heist and others, together with 10 bushwhackers, or as some say Ashby's cavalry, sent to Fort Delaware. These are sad and serious times, to see one after another arrested by one army & then another. . . . Gen. White,[31] who is in command here, seems to be ferreting out all things detrimental to the government. We lack, however, cavalry. It is hoped that a fresh supply may be sent on. Should Jackson ever return, the Unionists would I imagine suffer greatly. Mrs. Mary Campbell, who last received a pass to go to her husband who is up the Valley, was not permitted to proceed farther than Newtown. The Confederates sent her back. We are at a loss to know what it means. Whether Jackson has any force up the Valley, as it is thought by some . . . is difficult to say.

Laura Lee—August 28, 1862. The Yankees brought in prisoners this morning. It is so foolish of our men to be lingering around the town, just to show that they are not afraid, for they accomplish nothing else, except to be captured. The Union men are so vile as to betray where they are, and lead parties of cavalry to catch them. So many of the men refused yesterday to take the parole, that the Gen. has withdrawn it from those who took it, and waits further instruction from Washington.

Julia Chase—August 29, 1862. Quite a number of bushwhackers were brought in this morning and sent off, also a number of our townsmen, Mr. Casper Nott among the number. Charlie Crum expected to have been sent to Washington at the same time, but through the influence of Mr. Ginn he was released and we were all extremely glad. I had made up my mind to write to President Lincoln, had he been sent off, but a kind Providence interposed & he was restored to his family. They all feel under great obligation to Mr. G. and it is right they should. These are very sad & serious times indeed. When will the end come. There has been another raid by the rebels at Manassas, a few days after the one at Catlett's Station. Our officers seem very negligent and do not learn wisdom by experience. It is very warm and dusty, everything suffering for want of rain.

Laura Lee—August 30, 1862. The papers this evening contain his [Pope's] official report, in which he says that he has fallen back, but that he has whipped the rebels by doing so. The letters in the papers give a very different account from Pope. They say it had been a most daring and brilliant move on the part of the rebels, and that they have destroyed half a million dollars worth of stores at the Junction. Not withstanding the blockade, we have received one carpet and 200lbs. of sugar and some other things from Baltimore.

Julia Chase—September 1, 1862. We feel extremely anxious about the cars, as it is now after 9 o'clock and they have not arrived. . . . We are disappointed in not getting the mail and papers. As the 2 armies have been fighting for a week past, the result is anxiously looked for. Secessionists today say that Jackson is whipping the Federal army at a great rate & that McClellan has been killed. We place no confidence in the rumor. God grant that it may not prove true. . . . A great many of our Union people living in the country have had their horses stolen by . . . guerillas and they are obliged to flee here for safety. How long this state of things shall last, no one can say. There was a meeting appointed by Gen. White last week, for the citizens in town to consult in regard to these bushwhackers. . . . Mr. Robert Y. Conrad[32] proposed putting arms in the hands of the people & driving them out. Putting arms into the hands of secessionists the General did not approve of at all.

Laura Lee—September 1, 1862. There is the most intense anxiety and excitement here now. . . . Last night a letter came in which was written on the battlefield on Friday night. It said that there had been an awful battle, and that the Yankees had lost 10,000. This morning it is said here, that they have moved everything from Alexandria and burnt the long bridge. . . . The cars from Harper's Ferry did not come up last night, but no reason is given.

Laura Lee—*September 2, 1862.* ½ past 12 o'clock. Joy Joy!! These Yankees are going tonight! They are evacuating the place in the greatest haste. We are too excited to go to bed tonight, expecting our men in at any moment after 2 o'clock. . . . They have sent a large number of sick from the camp off towards Martinsburg in terror and confusion. The Union men have all gone. Cavalrymen are passing all the time. I was sitting quietly writing, when . . . I saw a bright light down at the depot. . .and found that the depot building, and all the warehouses which had not been burnt before were on fire. . . . The buildings were filled with commissary stores, and burned furiously. We had watched it for an hour when we saw a flash, and instantly a most awful explosion took place. It was perfectly terrific. We heard the shattered glass falling in all directions. . . . Some Yankees who say they have stayed to be captured, told Mrs. Baldwin that our men were not to come in until 10 o'clock tomorrow. I hope they will be in by daylight. I wish they were here now! Our only source of regret is that Jackson is not our deliverer, but he is at Manassas. We are able to enjoy their coming this time without any alloy. There will be no fighting, no killed and wounded to be unhappy about, and we heard this evening that Bob has gone to North Carolina, to see Lewis. So they are both safe. Thank God!

Julia Chase—*September 3, 1862.* What exciting times we have passed through since yesterday. Winchester again is in possession of the Confederates. Our troops evacuated last night and the Southern cavalry were ready to hop in. Marching orders were given out by Gen. White and his army left . . . before midnight. Many of the Union people left with them. . . . About 1 o'clock the depot was discovered to be on fire, and it, together with the warehouses were destroyed, burning all commissary & other stores, which was impossible to remove. About a half-hour after the fire broke out, the whole town was terribly alarmed by an explosion of the magazine at the fort, every one thought Winchester was to be shelled. . . . The people here are perfectly happy with joy, and have been going in crowds to the fort are coming in, with carts and wagons loaded. These people who hate and despise the Yankees so, are laying hold upon all left behind, and some will have more than they have had for a long time.

Julia Chase—*September 4, 1862.* We hear that the Federal cavalry are at Stevenson's [Depot] and have driven in the pickets. We look anxiously for them to make their appearance soon. The secession refugees, who have been coming home in great numbers, seem somewhat alarmed, and some are leaving town.

Laura Lee—September 4, 1862. I have scarcely the heart to write the accounts of our deliverance, for though the happiness of being free is very great, yet it is sadly marked by the accounts which our people bring of our losses in the late battles. Our dear friend Col. Baylor was killed last Saturday, while rallying and leading on a regiment (33rd Va.) which had faltered. He was one of our bravest and best officers, and so gracious and warm hearted, that we were all warmly attached to him. . . . Contrary to our expectations yesterday morning, no large body of our troops came into the town, only a few at a time of the cavalry, who went on out to the fortifications to take possession. It seems now that we have no troops in the neighborhood except a small cavalry force. . . . Col. Frank is Provost Marshall here, with only a battalion of men who came in last night. Everybody is in the greatest glee and excitement. The refugees are hastening home again, and the whole population of the counties around seems to be entered into the town, and all is bustle and congratulations. The accounts of our successes are wonderful.

Julia Chase—September 6, 1862. The secessionists say that Jackson has come over to Leesburg and crossed the river into Maryland. . . . If it is true that the Southern army have taken Maryland, it may have the desired effect of arousing every man & women in the whole country, and this is what we need—a united and determined people—who shall stand by their Country in their Country's hour of need. . . . Salt sold yesterday at $30. a sack. Bacon we hear at 30cts per lb. We are living in Dixie now. The Provost Marshall has issued orders that all persons in town & country who have taken things from the fort must send them back or their houses will be searched. I take it there will be but few secessionist houses who have not things stored away, tho' they hurried and got them out of town as fast as possible.

Laura Lee—September 6, 1862. A large body of cavalry came in today, just from Leesburg. They report that our army is certainly in Maryland, but what is the point of destination is unknown. This is a terrible state of suspense. We may hear at any moment of some great victory or reverse. . . . Many of the runaway servants have returned to their houses, some voluntarily, others brought in by the soldiers.

Julia Chase—September 7, 1862. Our town was thrown in considerable excitement this morning. Some of the cavalry dashed into town with the news that the Yankees were only a mile & half from town. Everybody was alarmed & for a little while there was a panic among the secesh and some of the soldiers. Several of the Confederates were wounded and a number of horses. . . . We hear of the Federals being at Charlestown & the places near. It would be quite a treat to see them dashing into town driving these troops out.

Julia Chase—September 8, 1862. There seems to be conflicting rumors in regard to the Southern army being in Maryland. A lady in passing this morning remarked that Burnside & his army of 10,000 had been taken & she hoped they all would be hung as high as Haman. Mr. Ginn was arrested this morning, but paroled to make his appearance at the Provost Marshall's office tomorrow morning. Mr. Joseph Jackson's house was searched for firearms & for the sutler who had been boarding there. A sword was held over his head and he was called upon to deliver up this person, or that he, Mr. J., would be taken & carried off further than when he was a prisoner. . . . These soldiers are going to the colored persons houses & taking all the clothing that they have in the way of shirts or blankets the Federals have given them. Also going to the poor people & taking what flour or other things that had been given to them by our troops. So much for Virginia chivalry. None but the Yankees do such horrid things.

Laura Lee—September 8, 1862. Yesterday was quite an exciting day. Just as everyone was ready for lunch, an alarm was raised that the Yankees were coming, and were only a mile from the town. There was a great panic. The soldiers were rushing through the streets to get their horses and arms, the wagons were loaded with their baggage and hurried off, the returned citizens all ran, and for half an hour the greatest confusion prevailed. By that time it was ascertained to be a false alarm, and the enemy, who had come for a few miles this side of Bunker Hill, had gone back. . . . I cannot realize that Col. Baylor is really dead. It is such a grief to us all. In all our hopes and anticipations of victory and freedom, he was always prominent. We sent letters today to Mrs. Baylor, who is in Staunton.

Laura Lee—September 9, 1862. Orders have come here today to prepare for the reception of 3000 sick and wounded from Loudon and Fairfax. They are coming in all the time, and the wagon trains are all on the way here, and an immense artillery force. This is to be the point of communication with the army in Maryland. We can hear no certain accounts from there, but all the reports are that we are prospering.

Laura Lee—September 12, 1862. Considerable excitement all day. Small bodies of troops coming in all the time. Gen. Hays has taken command,

and is organizing and arranging things rapidly. The fortifications are manned, and the troops arranged to catch the Yankees from Harper's Ferry, in case they should retreat. . . . They are surrounded, and Gen. Jackson marches down on them from Martinsburg tomorrow.

Julia Chase—September 15, 1862. Our town is filled with soldiers, and every house almost contains them. The pavements & cellar doors are lined with them—great many are disabled troops not fit for much duty. . . . We heard that Winchester was to be winter quarters for the army. God forbid it. Yesterday it was rumored that the two armies were fighting at Harper's Ferry. Gen. White has been reinforced . . . but probably not to the numbers that will be brought against him by the opposing [Generals] Hill and Longstreet. The result of this battle we leave in God's hands. No news has been received yet so far as we can learn. Heard on Saturday last that Father was in Baltimore. We trust he is well. Should this army remain all winter, there will be no hope of seeing him. Thursday has been appointed by Jeff Davis as a day of Thanksgiving and Prayer to God for the victories given to the Southern armies. We hope that the people of the North and West will be much engaged in prayer for our glorious cause, but if it is the will of God that the Independence of the South shall be recognized & our Country dissolved, we must submit, feeling that He knows best what will be for his glory & the good of this entire people.

Julia Chase—September 16, 1862. We feel ready to give up in despair, and have lost all hope that our armies will ever accomplish anything. Our country seems to be disgraced forever, and must prove a laughing stock & beyond to the whole world. Gen. White and his force have been obliged to surrender. It is said that 12,000 were under his command. . . . We expect to see Gen. White & his entire force paraded through our streets. It is said that some of our women intend visiting Gen. W., asking him for a pass. What won't these Secesh do. . . . When will our people, or leaders be prepared to save us from these mortifying surrenders & defeats. God grant this may be the last. Later— Thanks, thanks, good news seems to be on the wing. Our army has gained a victory in Maryland, we understand, taken 15,000 prisoners, cut a portion of the Southern army pretty badly, they losing one of their noted generals. It is almost too good to be true, but the news came from secession sources, therefore we can't doubt it. The Unionists have been very much down for months. It has seemed as if the Federal army had fallen asleep. . . . May the future show us that they have at last cast off their stupor and awakened to the fact that there is a mighty work before them before this rebellion shall have been crushed.

Laura Lee—September 16, 1862. The surrender at H. Ferry is a fixed fact. Gen. White and 11,000 men gave themselves up unconditionally. There was a severe fight in Md. Yesterday between Longstreet and McClellan, the particulars of which we cannot yet get, but the Yankees were driven back. Crowds of stragglers still coming in. Things are getting a little better arranged. We never knew what excitement and confusion meant until now.

Julia Chase—September 17, 1862. Wednesday. It is said that fighting is still going on between the two armies at Boonsboro. Our troops have been whipped again and 3000 prisoners taken. We are in hopes that this can't be true. 300,000 more men have been called out by the President, makes some 900,000 within the past 3 months. Would they had been called out a year ago, rather than our country should be destroyed.

Laura Lee—September 18, 1862. The reports tonight from the fighting of yesterday are terrible. It is said to be the bloodiest battle of the war.[33] Our loss is reported to be 20,000, but this <u>must</u> be a great exaggeration. Orders have reached here to prepare for 3,000 wounded, but where they are to be put no one knows for everyplace seems full now. Burnside was with McClellan with a force of 100,000. We must have the particulars tomorrow.

Laura Lee—September 19, 1862. After many wild and alarming rumors, we have just gathered from Mr. Boteler something like the truth. He is just from the army, and says that the battle of Wednesday was really the bloodiest of the whole war. McClellan with 100,000 made the attack. After fighting desperately the whole day, he withdrew a short distance, and sent to ask leave to bury his dead. . . . During the day and last night Gen. Lee crossed with his whole force, bringing everything, his sick and wounded, & stores, to this side of the Potomac. The reason is that the equinoctial rains are coming on, which always raise the river and there was danger of his being cut off from his supplies.

Julia Chase—September 20, 1862. Saturday. Oh, the horrors! horrors of war. Every heart must groan to think of the suffering that is in our midst. Some 3000 wounded soldiers are being brought in today, and our town is thronged with them. Poor fellows. I should suppose the secession ladies, who have urged and in many instances driven their friends into the army, must sicken when they see the distress brought upon these men. We have very cheering news in regard to our army, they routed & drove across the river the Southern army. God help them, and may we soon be delivered from this unholy war.

Laura Lee—September 20, 1862. This has been the most awful day we have ever spent. Directly after breakfast the lines of ambulances began to come in, and since then it has been an incessant stream. <u>3000</u> wounded men have been brought in. Everyplace is crowded with them, and it is perfectly heart-rending to know how much suffering and misery there is around us. We have been hard at work getting our cooking room established.

Laura Lee—September 28, 1862. Yesterday our army withdrew from the border, to within 12 to 6 miles of this place. . . . We have only withdrawn for the present to be near our supplies, though it is universally believed that it is only a question of days or weeks when our army will fall back from this place, as it will be impossible to winter here.

Julia Chase—September 29, 1862. Our town is all alive with troops, wagons, & c. Such confusion and noise. Several thousand soldiers passed through en route to the army, which lies between Winchester & Bunker Hill. A great number of these men are barefoot and unarmed. Suppose, however, sufficient quantity of arms has been captured from the Federals, to supply them. If these men are not shod before cold weather sets in, it will be rather hard for them. We thought yesterday that the army was falling back, southward & that the Federal army would probably be here before the close of the week, but it does not look like it, but that they are to remain here for some time. Mr. Denny is asking $1.00 per yd for calico. Says if he can't get that price here he can at Staunton. Sugar, if there is any in town, sells at $1.25. Should the army remain here this winter, we shall certainly suffer very much, indeed there will be some danger of a famine.

Laura Lee—September 30, 1862. No movement in the army. The town is crammed with soldiers of every description. There are 24 hospitals, besides hundreds of patients in private houses. The cooking room is in vigorous operation.

CHAPTER THREE

October 1862–March 1863

"We live in a constant state of hopes and fears"

The late fall and winter of 1862–63 was a discouraging time in the lives of Julia and Laura. Both women were disheartened over the constant state of uncertainty and fear they had to endure as the forces of each side occupied and retired from Winchester repeatedly during the latter months of 1862. Adding to Julia's dismay were the constantly changing circumstances that prohibited her father from returning home. Then at the start of 1863, Laura and her fellow Confederate supporters had to endure an extended Federal occupation of the city and the harsh conditions that ensued.

Although no major fighting occurred in the Valley, both women intently followed the actions of their military forces. The Federal defeat at the battle of Fredericksburg in December led Julia to question the bravery of the Federal army and she wondered if there was a military leader in the North who would be able to lead them to victory. Following the occupation of Winchester by the Federals in December, Laura readily acknowledged that everyone was more depressed than ever before. Food shortages added to the bleak picture and ensured that the winter would be a hard one.

Julia Chase—October 1, 1862. We are having exceedingly warm weather, more so than some weeks this summer, and very dry and dusty. What a busy industrious army the southern one is, always on the move. Seems to me that if the Federals were as energetic our cause would be much more prosperous. We had hoped to see the rebels retreating ere this, but the prospect is rather poor, tho' they can't remain long, as they have no forage for their horses and have brought up everything. The country is indeed barren in this portion.

Julia Chase—October 4, 1862. Oh dear! But a small portion of the artillery have moved off towards Staunton, and it is said that when the army leaves, a sufficient force will remain to guard the town. Are we to have these dirty, filthy creatures here much longer. . . . The worst of all, we hear that the Federal army is just crossing over the river into Virginia at Shepherdstown. We have been hoping against hope. The Union refugees will never be able to get back if this state of things continues much longer. Poor Father, he, I imagine, is very much discouraged at the state of affairs. Will a bright day ever come? We are paying Richmond prices for articles now. 75cts & a dollar per lb. for butter. A market man had 2 small chickens for sale, $1.00 a piece, everything else in proportion.

Laura Lee—October 4, 1862. I am so constantly occupied that I cannot find the time to write four days today. Things remain in status quo since my last entry. Our army has been resting and filling up and is said to be now in finer condition than it has ever been. Things seem to indicate a movement towards the border before long.

Laura Lee—October 5, 1862. There has been no movement in the army, and not even any rumors. I feel all the time as if we must be prepared every moment for something tremendous, either to be left to the Yankees, or an onward movement, and a terrible battle with all the painful and heart-rending scenes which follow. It is wonderful how we can keep up anything like cheerfulness with the prospects before us. Winter is almost upon us, and scarcely enough fuel to be procured for cooking. All kinds of provisions are enormously high and scarce.

Laura Lee—October 6, 1862. Tonight we hear that our army is preparing to move southwards. I have known that it must be so, but it is terrible to feel that our brief dream of freedom is to end so soon, and for so long, for any move now is for the whole winter. Sad and dreary is the prospect before us, in being separated from all our friends, and unable to hear any true accounts. I know that the enemy are preparing to make a desperate effort against us this winter, and feel appalled and almost despairing, except when I can realize that He who has helped us thus far is still all powerful to save.

Laura Lee—October 8, 1862. Working hard at the dispensary all day. Everything quiet, and no move as was expected yesterday. The hospitals are still full though many sick and wounded are sent to Staunton each day. . . . The heat and dust are unprecedented at this season of the year, and would be intolerable, except that such a season is much better for the army than a damp and rainy one would be.

Julia Chase—October 11, 1862. The warm days have passed, and fall, with its winds and frosts are upon us. Everyone is looking out for their winter supply of wood. It is selling at $10.00 a cord and it is thought before long it will be up to $15.00 or 20. Should this army remain, I don't know what will become of us. Butter still keeps up, honey the same price. Cornmeal $2.00, bacon 50cts a lb.

Laura Lee—October 14, 1862. Still rushing through life, with scarcely a moment to pause for even thought. It is a disheartening sort of existence and one which I cannot wish to last for very long. We have a house-full to provide for, and visitors until late every night. . . . We have had three days of rainy, cold weather, but it is warm and bright today. The army is still quiet. J. E. B. Stuart[1] made a raid through Md. to Chambersburg, Pa. He is said to have captured 2,000 horses, burned the depot building, and returned through Hagerstown with the loss of only one man wounded. The poor men at the hospitals are dying fast, and things are most distressing and depressing.

Julia Chase—October 18, 1862. We heard last evening that cannonading had been heard throughout the day in the vicinity of Harper's Ferry. The Confederates have been driven out of Charlestown and a part of the town destroyed. We hope for something better before long, and that the rebels may be on the retreat.

Julia Chase—October 19, 1862. Stuart's cavalry made a dash into Pennsylvania last week and captured, we hear, some Unionists, also a number of horses. . . . God be praised, the Federalists have gained a victory at Corinth,[2] for and as the southern generals admit, our officers have laid a trap for them and defeated them with a pretty heavy loss. We are so shut out from the world now, that we know little of what is going on, excepting what we hear from the Richmond papers. They sell for 15cts apiece and only half a sheet on common yellow tinged paper, as if they were years old. So much for Dixie. I think Dr. Boyd labored under a great mistake when he said that much suffering would occur should the Federal army remain. He ought to have reversed the order of things, which would have been nearer the truth. The Richmond paper speaks of the inhabitants of Norfolk being in a starving condition, that some of the women & children had gone to Elizabeth City for bread. Will the people ever come to their senses? God only knows. President Lincoln, it is said, has issued a proclamation[3] that after the 1st of January all slaves are to be freed in the disloyal states. I can't reconcile it with his Inaugural when he said that he did not intend, or that Congress had any right, to interfere with slavery in any of the states. The only light in which I can see <u>right</u> is, that the slaves are in the way of putting down the rebellion in that they are tilling the soil while their masters are in the army fighting against the U.S. Government. There have been a number of the troops taken with the small pox, and a portion of Longstreet's division have encamped some miles the other side of town on that account. It would make sad havoc should it spread. There have been a great many deaths in the hospitals, and the men have lain out of doors for days and nights unburied—are unable to procure planks to make coffins.

Laura Lee—October 19, 1862. Day after day passes without my finding time to write even a few lines. Since I last wrote we have had two rains, and the weather has become very cool. We have the greatest difficulty in getting even the smallest quantity of wood. Last Friday quite a large body of the enemy crossed the river, and . . . took possession of Charlestown. Every preparation was made to give them a warm reception. The baggage was packed, and the army moved forward, but the next day the Yankees retreated, and all is quiet again. . . . We still have numbers of visitors, and everything is very pleasant except the hospital duties which are awful.

Laura Lee—October 25, 1862. Things have been quiet during the past week. We have been very busy at the dispensary, and getting the house put into wintertime. . . . There is no certainty as to the movements of the army. It is reported that McClellan has sent a large part of his army back to Washington, and if that is the case ours will not tarry much longer here. Almost everyone seems to think that a force will be left to keep this place, but no one can possibly know what will be. All depends on the movement of the enemy.

Julia Chase—October 26, 1862. A cold rain storm today. Hard upon the soldiers, especially those without shoes or blankets. There are 51 dead soldiers lying unburied in the graveyard. Why it is they are not properly cared for I can't say.

Julia Chase—October 28, 1862. A portion of Longstreet's[4] division passed through the town today in their march to Staunton. 12 pieces of artillery. We are glad to see a move of some kind. Sugar is selling at $2.50 a lb. pins $1.00 a paper. Hard soap $1.00 a lb. Wood $12.00 a cord. What ruinous prices—but no one scarcely seems to place much value upon the money now in circulation.

Laura Lee—October 28, 1862. The enemy are said to be building pontoon bridges at three points to cross. Hunter McGuire brought Gen. Jackson to see us this morning. I was not in the room, and so missed seeing him. The paper last night reports that Galveston is taken. I am prepared to hear at intervals during the winter that Charleston, Savannah, Mobile, and Vicksburg are all in the enemy's hands. It is an awful prospect, but I know we must have a terrible struggle with the new army which Lincoln has raised.

Laura Lee—October 29, 1862. Another division of Longstreet's Corps marched through town this morning, making the third which has passed. The rest of the Corps are to follow tomorrow. Jackson remains on the border for the present, but for how long, who can tell?

Julia Chase—October 30, 1862. The troops are on the march again. 26 regiments of infantry, with 17 pieces of artillery passed through town en route to Culpeper—so says one of the soldiers. The Federals were at Pughtown yesterday, merely a dash of the cavalry I suppose. Would that we could see them coming into town. We are having charming weather now—Indian Summer. The armies ought to improve it and I hope to hear of great victories. Galveston (Texas) has been taken by the Federals, so the Richmond papers say. Mr. Aaron Griffith[5] was arrested a day or two ago. It is thought he will be dealt with pretty severely. His horses, together with one belonging to his daughter, have been taken by the rebels. They say his property will be confiscated. The secessionists will only have to suffer when the Federals have possession of Winchester. The Marylanders who joined the Southern army when it was in their state, are now guarding the town.

Julia Chase—November 2, 1862. This is the most quiet Sabbath we have had for some time. But few troops are about Winchester, tho' a portion of Jackson's army are near Berryville. The Federals were at Hog Creek, little nearer town, on Friday last. Mrs. Legg buried her youngest child yesterday. Potatoes $5.00 a bushel.

Laura Lee—November 3, 1862. We are to be left to the enemy! All of Jackson's Corps except one division, have crossed the country to join Longstreet about Culpeper. There has been fighting, how serious we cannot learn yet, but there is a rumor tonight that Gen. Longstreet is killed. Jackson's old division is camped four miles from here, and we expect tomorrow to see them march through to leave us again. It is a solemn time to me though the girls are gaily laughing and talking to a roomful of young officers.

Julia Chase—November 5, 1862. Fighting is going on between the 2 armies. It is reported that Gen. Longstreet is killed, but we don't credit it much. A portion of Stuart's cavalry have fallen back to Winchester. They have been encamped between Martinsburg & Bunker Hill. Jackson is said to be in a tight place, but it is not the first time that he has been so situated and made his escape, so we have no hopes of hearing of a surrender or defeat.

Julia Chase—November 7, 1862. The first snow of the season and quite a winter's day in appearance. Mr. Crum has lost his second daughter of Dyptheria. Miss Rebecca Neal is also dead. . . . How many of our Winchester people have died since the war commenced. Mr. Griffith was released on Monday last, which is very gratifying to his friends. We heard a night or two ago that others of the Union people were to be arrested. When these troops leave, God forbid that the Unionists should be at the mercy of these rebels.

Laura Lee—November 7, 1862. Jackson's Corps is still near us at different points, a few miles in the rear of Winchester. Gen. Stuart still occupies the town with his Maryland brigade. The indications that he will remain here are quite encouraging. . . . Today we hear that Longstreet's Corps is passing on to Richmond, to meet the demonstrations which McClellan is making against it by way of Fredericksburg.

Laura Lee—November 8, 1862. We are expecting a very serious disturbance in the course of a few days in our household. Sister Lib insists that we shall send Emily away to a safe place, and we expect that she and Sarah will both rebel at the idea. Mrs. Burwell intends to send Betty, and we shall be left with no servant but Sarah if indeed she does not insist on going with Emily.

Julia Chase—November 9, 1862. There is considerable stir in town today. Orders have been received for all to leave. The commissary is packed & many of the secessionists have left, others going, expecting before tomorrow's sun that the Yankees will be in. God grant it may be so, tho' we heard this morning that Gen. Jackson was going to make Winchester his winter quarters.

Laura Lee—November 10, 1862. We live in a constant state of hopes and fears. Yesterday there was a perfect panic. Gen. Stuart received orders to keep himself in readiness to move immediately. Necessarily most of the people interested to leave here took their belongings and went off at once. . . . We had just made arrangements for them to go the next day or two . . . when Lute . . . came running in to say that Jackson's whole army was coming back here for winter quarters. . . . True enough in half an hour Jackson's old division marched through followed by a regiment of artillery, and all their heavy baggage, and settled themselves a few miles from town on the Martinsburg Road. The other divisions have come up and camped on different roads near the town. Some think they have come to stay for the winter, others that it is only for an expedition to get commissary stores at Martinsburg. Gen. Jackson has taken a house for headquarters.

Julia Chase—November 11, 1862. Monday. Alas! Alas! While we really hoped and expected to see the Federals this morning—here comes a long train of wagons, followed by Jackson's division, who (they say) are to remain all winter. . . . There is no prospect <u>now</u> of seeing <u>any</u> of the Union refugees. Our heart sickens when we think of it, and we had hoped never to have had this army back again.

Laura Lee—November 11, 1862. They are bringing large quantities of stores to town today. The <u>Baltimore Sun</u> says that Lord Lyons has arrived with the ultimatum of England and France, and that there is immense excitement in the Northern cities. The late elections have given the democrats large majorities.

Julia Chase—November 13, 1862. Gens. Hill & Ewell division, we hear, are marching here from Strasburg. It is said they are making preparations to march into Maryland. Should such be the case, may they get a good whipping. The railroad from the Ferry to Baltimore is being destroyed by the Federals. Gen. Geary made a raid into Jefferson County and took every thing he could lay hands on in the way of sheep, cows, chickens, & c.

Julia Chase—November 15, 1862. There seems to be no prospect of this army leaving very shortly, tho' we hear there is a large force of the Federals at the Ferry. Some skirmishing has taken place at Charlestown. If it is true that the Federal army is at the Ferry, we wonder at their slowness in driving the army from here. Would that we could see them skidaddling in great haste. . . . Bleached cotton selling at $1.50 in Richmond. Potatoes are selling at the rate of $8.00 a bushel.

Laura Lee—November 15, 1862. Things remain quiet. The report of recognition has not been confirmed, but it is certain that McClellan has resigned, and that there is great disturbance and dissention in the North in consequence.

Julia Chase—November 18, 1862. Gen. McClellan has been superseded by Gen. Burnside.[6] The secessionists here say that McClellan and staff have been arrested as traitors. If such is the case, may their fate be like that of Arnold. This may account for the inactivity of the Federal army for the past three months. God forbid that all our generals should prove traitors. We feel satisfied that this rebellion will never be crushed, until all traitors are removed out of the army.

Laura Lee—November 20, 1862. The whole army is ordered off, to move tomorrow to Richmond. The Marylanders are said to be left here for the present, but of course will fall back when there is any demonstration against this place.

Julia Chase—November 21, 1862. The troops are on the march today, going up the Valley. 10 regiments of infantry, with 29 pieces of cannon, passed by this morning, tho' the greater portion passed from the other streets.

Laura Lee—November 21, 1862. The army marched off this morning. Gen. Jackson goes tomorrow. Sandy P. came last night to say good-bye, and again tonight. . . . The Marylanders are all who stay.

Julia Chase—November 22, 1862. Gen. Hill's division that had camped near Berryville came through town en route for Richmond. There are but few Marylanders left to guard the town, with Funston's Legion of 3 or 400 cavalry. We would rather see none left at all—but hope the Federals may dash in and cause a skidaddle. We don't know that any are very near, tho' we hear that they are at Martinsburg and also on the Romney Road, down to Pughtown. It is said that fighting has been going on near Strasburg, probably skirmishing only.

Julia Chase—November 23, 1862. Our town is very dull and quiet since the army left, tho' it is said that Jackson's army will be here shortly, as they have been whipped badly and are unable to get up the Valley. We doubt the correctness of this, however, but hope that the whipping part is true.

Julia Chase—November 25, 1862. It is to be hoped we shall hear no more of the thieving Yankees, after the acts of today. All the tobacco, from the citizens of our town, whether friends or foes, by the order of Gen. Jones, has been taken, or rather stolen, and carried just out of town and burned. The loss will be right heavy to some individuals. . . . There are some, however, I imagine, who have it concealed but deny the fact and have escaped the clutches of the rebels.

Julia Chase—November 26, 1862. Cold and windy day. The Richmond papers say that Gen. Burnside had demanded the surrender of Fredricksburg by a certain time or it would be shelled. . . . It is thought, however, that the Federal army will not hold F. but advance onward towards Richmond. God grant that this winter's campaign may be more successful than the past year has been to the army of Virginia under McClellan. . . . What is needed most is that our generals should be industrious and untiring in their efforts. Out town is still in possession of the Confederates; we do not hear of any Yankees very near us.

Laura Lee—November 26, 1862. Things are quiet, though everyone expects we will be left shortly. Alfred came in this evening. He says that the Yanks have all left Loudon, but that they behaved outrageously there, stealing and destroying everything.

Laura Lee—November 27, 1862. At the dispensary today. There are but two hospitals now to cook for, the York and the Union and only about 5000 sick. They are being sent off as fast as they are able to be moved. . . . We hear many rumors of Burnside advancing on Richmond, but nothing reliable.

Julia Chase—November 29, 1862. A courier has brought word that the Federals are at Berryville and advancing this way. Orders were then given to evacuate Winchester, and about 5 o'clock the infantry passed through town in the direction of Berryville, as if to engage the Yankees, but in the course of an hour returned again. The cavalry were then all out, flying in all directions, & by 8 P.M. their baggage wagons & c. passed by en route for the Valley. Our hopes were quite high, as we fully expected by morning to see the Federals in possession of W.

Laura Lee—November 29, 1862. We have had a great panic today. About 10 o'clock two regiments of Yankees dashed in upon the camp of White's battalion of cavalry below Berryville. The whole party ran off up here, leaving their camp to the enemy. Gen. Jones ordered them back at once, and went at their head. The Md. Battalion was ordered out, and passed through the town cheering and singing, but about dark were sent back to their camp. It is not known yet whether this is only a raid, or a real advance upon the town.

Julia Chase—November 30, 1862. Sabbath. Our hopes are all dashed to the ground; the orders have been countermanded and the troops are to hold our town again. Only a few Federals came into Berryville, though we can't but hope it will not be long before we shall see them among us. We have come to the conclusion not to expect anything until we see it with our own eyes.

Julia Chase—December 2, 1862. The troops are under marching orders. It is said the Federals are approaching in three directions and are hurrying their wagons as rapidly as possible for fear of being cut off. Great many secessionists have left, some taking their darkies with them. We shall expect to see the Yankees tomorrow certainly.

Laura Lee—December 2, 1862. All is perfect stillness. Every soldier gone except the sick at the hospitals and the nurses and surgeons in attendance on them. Gen. Jones ascertained that a whole division was advancing rapidly upon the town, and at 8 o'clock ordered a retreat to Strasburg. We had a good many soldiers in to get supper, belonging to a battery which was waiting in the street for orders. Several of them came into the parlor to write letters to leave for us to send to Maryland. . . . Afterwards we secured the silver and valuables. The flag had been attended to before they all left us. Nettie is quite sick tonight from agitation and distress and apprehensions of the Yankees. We expect them in early tomorrow.

Julia Chase—December 3, 1862. This is a charming winter's day—fine for army movements, but no signs of the Federal army and I doubt they are coming. We don't understand this move on the part of the Confederates at all & it is said also that the whole southern army are coming back. Father has been at the Ferry for several weeks, is very well, but like the other refugees very impatient to return home. The time appears very long to all of us.

Laura Lee—December 3, 1862. To our great surprise the enemy have not come in today. Our pickets are still below the town, and report them as only 6 miles off encamped at the Opequon. We are very glad of the day's respite, as it has enabled us to remove all the dispensary furniture and supplies to safe places. The ladies will now have the things prepared at their own houses and take them to the hospitals. . . . Just a month ago we walked out at sunset one evening . . . to the fortifications, and stayed to watch Jackson's camp fires and returned by moonlight. We thought then we would be left in a few days. Well, we have had three happy months and must be grateful for them, and cherish the pleasant remembrances they have given us. One of our greatest sources of trouble is that we shall have no more letters from our dear ones. All accounts agree that there must be a battle at Fredericksburg before many days, and we can hear only rumors and Yankee accounts of the results.

Julia Chase—December 4, 1862. Everyone is on the lookout for the Federals, as they encamped 2 miles from town last night. We hope to see father before very long. Later, the long looked for have come at last, but everything appears mysterious to me. The Federals, before coming into town, demanded of the Mayor the surrender of the town. An hour and a half was given to all citizens or soldiers to leave if they wished. Then . . . the Federals entered very quietly and orderly, cheering a Union flag, which was waved as they passed on by Fort Hill. They remained in town but 2 hours only, to the disappointment of the Unionists and great joy of the secessionists. . . . Some of the officers told the ladies they did not come to stay, but a large force would be here shortly and hold the town. We pray it may be so. Quite a number of Union men left and some Negroes. . . . Mrs. Gibbon's Union flag was demanded by some of the cavalry men, but she positively refused to give it up, they threatening to burn her house up, but we don't believe they would dare do that.

Laura Lee—December 4, 1862. We lead the strangest life of excitement and change which can be imagined. For three hours today we were in the hands of the Yankees, and again we are free! This morning at 10 o'clock they were said to be still several miles off, and it was such a charming day that we determined to have one more long walk before they came, so Lute, Lal, Liggie Tidball, Anna Jones, and I walked out to the fortifications and wandered about for two hours. When we reached home we found that a cavalry officer . . . had just come in to demand the surrender of the town. . . . At ½ past 12 they began to come in, and marched across the end of the town, straight from the Berryville Road to the fortifications. . . . We heard nothing more of them until 3 o'clock, when someone came in and said the Yankees have all gone. We thought it was only a wild rumor, but soon found it was quite true. They threw some shells across the town at our pickets, and then marched off in the greatest haste down the Martinsburg Road. We were afraid that our men would not hear it in time to pursue them, that Mary, Lute and I walked out to give them the information. They had heard the rumor and . . . sent couriers up to Gen. Jones at Strasburg. We expect all his command back tomorrow. It is still a mystery why the Yankees should have come at all, to stay so short a time. They did no havoc to anything or anybody.

Julia Chase—December 5, 1862. It seems like a dream that the Federals have really been in Winchester. Gen. Jones' force have all come back again, tho' it is said they do not expect to remain long. We shall look for the Yankees very soon. Gen. Burnside, it is said, is marching on Richmond with a large force and says he will either take the city or be taken. We like to hear our generals talk that way & hope their actions may verify their words. The secesh say that Jackson's army will be back again shortly. I for one don't believe it. Today we are having a cold snowstorm and it feels more wintry than any day of the season. This is hard weather upon the soldiers.

Laura Lee—December 5, 1862. Several companies of cavalry came in during last night, and more this morning, and about 10 o'clock the battalion came and went into quarters in the town. The enemy are back in Harper's Ferry. . . . It has snowed all day, and is now the most brilliantly beautiful night. But oh, the poor soldiers out in the snow!

Julia Chase—December 9, 1862. Yesterday our house had a thorough search for Yankee cloth. The secesh are so accustomed to taking things, that they judge all Union people by themselves. No Union cloth or any thing approaching it could be found on these premises. It is said today the Federals are evacuating Harper's Ferry. Don't think it true.

Julia Chase—December 13, 1862. The troops have left for Front Royal. News came last evening that the Federals were at Middletown. Whether advancing to Winchester, cannot say. We do not expect them here this winter, but would welcome them very gladly, so our friends could return. Heavy cannonading has been heard, as if from Fredericksburg. The last accounts from Gen. Burnside's army was unfortunately "all is quiet," the same thing we heard so long from McClellan when near Richmond. . . . Everything, so far as we can judge for our country, seems very unfavorable and dark. We cannot expect successes while the people are so divided, and we sincerely hope that ere long a leader may be raised under Providence that shall be enabled in a great measure to crush this rebellion, and more unity of action among our generals. The surrender of Harper's Ferry some time ago was a disgrace upon our country, as well as the evacuation of Winchester.

Laura Lee—December 13, 1862. Another stampede! Today we witnessed the fifth evacuation of Winchester. Directly after breakfast Capt. Williamson came in great haste and excitement to say that they were ordered to march at once to Front Royal, as the Yankees were advancing on Strasburg to cut them off. . . . By eleven all were gone. Post Office, Telegraph and everything, and here we are high and dry, perfectly isolated, belonging to neither Yankee nor Confederate Government, for there is not a single official belonging to the latter remaining here. There is a report today of a fight on Thursday at Fredericksburg in which we drove them back with severe loss, but we fear we shall not be able to hear the particulars before we are entirely cut off.

Julia Chase—December 14, 1862. We heard a few days since that father had gone to Baltimore. We have given up the hope of seeing him this winter. . . . The news is that the two armies have been fighting for 3 days.

Julia Chase—December 15, 1862. The secessionists are in full glee this morning. According to their report, the Federals have been cut to pieces, and that the slain are laying in piles, one above the other, that 10,000 of the National forces had gotten on a high bluff and great slaughter had been made against them.[7] God Almighty knows whether this be true or not. If so, it appears to me that our Country's cause must be a very unholy thing, which would account for the reverses the National Army have met with since the war broke out. Some think this battle will decide the fate of the South and that peace will be declared. We would be much better pleased if peace should follow, to hear of our armies making at least one grand struggle before. To think that the Federal soldiers must bear the name of being cowards, a disgrace to all nations, is rather revolting.

Laura Lee—December 15, 1862. The move of Saturday proves to have been from a mere panic. There are no Yankees within 40 miles of us. Gen. Jones is quietly reposing at Middletown, and it is supposed, and by a good many people hoped that he will not return here to keep us in a state of constant excitement with his panics. The fighting at Fredericksburg was continued on Thursday and Saturday. Rumor gives us a decided victory, but as yet we can hear nothing certain, and we are wretched until we hear the particulars and know if our friends are safe.

Laura Lee—December 17, 1862. Our victory has been far greater than we had dared to hope. The enemy was repulsed at every point, and driven back across the river with fearful loss. Our loss comparatively small, 5,000 killed and 2,000 wounded. But how terrible even this. . . . We received a letter today from Anna, the first for nine months. It was a great happiness to see her handwriting once more, though her accounts of things in La. are most deplorable. We saw a <u>Baltimore Sun</u> today of last Monday. It was very gloomy and admitted a terrible defeat, but as usual claimed that we had overwhelming numbers, 200,000 against their 40,000. How absurd!

Julia Chase—December 22, 1862. The secessionists seem uneasy this morning. It is said the Federals took possession of Strasburg last evening. The pickets extend below Middletown. We don't know whether they are advancing on to Winchester or not. We hear that Mr. Graves has been taken together with the mail. If true, it will probably go hard with the old gentleman. . . . The loss of the Federals in the late battles at Fredericksburg, is estimated at 10,000 killed, wounded and missing. What a sacrifice of life. It must be very discouraging to a national soldier who leaves the comforts of home for defending his country, to think that there is no commander in the whole Federal army whom he has perfect confidence in. May Providence raise up a leader like Joshua of old, who shall be enabled to crush the enemies of our beloved country.

Laura Lee—December 22, 1862. Yesterday intensely cold. I was not well, and did not go out. Prayer meeting here at night. Today another panic. . . . A report had come that 6,000 Yankees had crossed to Strasburg, captured old graves and the mails, and were advancing rapidly on this place. Mr. Burwell came in about 10 o'clock and said they were certainly only two hours march from here, but now at 11 p.m. we have heard no more of them. I believe it a false report, but still it has driven all of our soldiers away and we will have a solitary Christmas.

Julia Chase—December 23, 1862. The Federal cavalry took possession of our town this morning. We hope they are going to remain, so our friends may return, if no more. Later—A portion of the cavalry left town for the purpose of foraging. Most of persons thought they had gone for good, the Secesh were in full glee, jumping & clapping their hands at a terrible rate.

Julia Chase—December 24, 1862. A portion of Gen. Milroy's[8] command arrived today. The troops number about 4000. Quite a number of Unionists left for Maryland today in order to get groceries. Should these forces remain we shall look for father and other Union refugees. I shall start for Harper's Ferry this afternoon via Martinsburg, in case father may not return home, he can get some things he needs, and that I may see him.

Laura Lee—December 24, 1862. These wretched, horrible Yankees are here again! This morning while we were at breakfast, some hundreds of cavalry came in. They have opened a Provost's office, and put out pickets, and tomorrow Milroy's whole command will be here. What a Christmas! Christmas Eve. We made a feint at preparing for Christmas today, in the way of a few cakes and pies, and a little jelly. . . . We dressed the parlor very prettily with evergreens, and have continued to be reasonably cheerful, notwithstanding the adverse circumstances of our town being full of Yankees. Several thousands came in this morning, and this afternoon they have been searching houses for rebels and arms. They say they have brought no provisions, but intend to live on the citizens. They will not live very long if that is their only dependence.

Laura Lee—December 25, 1862. Early this morning they began to search houses for bacon, arms, and liquors. The Gen. ordered the citizens to furnish 2,000 rations of bacon, and they are taking all they find. They have not been here yet at 1 o'clock. We went to the Lutheran Church this morning, and had Christmas music from our own choir. The girls dined at their fathers, and now have gone with Mary and other ladies to take a treat of cakes & jelly to the men at the hospital. It is reported on every side that these Yankees are to leave here tomorrow, but it is too good news to be true.

Julia Chase—December 26, 1862. Was unable to accomplish anything I desired by going to Martinsburg. Father had left the Ferry for Baltimore, but the impression in Martinsburg is that our troops will hold Winchester for some time. If so, we shall expect to see father in a few days. . . . Yesterday, Christmas, was a charming day, more like Spring. We shall, however, expect a change before long.

Laura Lee—December 27, 1862. These wretches have settled themselves here, and are tyrannizing over us in the most shameful manner. They are bringing quantities of commissary stores, but have no tents and their Gen. says that when the weather gets bad, he intends to put the soldiers into every house in the place. . . . The soldiers have laid waste to Col. McDonald's and Mr. Wood's places, tearing down every outhouse and fence, breaking into the cellars and pantries, and carrying off everything that they had for their winter provisions. They were on the point of turning Mrs. McD. out of her house to take it for a hospital, when the Gen. relented, and stopped it. We hear nothing more of our forces near here, and are afraid that Gen. Jones is satisfied with giving the Yankees a scare, and has gone back to leave them in peace. . . . We can hear nothing from our army except that all is quiet.

Laura Lee—December 30, 1862. A damp, drizzling, disagreeable day. Not a word of news except a report that Gen. Jones' command has gone back to Woodstock. This noble Gen. here headed a party yesterday, who went out on a chicken stealing expedition. They returned laden with all the poultry from the Lupton neighborhood. They took besides all the provisions the people had, even the fresh pork they had just salted away for the next year. These are the worst villains we have ever had here.

Laura Lee—December 31, 1862. New Year's Eve. A sad and dismal time, weather dark and gloomy, and everyone more depressed than I have ever seen them. We are told that tomorrow emancipation is to be proclaimed from the Courthouse, with the ringing of bells, and that the soldiers are to be quartered on the citizens without distinction. They do not have wood from the country, but tear down the few fences that were left, and the outhouses and wooden buildings around the town. They have torn the [Winchester] Academy to pieces, and are now destroying the Market House. There seems to be no hope of relief from our dismay.

Julia Chase—January 1, 1863. Clear but cold today. Some prisoners brought in this morning. Father is still at Baltimore, we hope to see him soon. According to the President's Proclamation, all the slaves are to be freed from today. This will give great dissatisfaction to slaveholders but joy to the Negroes. I doubt whether they will be better off by their freedom.

Laura Lee—January 1, 1863. We feel quite inspirited tonight. It is said that our Jackson has turned his face in this direction, and is coming, and though I do not believe it yet, it is pleasant to hear even the rumors of such happiness. Gen. Milroy arrived today, and says he shall quarter 26 soldiers in every family where they refuse to take the oath. . . . The Baltimore papers record a new raid of Stuart's and various successes we have had in the South and West.

Julia Chase—January 3, 1863. We heard from father tonight that he will not return home for the present. I shall then go to Baltimore that I may see him. Gen. Milroy, with his troops arrived here on the 1st. We feel now as if they intend holding the town. We hope they will at least remain this winter, if the Balto. & Ohio R. Road is to be protected. Winchester would be the key to that road. A heavy battle was fought . . . in the vicinity of Murfreesboro between the 2 armies commanded by Gen. Rosecrans and Gen. Bragg.[9] The result so far seems favorable to the Union. The battle is still raging and our losses severe. . . . The little Monitor has been destroyed near Cape Hatteras. As usual there is nothing important from the Army of the Potomac.

Julia Chase—January 5, 1863. The Richmond papers claim a victory for the South in the late battle at Tenn., while the Northern papers admit a great victory for them. So far as we can judge, it was favorable for the rebels the first day, and the Secesh as usual consider the result as decidedly against the Federals. The weather has been very pleasant up this far, fine for army movements. Why is it the Army in Virginia remains so inactive. Are they ever to do anything. God have mercy on those upon whose shoulders the fault lies, and stir them up speedily.

Laura Lee—January 5, 1863. Yesterday Lincoln's proclamation came in the papers, but thus far we have seen no effects of it. There are still rumors of an advance of our men on this place, but one of the authorities is Mr. Boteler, which makes me doubt the whole thing. The Yankees are bringing large quantities of commissary stores, and the sutlers are opening goods. We intend to take advantage of the opportunity to get a good supply for the boys. We have sent in three or four ways for things from Maryland which we hope to get. As these wretches are here, we want them to stay long enough for us to get things for our men when they come back. The Baltimore papers report a terrible three days battle last week in Tennessee, in which, of course, they claim a victory, but acknowledge an immense loss of men.

Laura Lee—January 6, 1863. There was fighting yesterday at Romney, in which the Yankees were worsted. They sent up reinforcements today from here. The reports that Jackson is coming still continue. The enemy has been again repulsed at Vicksburg. It is snowing tonight, though not very cold, but it is dreadful to know that so many of our men are without shelter.

Julia Chase—January 7, 1863. Thanks to a kind Providence, father has at last returned after an absence of 4 months. He is looking very well indeed and has enjoyed good health since he left home. May he be permitted to remain with us always. We had quite a snow storm yesterday. Today is cold and looks more winterish than any of the season.

Laura Lee—January 7, 1863. Milroy has had the freedom proclamation posted up all over town, and the men and even the officers are going about

among the servants reading it to them, and assuring them that they are perfectly free. Thus far ours have given no sign of any change, but I suppose
they are all waiting for some bold spirit to take the initiative. The papers
today give a most confusing account of the terrible five days fighting in
Tennessee, and though they claim to have gained the advantage in the end,
we gathered very conclusively that it was no victory to them. . . . These
miserable Yankees captured a large package of letters yesterday at Newtown,
which were being brought here.

Julia Chase—January 9, 1863. More snow this morning, after moderat-
ing it turned into rain, tho' tonight the stars are shining. The walking will be
very slippery tomorrow. Gen. Milroy made a speech in honor of West Virginia. The cavalry, artillery & infantry turned out. Had it been pleasant, there
would have been a fine parade. A secesh lady remarked as they passed by, "Oh
what perfect nonsense, they only want to show their force, as if Jackson could
not drive them all out." We hear that the rebels are all around us, but we don't
believe all we hear, tho' the secesh would like much to have it so.

Laura Lee—January 9, 1863. The papers today are teeming with
accounts of what they claim to be their victory in Tenn. And though they
have nothing to show for it except that our forces have fallen back, and they
are following, I cannot help being very uneasy, lest this last battle should
prove like the Shiloh fight, ours first, and then theirs. Gen. Milroy went to
Kiger's today and actually turned the family out of the house, and took possession of it for headquarters. The Yankees captured a large mail yesterday,
which had been sent down the Valley, to be smuggled in.

Julia Chase—January 12, 1863. Charlie Miller and I will leave for Baltimore tomorrow to be absent a few days.

Laura Lee—January 12, 1863. The papers give Gen. Bragg's dispatches
to the very last claiming a grand victory. Afterwards he withdraws in consequence of the reinforcements the enemy were receiving. At Vicksburg,
we were again successful in repulsing them. . . . Our cavalry is around us in
various directions picking up prisoners and wagons. They are more strict
here than ever before. None is permitted to leave town in any direction
without taking the oath, and no supplies are allowed to come except on the
same conditions.

Julia Chase—January 16, 1863. Returned from Baltimore this evening.
When within four miles of home, were obliged to halt until a regiment of
infantry passed by. Rumors were afloat that the Confederates were on the
Martinsburg Road, but we saw nothing that looked like secesh.

Laura Lee—January 17, 1863. Gen. Milroy is trying to starve us into loyalty. No one is permitted to bring supplies from Md. except on taking the oath, and then only for their own use. The sutlers are strictly forbidden to sell to the citizens, and all means are used to make us suffer to the utmost. The soldiers are tearing down every unoccupied house, and carrying the wood and roofing to the fortifications, to build huts and stables. The [Winchester] academy and Quaker meeting houses are destroyed, and numberless smaller houses and stables and barns. The poor old town is rapidly being demolished.

Laura Lee—January 21, 1863. Nettie very sick all day. Burnside reported to be again crossing the Rappahannock. Numbers of servants are leaving everyday, free as well as slaves. Even Randell Evens is going. The Yankees tell them President Davis has ordered them all to be killed.

Julia Chase—January 22, 1863. This has been a very gloomy week, a storm of snow and rain has prevailed for several days. Rather unfavorable for army movements, tho' there are rumors in the paper that Burnside has crossed the Rappahannock and a battle is progressing, and Gen. Hooker mortally wounded.

Laura Lee—January 23, 1863. It was not true that there was fighting yesterday, but the papers insist that Burnside is moving to cross the river for another attack. They are also moving on Wilmington and Charleston. We have had a long spell of wretched weather, rain, snow and sleet, everyone is kept in the house, and everything is sad, discouraging and depressing.

Julia Chase—January 24, 1863. There is no truth that the Army of the Potomac have crossed the river, the storm having prevented it. The rebels have surrendered the Post of Arkansas to the Union army. Nearly 5000 men taken prisoner, with small arms & c. Gen. Butler has been assigned to N. Carolina. We shall expect to hear stirring news from that quarter ere long, and God grant we may hear of the fall of Charleston before many weeks. Today is the most pleasant of any we have had for a week past. The walking has been awful.

Julia Chase—January 27, 1863. Gen. Burnside has resigned his commission & Gen. Hooker[12] now commands the Army of the Potomac. God have mercy upon that poor army and indeed the whole country. Everything looks dark and discouraging, and it seems as if the fault laid at the gates of Washington City. When will our authorities awake from their stupor, or madness as it sometimes appears to us. How much wisdom and strength is needed for our rulers and all in authority.

Julia Chase—January 28, 1863. The blacks are leaving in great numbers, and probably in the course of a few weeks there will be but very few left. We shall be at a great loss to get anything done. We are having a very severe snow storm, reminding one of those Northern snows. It has drifted in some places 2 feet or more.

Laura Lee—January 28, 1863. Burnside is removed, and Hooker put in his place. Franklin and Summer are also removed. Expeditions have gone against Vicksburg and Galveston. We are in the midst of a great snow storm.

Laura Lee—January 29, 1863. Gen. Milroy's last exploit has been to send a Negro man with an escort to Mr. Lewis' to take possession of the man's wife and children, and also a wagon and horses to carry them off with. They took Mr. Lewis' best carriage horses. Gen. Milroy told a girl the other day, when she went to him to ask for a pass, that Hell was not full enough of rebels yet, and would not be until more of these Winchester women went there. Dignified: That for a "Federal Officer." The blockade is strictly enforced with regard to everything, but smuggling is successfully carried on.

Laura Lee—January 31, 1863. Milroy issued an order today forbidding either flour or wood being sold to any except loyal citizens. One of the sutlers was arrested today, and his large stock of goods confiscated, as a punishment for selling to the citizens.

Julia Chase—February 1, 1863. Attended the funerals of Mr. Schultz & Mr. Hoff this afternoon. The house much crowded, sad sight to see two corpses side by side—pleasant in their lives and in death not divided.

Laura Lee—February 3, 1863. We were aroused last night in the middle of the night by a large body of cavalry, which had just come. They dismounted and picketed their horses, and kindled fires in the middle of the street all around, and . . . were stamping and shouting and breaking down fences to burn all the rest of the night. It was surprisingly cold and snowing and the poor wretches must have suffered terribly. They say today that some of our men are at Front Royal.

Julia Chase—February 4, 1863. Another stormy day of snow and rain, the weather very cold.

Laura Lee—February 4, 1863. These villains are tearing down all the fences to burn. They are established in Dr. Baldwin's garden, and have burned all his fencing, and are now working on ours.

Julia Chase—February 5, 1863. A raid was made this afternoon on the stage coming from Martinsburg. 17 bushwhackers attacked one of the stages, capturing all the passengers, but one, a Lieutenant, who gave the alarm to the nearest pickets, thereby making his escape, also a lady that they left in the stage, took the horses and made tracks. . . . It is said that the blockade has been raised at Charleston by the rebels, an ironclad having made its escape. The Richmond papers of the 3rd make no mention, however, of the fact.

Laura Lee—February 5, 1863. Another terrible snowstorm. The thermometer 4 degrees below zero. This is the most severe winter we have had for many years. It is so dreadful for our soldiers. These vile Yankees are still in Dr. Baldwin's garden, and have burned almost all of the fence between us. Mary and Mrs. B. both applied to the Provost today to stop it, and he promised to do so, but they are still burning it as fast as they can. It is too hard! We can have no garden next summer without a fence, and there is no possibility of getting planking rails to make one.

Laura Lee—February 6, 1863. Splendid news today! Our gunboats went out of the harbor at Charleston on last Sat. 31st Jan. and sunk one, burnt four and dispersed the remaining nine of the blockading fleet. The Consuls admit that the blockade is fairly broken. The enemy has been repulsed at Savannah and also at Stone Island on the 1st and 2nd of this month. Mr. Barton's last remaining servants are to go tomorrow. Kiger who was coming in with letters was caught, and the letters read and sent to the persons they were addressed to, but with a stern order from Milroy to forbear sending letters secretly, as the persons who take them shall be severely punished.

Julia Chase—February 8, 1863. Quite pleasant today, the snow melting fast.

Laura Lee—February 11, 1863. These vile fiendish wretches, not content with encouraging and persuading the servants to go off, force off those who are unwilling to go. They send parties of cavalry through the country, who seize wagons and horses and fill them with the Negroes who have chosen to remain at their homes and bring them away in spite of their entreaties to the contrary. The Yankee Government attempt to deny the breaking of the blockade. They are preparing to attack Charleston immediately. I do so dread the result.

Laura Lee—February 14, 1863. Mrs. Baldwin went again to Milroy to complain that his orders were disregarded, as the men were still burning our fence. He flew into a great passion, and in the course of the conversation told her in so many words that <u>she lied</u>, and ended by ordering her out of the room. The brute!

Laura Lee—February 16, 1863. Mrs. Burwell has returned from Balt. With plenty of nice things for the girls, and some too for the boys. . . . Last night a report reached here that the enemy has been again repulsed at Vicksburg, but there has been no confirmation of it today. It is said that there is a Negro regiment on the way here.

Laura Lee—February 20, 1863. We went out this afternoon to buy boots, shoes and clothes to have for our men when they come back. We began by getting two pair of boots and the same of shoes, but we can only bring them home one pair at a time, as it is in direct opposition to the orders to buy anything for soldiers. But it is a great pleasure to circumvent the Yankees, besides the comfort of supplying our men with things they so much need. Another large sum of money came to us today from Balt. for the very purpose.

Laura Lee—February 25, 1863. We spent yesterday evening at Mrs. Tuley's, with the Sheppards. It was the first time we had been out for nearly a year. We got some more clothes today for our soldiers. There are many rumors of our troops advancing on this place, but I do not credit them at all. As a necessary consequence of them, however, more of the servants are going off. I am very much afraid Sally is going to take Betty and Matilda.

Laura Lee—March 2, 1863. The soldiers are scouting through Clarke Co., and bringing in large numbers of Negroes who had been satisfied to stay at their houses. There are hundreds waiting here to be sent on to [Pennsylvania]. Ours still are vehement in their loyalty, but there is no faith to be placed in one of them. We have just accomplished quite an adventurous feat in hiding away a large quantity of contraband articles in a house which was full of people, but one of whom knew of our design. We found it was becoming unsafe to keep them here.

Laura Lee—March 6, 1863. All Mrs. Tuley's servants went off this morning except one little girl. We spent this evening at Mr. Sherrards with Mary Baker and Mrs. Stephenson, and the party ended up in something of a row. The girls were singing Southern songs (as they are in the habit of doing nearly everyday) and some soldiers who were standing at the window chose to take offense, and sent in a very rude note and then climbed on the roof . . . and nailed up a Union flag. They warned us that they would guard the house all night and not allow anyone to leave it. Some of the ladies were frightened, but I was not at all so as I knew they were acting without authority. At last we sent over to the Provost to complain, and the sergeant of the guard came and was very civil and escorted us home safely at nearly 11 o'clock.

Laura Lee—March 9, 1863. Those hateful Stars and Stripes are still waving over Mr. Sherrard's house. It is a piece of malicious spite in that the Provost not allow it to be taken down. There is nothing new today, but various rumors that our men are coming.

Laura Lee—March 11, 1863. Mr. Seever's last servants are off today. Our only excitement and amusement consists in buying everything we want without a permit. New and very strict ordinances are out today. Everybody's permit is revoked, and none are given without the oath being taken. The sutlers are forbidden under heavy penalties to sell without a permit, yet Mary has bought today 100 herrings and 25 pounds of molasses. The soldiers are forbidden to sell to citizens and they have to be very secret about it, but everybody manages to get what they want. We have bought from them from time to time 8 fine hams, as much coffee as we want, and very nice soap. We have the contraband goods so safely distributed, that nothing will be found here if the house is searched.

Laura Lee—March 16, 1863. Yesterday we had another terrible storm of snow, hail, with severe thunder and lightning. In the midst of it some reinforcements came in. They say 5,000 but, of course, they exaggerate the number. It is evident they intend to fight for this place if our men do come. . . . Mary goes on buying everything. She has nearly 100 pounds of coffee, as much of sugar, a good supply of molasses, herrings, oil, dried fruit, and other items, besides several hundred dollars worth of clothing for the soldiers. I have plenty of clothes for the boys of every kind. Nice gray cloth for a suit for Bob too.

Laura Lee—March 17, 1863. I feel perfectly exhausted tonight with two days fighting with the Yankees. Yesterday after I had written we were in Nettie's room quietly reading to her when Lute came in and said she was afraid we were to have trouble. Three officers had come to the door where she was and inquired if these rooms in the wing were occupied. She told them yes and they asked how and if they could be vacated. She said by ladies, and that it would be very unpleasant for them to be turned out of their rooms. They said they would be as certain and walked off. Just after dinner they came back with an order from the Provost Marshall, that Col. Staunton should take such rooms in Mrs. Lee's house as he found suitable. We demonstrated most vehemently and told them that our sister was very sick and it would be risking her life to move her. Col. Staunton said then he would not by any means have her moved, but would take the parlor and dining room. We were horrified at this, and said rather than that, we would

move her into the dining [room] for the present, and give them the other
rooms, but he said he saw we were not inclined to be accommodating, and
that he would have the large rooms. He and some of the men with him
were most insolent and insulting in their manner. They said we need not
say a word, that we had heard the orders, and that such and such pieces of
furniture might be moved, others would be left, the parlor carpet might be
taken up, the other must be left down, and ended by saying "we will
occupy these rooms in two hours." Mary went at once to Milroy. He was
not uncivil, and said he would speak to the Provost and he said he would
endeavor to persuade Col. Staunton to be satisfied with the smaller rooms.
This was a reprieve, and Nettie would have to be moved in any event, we
determined to vacate the little rooms, hoping they would not be so audacious as to refuse to take them when they were ready for them. The neighbors were all very kind, and the rooms were soon empty, but our
persecutors did not come again until this morning, when one of them came
with six soldiers to move the furniture from the parlors as they were determined to have them. Again we fought them off with words, and the man
said again he would talk to the Col. We heard no more until 4 o'clock
when Col. Staunton came again and said he preferred the large rooms and
would have them. Mary and the girls again resisted and remonstrated and at
last successfully, for very shame's sake he had to yield, and said he had been
outgeneraled, and that he would come tomorrow and take the small rooms.
This was such a relief from being turned out of the parlors that we are quite
satisfied. These wretches are quartered on many of the families in the town.
. . . Someone heard Col. Staunton say that as Mrs. Lee had been the head
of the cooking room, he would see if he could not be the head of Mrs.
Lee's house. This is the secret of his persecution of us.

   Laura Lee—March 20, 1863. Our new inmates keep very quiet and we
do not see them at all. It is very cold and snowing again. . . . Many of the
letters that came yesterday give the most cheering accounts of the condition
and prospect of our army. The papers today report that the Yankees have
made their grand attack on Port Hudson, and have been repulsed, losing
another gunboat.

   Laura Lee—March 23, 1863. This is the anniversary of the battle of Kernstown. We have vivid recollections of the horrors attending our first experience
of a battle. Our Yankees are all off again. They were ordered back to Harper's
Ferry, and went this morning to our joy! We cannot understand why the reinforcements which were sent in such haste, have been sent off so soon.

Laura Lee—March 26, 1863. We have had another encounter with these creatures. Tonight, while we were at tea, a party of soldiers came, ringing furiously, and demanded to come in to search the house for a rebel soldier who had escaped from the guard house. They went all over the house, and they continued their search at the different houses on the street. Our hope of release is indefinitely postponed. Our forces in the Valley have fallen back to Harrisonburg.

Laura Lee—March 30, 1863. No news from anywhere today except rumors that our friends are coming <u>sometime</u>. Mr. Bell, the "rebel" for whom they were searching last week, has made good his escape. . . . I feel quite cheered by the prospect of having our garden fence put up, and being able to cultivate the vegetables on which so much of our comfort depends.

CHAPTER FOUR

April 1863–September 1863

"There is a wail of woe throughout the South"

As the spring of 1863 got under way, Laura and the rest of the Confederate citizens in Winchester continued to cope with the harsh reign of Federal commander Gen. Robert Milroy. In command of the city since January, Milroy had instituted a number of acts, including banishment from the city, to make life as miserable as possible for those who supported the Confederate cause. Laura described his rule as a perfect reign of terror.

As before, the two women continued to follow the events of their military forces, both in Virginia and the Western Theater. Laura mourned the death of Jackson following the battle of Chancellorsville, and in the aftermath of the twin defeats of Gettysburg and Vicksburg, she admitted that events were not going well for the Confederacy. After having suffered through so many defeats, Julia finally rejoiced over the Federal victories and hoped that before long, "Charleston, that nest egg of treason," would be in Federal hands.

Laura Lee—April 1, 1863. Our invalids are all better today. Mary bought a great many things this afternoon. The sutlers never even alluding to a permit. I got a new bonnet. Quite an important event.

Laura Lee—April 4, 1863. The sutlers are disregarding the orders and sell quite freely without permits. Mary got today molasses, potatoes, oil, fish, and beans. O, if we only had more money! Milroy had a grand parade and review today. They say they have nine thousand. People who have watched say there are not more than five thousand. We heard tonight, to our sorrow, that Col. Staunton's regiment is ordered back here. We fear he may choose to fix himself here again. The troops at Fredericksburg are moving, preparatory to another battle we fear. Such weather! Snowing again tonight. The attack on Port Hudson is a complete failure and Banks has gone back to New Orleans. . . . Milroy told Mrs. Tuley, all you women can be very polite and pleasant when you come here to ask favors, and then you go away and call us Yankees "trash." It was most amusing to hear.

Laura Lee—April 6, 1863. About two o'clock a Capt. and a private came here and said they must search for contraband goods which were reported to be concealed here. We told them they would find nothing of the kind here and sure enough they did find nothing of the kind, though they were walking over and around and among any quantity all the time, but they were none the wiser. The Capt. proved to be the deputy Provost. He was quite civil, and gave us a certificate that the house had been searched and nothing contraband found. Mrs. Logan has had a dreadful time. They have taken possession of almost all of her house besides sending away a wagon load of furniture. Mrs. Burwell has gone to Baltimore again, to bring our things which we are so anxious to get, as then we will be quite ready for our friends.

Laura Lee—April 7, 1863. The most shameful outrage which has yet occurred here, was perpetrated today. Mrs. Logan,[1] her three daughters and two sons, were sent off today, after a few hour's notice, without any charge against them except a suspicion of having goods concealed. They were per-mitted to take their clothing but nothing else, not even a teaspoon or enough provisions to dine on. Mrs. Milroy and her family arrived before the Logans left, and she laughed very much and ran into the house saying she believed she was mistress here now. Even the officers who had been con-ducting the proceedings were shamed, and begged her to desist for a little while. . . . The house is one of the handsomest in the town and well sup-plied with provisions of every kind and plenty of groceries, all of which Mrs. Milroy took into immediate use. They hung a Union flag over the door while the family was going out and then took it down. Mary has been very sick for a fortnight with erascpallus [erysipelas] and is not fit to leave the house in such weather as this. It may cause her death. Milroy says this is only the beginning of this sort of thing and there is no telling where it will end.

Laura Lee—April 8, 1863. We are in a rather shaky site just now. We are assured on all hands that we are one of the five families to be sent off tomorrow. One of the charges against Mrs. Logan was that she had a prayer meeting on the rebel fast day. It was not true of Mrs. Logan, but we were the offenders on that point, and if they hear it, nothing is more probable than that they will make it a pretext for sending us off. We hear that the Provost says that he found nothing suspicious here, but that he is certain that Mrs. Lee has bought things and secreted them in other people's houses, and that he will search until they are found. . . . The Singletons, Sherrards Williams, Conrads and Lees are the families selected to have the honor of suffering for the cause.

Laura Lee—April 9, 1863. There is a perfect reign of terror here now. These wretches are searching everywhere again for arms and contraband goods and are rude and insolent almost beyond belief. We had quite an alarm this evening. They have searched poor Mary Macky's house three times today, the last time it was for Mason's furniture and papers. This touches us very nearly and made us the more uneasy, as one of them said they had captured a letter to Mr. Mason's daughter, Miss Ida. Lute had sent a letter to Ida only yesterday and we dreaded that that might be the one. I went to the person who was to send it and found to our great relief that it had not yet been sent. It is a wretched state of apprehension in which we live, and yet we are willing and glad to bear it all and live on the hope of deliverance. They went around again for spades, hoes, picks and wheelbarrows, taking all they could find. We escorted our wheelbarrow away tonight.

Laura Lee—April 16, 1863. Since this day [a] week ago I have been very sick with a severe attack of erasepalsis in the head and unable to sit a moment. I can now only write enough to note down a few things which have occurred since. On Tuesday, Mary Magill[2] was sent beyond the lines on half an hours notice, because of a letter she wrote describing the Logan affair <u>with remarks</u> which fell into Milroy's hands. On Wednesday night a party of 23 Negroes (all women and children except one man) were carried in a wagon to Mr. Singleton's and he was ordered by the soldiers . . . to show them to his best rooms, as they were to be quartered on him. His opposition and remonstrances were in vain. The soldiers fixed them in the house. But after they had gone away, the Negroes, who seemed very humble and shocked at what had occurred begged that they might go into the kitchen, which they did as many as might go into the kitchen, and the remainder slept in the dining room.

Laura Lee—April 21, 1863. I am better now and able to sit up. Last Saturday, just after dinner, one of those vile gray scouts came and told Mary to have two or three rooms prepared for some families who would be here in the evening. Mary went at once to the Provost Alexander, and he told her, yes, he had sent the message that he had orders to occupy rebel property, and she was the most outrageous rebel in the town, and it was the very least he could do to her. He was not rude in his manner but rather jocular.

He said that she had showed so much delight when her other Yankees left, that he wanted to give her the opportunity to be delighted again. He said he would send a Mr. & Mrs. Clark here Sat. evening or Sunday morning, but here it is Tuesday and we have heard nothing more of them.

Julia Chase—May 1, 1863. A battle has commenced between the 2 armies at Fredericksburg and the town of F. is in possession of the Federals. Gen. Hooker has drawn the enemy out from his entrenchments and is determined that he shall fight on fair ground.

Julia Chase—May 4, 1863. The weather quite warm and Spring like. Heavy fighting has taken place between the two armies & the rebels claim victories of Saturday's & Sunday's fighting,[3] great loss of life on both sides including many officers. . . . The Federals have fought well up to this time, and every heart is in anxious state of mind as to the result.

Julia Chase—May 7, 1863. The papers mention the death of rebel A. P. Hill,[4] also that Stonewall Jackson is severely wounded; we doubt, however, the truth of it, as we have heard such reports before. Everything so far as we can judge from the papers are quite encouraging and God grant that when the battle is decided it may be in our favor.

Julia Chase—May 8, 1863. This has been a very stormy week, rather unfavorable for army movements. 2 regiments of infantry left this morning for Western Virginia. The late raid by the rebels on the Balt. & Ohio R.R. caused much excitement in that portion of the state; we hope they may not be allowed to destroy any more property. . . . Later—Are we ever to have success in Virginia. Gen. Hooker has re-crossed the Rappahannock, having met with a sad reverse. Oh! How much sadness will be in the land in consequence of this defeat. We were led by the papers to believe that everything was so favorable for the Union army, and just when our hopes were at the highest they are dashed completely to the ground. The secesh are very joyous & well they might be, rather taunting in their remarks to the Unionists. Great God! Shall this thing always be.

Laura Lee—May 9, 1863. After another week, I am just able to sit up and try to take an interest in what is passing. It is now four weeks since I was taken sick, and I am still perfectly prostrated. Great events have occurred in the past ten days. On the last day of April the Yankees completed their crossing of the Rappahannock, and on . . . the 2nd, 3rd, and 4th of May there were terrible battles of greater or less extent in which we have been again successful. We have argued all the week from the tone of the papers that they have had no victory, but yesterday they were forced to admit that they had been defeated and had re-crossed the river. Gen. Jackson is wounded, but we hope not seriously, as he is reported to be still on duty. Our loss is said to be heavy. . . . A great many of the troops have left here, and many persons think they are going to leave here altogether. The town is in the most terrible condition. There is scarcely a house where there are not one or more sick, and in many cases four or five. Sarah and Betty are both in bed with the fever and Emily all the time poorly.

Laura Lee—May 12, 1863. I am improving, but very slowly. I took a short drive on Sunday and spent the evening downstairs yesterday. The Yankees profess to make very light of their late defeat and claim that Stoneman's raid upon the railroad, when he burned a bridge within a few miles of Richmond, was quite as great a victory as ours on the Rapp. The sickness here continues to a terrible extent, though as yet there have been very few deaths. We cannot get the proper medicines, and what we do get is by stealth as Hartman's store is closed, and he is forbidden to sell but he manages to slip out whatever he has that people want. Nobody will risk their lives by using the medicines from the other druggists.

Julia Chase—May 14, 1863. The papers speak of the death of Gen. Jackson, from wounds received in the battle at Chancellorsville. The Richmond papers do not admit that he was killed by the Yankees but that his own men killed him in the confusion of the fight. His death will be felt greatly by the South. Great deal of sickness still in town and many colored have died. . . . Rain since dinner, and a great change in the weather, very cool and windy.

Laura Lee—May 14, 1863. Dreadful news today. There is a report in the papers that Jackson died last Sunday from his wounds. It is too terrible a blow to believe it except on certain information, and many persons disbelieve it entirely, but the circumstances are given with such minuteness, that my reason tells me there is no hope.[5]

Laura Lee—May 15, 1863. Gen. Jackson is dead! There is a wail of woe throughout the South.

Laura Lee—May 20, 1863. The Yankees have released Dr. Boyd's house but have taken Nat Bent's as a hospital. The last act of oppression is an order to all persons renting property from disloyal citizens to pay their rent to the Provost Marshall to form a fund for hospital purposes. This afternoon Julia Clark was walking on the street and had a crape rosette on her shoulder as a badge of mourning for Gen. Jackson, when one of those odious gray scouts stepped up to her and told her that the rosette was an insult to their soldiers and must come off, and he put out his hand and tore it off her dress.

Julia Chase—May 22, 1863. Mr. Trenary buried his wife today, also a daughter the early part of the week. The soldiers at the hospital are dying off very rapidly. Our town has been in a dreadful condition but it is now undergoing a cleaning which will be of much benefit.

Julia Chase—May 25, 1863. The armies of Grant & Johnston in the S. West are engaged in battle and if the papers are correct we expect to hear of the fall of Vicksburg[6] very soon, should such be the case the army in Virginia & further south would be cut off from all their supplies, however, it may turn out a second Fredericksburg, if the Federal forces should fail there it seems as if this putting down the rebellion will be perfectly abortive.

Laura Lee—May 25, 1863. This is the anniversary of the battle of Winchester, the day when our men marched in so triumphantly, and now both of our heroes, Jackson and Ashby, are gone. I am so glad that our men did not go to Clarksburg in their late expedition to W. Va. Wherever they went the people are compromised with one party or the other. Eight wagon loads of women and children have been sent through here in the last few days from there, for having given food or information to the "rebels." On Saturday Anna Jones was followed by a mob to make her take off her badge of mourning. Things here have improved considerably. The town has been quite thoroughly cleaned up, and Milroy has allowed whiskey, which was absolutely necessary to the lives of the sick, to be bought and sold. . . . No news from the Valley, but very bad news from the South. We have had several reverses around Vicksburg, and now there is scarcely a hope that Vicksburg will be able to hold out much longer.

Julia Chase—May 28, 1863. Very pleasant but exceedingly dry and dusty—rain very much needed for the gardens.

Laura Lee—May 30, 1863. Reports coming down the Valley say that Gen. Lee's army has crossed the Rappahannock and is advancing on either Washington or Maryland. Here Milroy is doing as usual. The Singletons' house was taken for a hospital yesterday. The family were notified that they would be sent through the lines today, but afterwards they were permitted to remain and seek shelter with some of their friends. . . . Two surgeons went to Dr. Robert Baldwin's yesterday and went over the house to see if it suited for a hospital. They said it would answer and that they would probably take it. The poor old Dr. is in the most dreadful state from asthma and heart disease and liable to die at any moment. They have heard nothing more today and we hope that the men were moved by some feeling of humanity and compassion. They do not really require so many hospitals, but it is part of their purpose of oppression to occupy every rebel property.

Laura Lee—June 4, 1863. The order taking Mr. Singleton's house has been revoked and they are left in peace for the moment. They did not turn poor old Dr. Baldwin out of his house, but were satisfied with taking his dining room, where they hold a Court of Inquiry. We received a letter from Flora on Monday telling us that they had sent the money by private hand to Martinsburg and we may hope almost certainly to receive it. This will be a great relief, for we were beginning to fear that our money would give out entirely and it is impossible to collect any. We can never forget the affection and kindness of those dear children in our time of trouble. There is much talk of Gen. Lee's advance, but we can hear nothing certain of the movements of our army. Vicksburg still holds out and great hopes are entertained that it will be saved. The sick in town are improving and few new cases.

Julia Chase—June 5, 1863. The papers speak rather encouragingly in regard to Grant, that he will be enabled to take Vicksburg but that time will be required. It is thought that Gen. Johnston is trying to get possession of Memphis, thus getting in the rear of Gen. G.

Laura Lee—June 9, 1863. Our life is so monotonous that there is nothing to record from day to day but the same oppressions and tyranny. The sickness has almost disappeared, at least as to new cases, but the invalids are very slow in recovering strength. The money which we expected has not come, to our great disappointment. . . . It is still a mystery what has become of Gen. Lee's army, but all admit that some great move is on hand. . . . This morning a servant man who Dr. Baldwin had hired at Christmas from Dr. Page. . . came with a soldier to demand his wages, saying that he had an order from Milroy. The Dr. swore at him and drove him off, but they are afraid that if he really had an order they will enforce it.

Julia Chase—June 10, 1863. The siege of Vicksburg is progressing satisfactorily according to the latest advises. A cavalry fight took place yesterday between the Federal cavalry & that under the rebel Gen. Stuart on the Rappahannock. Stuart has been massing a large force of cavalry at Beverley's Ford, as is supposed with the intention of making a raid. They attempted to cross, but were repulsed by our troops driving them back after an obstinate fight, holding the south bank of the river. Dr. Robert Baldwin was sent out of the lines today, his wife accompanying him. We hear that it was the intention of taking them as far south as Middletown, but that Mrs. B. talked so outrageously that they were landed at Newtown.

Laura Lee—June 10, 1863. Another shameful outrage to record today. Dr. Baldwin was notified that he was to pay Remus 40 dollars, and he was given twenty minutes to decide about it. He told the soldiers that it would not take one minute, that he would not pay a cent to save the whole Yankee nation. He was then notified that he would be sent through the lines in an hour. The noble, brave, old man would not yield and though his friends made every effort, and would have paid the money without his knowledge, nothing availed, and he was sent off in the afternoon. Mrs. Baldwin went with him. . . . All the neighbors collected around the house to say goodbye. They went off in fine spirits, but it is a cruel, cowardly act to send an old man sick and diseased out into the world.

Julia Chase—June 11, 1863. Henry Griffith, son of Mr. Aaron G. died this morning of the fever. Today's paper says that the cavalry forces of the Army of the Potomac gained a glorious victory over Gen. Stuart and discovered his arrangement for a raid into Maryland & Pennsylvania. . . . Reports from the rebel lines say that Vicksburg has fallen, but it is not credited. It was reported a day or two since that the rebel forces were in the Valley of Shenandoah but none have been found between here & Strasburg.

Laura Lee—June 11, 1863. We have heard from Dr. Baldwin. Those wretches put them out on the side of the road beyond Kernstown. They were fortunately near enough to a house for the Dr. to walk to it, and the people were as kind as possible and kept them all night, and sent them on this morning. . . . The money from Clarksburg, $100.00, arrived this morning. We are very glad and thankful. These Yankees are in a great fright. There are reports of our forces in the Valley. They sleep on their arms every night.

Julia Chase—June 13, 1863. What exciting times we are passing through since Friday. Skirmishing commenced on that day between the Confederate cavalry & Federals. . . . Yesterday, Saturday, fighting continued all day and cannonading was going on through all its hours. The rebels are coming we hear in great force, Ewell's division (formerly Jackson's) it is said being here. The town is all in an uproar, wagons lining the streets all the day, cavalry & infantry passing by, the secessionists very joyful flocking to the sutlers, buying up all they can for their friends, while the Unionists are in an anxious state of mind. Reinforcements are looked for tonight, but not to the number requisite. God in his mercy, grant that Winchester may not be given up to the rebels, we dread their appearance. . . . We don't see how Gen. Milroy can hold out & it is thought he is completely surrounded, we hope, however, he may be enabled to cut his way out. . . . It is said that Gen. Lee's whole force is in the Valley, Gen. Hooker in his rear, how true it is we can't say, this week will decide very important events, either for or against our Country's cause. The armies are drawn up in line of battle just at the edge of town, at Mr. Kohlhousen's—also Mr. Geo. Baker's. Oh how sad and dreadful the thought to think that these men who ought to be living on brotherly terms are arrayed against the other. When will the shedding of blood stop?

Laura Lee—June 13, 1863. This is almost an exact counterpart of May last year. They were moving commissary stores all night and again today. There was a smart fight within two miles of town this morning, but now at 3 o'clock they have retired. They say that the rebels are approaching by several roads. . . . The soldiers say they will certainly burn the town this time, and we thought as a prudential measure we would bring down our trunks from upstairs where we keep them already packed. The firing was voracious at about 4 this afternoon from the Fort. They fired for half an hour shelling the woods around the town, but there was no response. The wagon trains have gone off and the general impression is that they will evacuate tonight. I do not believe it. I am afraid they will stay to fight. A great many wounded were brought into the hospitals this evening, which is some little assurance of safety, not withstanding their threats. It is strange how we can get accustomed to such things.

Julia Chase—June 14, 1863. The Rebels took possession of our town at 5 o'clock this morn. And we are now in Dixie. Oh what a sad, sad day this has been to us. Gen. Milroy left the fort during the night but with the loss of 3800 taken prisoners, and 300 wagons heavily loaded, besides a great many horses. This is considered a glorious victory by the Rebels.[7] Their forces were between 30 & 40,000 against 6000 effective men. . . . Had he removed his army train, it would not have been so bad, but to have so much captured, it is outrageous. The Federal Government have from the commencement of the war, fed, clothed & supplied with arms the whole Southern Army. Is this state of things to continue forever? If so, much better have peace now than to go sacrificing men & property. The Rebels say they are going on to Maryland.

Laura Lee—June 15, 1863. Oh, this joyful day! The skirmishing continued during all day yesterday to the east and south of town, but it proved to be only a feint to draw off men from the real attack by our batteries shelling the fortifications from the rear. It was entirely unexpected to them, for they had no idea how large a force we had and thought the attack would be entirely in the front. They soon turned their guns and returned fire, but were forced to abandon the first two forts in less than half an hour. . . . They carried the field pieces with them and ambulances and all crowded into the other two forts. There were large numbers of contrabands up there who had sought refuge there. The Yankees boasted that they were impregnable, and of their threats that they would destroy the town. The fire from our batteries was now directed to the last two forts and was tremendous. It was answered with equal rapidity from their field batteries as well as their siege guns. About 7 o'clock Mr. Brown sent for us to come to the top of his house, from which we could see the whole scene perfectly. It was a grand but terrible sight. We could see the flash of every gun in the forts and the shells from our batteries exploding in the air directly over them and falling in among the unfortunate creatures crowded in there. The incessant firing continued until after 8, and when a La. regiment charged with bayonets upon the third fort and drove the Yankees helter skelter out and into the fourth. By this time it was dark and both sides ceased firing. . . . We were worn out with fatigue and excitement and went to bed expecting that today would bring a repetition of the same scenes. This morning at 4 o'clock we were roused by musketry at some distance, and some persons who were already about, called out that the Yankees had left the fortifications and were fighting below the town. We looked out and saw a few soldiers in gray clothes and then everybody went crazy. We tossed on our clothes, and men, women and children ran up to Fort Hill to see and hear what was going on. Our men were already bringing in crowds of prisoners. . . . Milroy and his staff and a smaller portion of his troops escaped, having cut their way through. It is the greatest disappointment to all classes that he was not taken. The whole of Ewell's Corps are here surrounding the town and those who had been on the south and west of the town soon came pouring through to join in the pursuit. The people were perfectly wild with delight and excitement and the troops no less so. They gave the regular Confederate yell in a way that astonished the Yankees in the hospitals. The Taylor Hotel porches were crowded with them eagerly looking on. Hundreds of women were down on Main St. bareheaded, waving and cheering. . . . When all had passed we came home to have breakfast prepared, and the rest of the day has been spent in receiving numbers of our friends and in working hard, as the servants are as crazy as possible and can not be kept out of the street long enough to accomplish anything. We have listened to the most exciting descriptions of the fighting of the past three days. Dr. and Mrs. Baldwin came home this morning and had quite a triumphant reception. The country people are flocking in in crowds and it is quite a gala day. . . . We have taken 5,000 prisoners and even more stores when Banks ran from here, for nothing was burned this time.

Julia Chase—June 16, 1863. We hear that Gen. Lee has possession of Arlington Heights & Longstreet has entered Hagerstown . . . but we don't believe a word of it. In all probability Stuart has made a raid into Pennsylvania, and that there will be a desperate struggle on the part of the Southern Army, there is not the least doubt; they have taken the aggressive, and we expect to hear of Washington being taken, also that they will invade the Northern States; if this will not open the eyes of the whole Nation and call forth all their energies nothing will. A secessionist says that from this point to Manassas is lined with troops but the Secesh do not always confine themselves to the truth. All the sutlers, with their goods, were taken at the fort, F. Meredith & J. Ginn among the number.

Laura Lee—June 16, 1863. Capt. Williamson came to breakfast before we were up. He waited very patiently. A number of the young men have been already by to get boots, shoes and clothes. They seem perfectly delighted with them and say they are invaluable to them. Major Green told us last night that he was going to bring Gen. Ewell and Gen. Early[8] to see us this evening, and Mary asked him to bring them to tea. He came this morning to get a box containing a pair of elegant boots, gloves, socks, handkerchief and nicknacks, which had been purchased to present to our lamented Jackson, but which were now sent to his successor, who had so worthily filled his place. Major Green said the gentlemen would come with pleasure. They were to be present at 5 o'clock at the raising of the Confederate flag at the fortifications. . . . Late in the evening Dr. Green and Capt. Brown came with Gen. Ewell's carriage to take us to the fortifications to see the flag raised. We had a charming drive and came home to tea with the two generals and most of their staff officers. We had tea in the yard, and then for an hour Gen. Ewell was receiving and sending dispatches, while we sat on the front porch with the officers who were not engaged with him. . . . Altogether it was a very pleasant evening.

Julia Chase—June 18, 1863. There seem to be very few troops about town, and have conducted themselves much better than heretofore. The

Union people, we think will not be disturbed, as the secessionists received so many favors from Gen. Milroy, tho' some who conducted themselves so dreadfully were punished. We have no fears. We are in the hands of the Almighty.

Laura Lee—June 18, 1863. More rumors today that we have taken Harper's Ferry and 4,000 prisoners and that Gen. Lee has again fought Hooker at Manassas gaining a great victory and driving him back towards Washington. A portion of our troops have been in Penn. for two days. Gen. Ewell told us in leaving the other night that the hardest fighting of the war was to be done now, and that we must all pray for them.

Julia Chase—June 20, 1863. Is there to be no end to the prisoners and stores that are captured by the Rebels? Is the whole Federal army asleep or lain down their arms? We should judge so. Some 49 wagons are passing by with captured stores from Maryland. Seems to us that the Federalists are just giving everything over into the hands of the Rebels. When will they rouse from their stupor? Are there no brave soldiers in our army? Are our Generals so stupid that they permit these things. God Almighty, stir them up, and may they be awakened to a sense of their inefficiency and help them to make a bold strike into this Rebellion. It is said that Cumberland, Williamsport, Hagerstown, Greencastle and Carlisle are in possession of the Rebels, passing along unmolested, without the least opposition. . . . Unless our soldiers and officers enter the war with heart and soul, determined to do their duty to their Country, and as soldiers, they will never gain a victory. There is too much drinking and money making to accomplish much, and how can we expect victories while such things continue.

Laura Lee—June 22, 1863. Today more reports about Hooker's advance. There must be another terrible battle. Major Mills and Capt. Garden dined with us, and just as they were leaving, Mr. Lawley arrived with his friend Col. Fremantle[9] of the Coldstream Guards. They bring bad news of Vicksburg. It is feared it cannot hold out.

Julia Chase—June 23, 1863. The rebels under Gen. Ewell are in Pennsylvania and are accomplishing their object in capturing horses, Negroes & cattle. We had supposed that something would have been done there on the part of the unionists, but so far as we can learn the rebels have marched through without the least resistance. Great God! How long shall this state of affairs continue. Hast thou given up the people of the North to their own destruction, is there no hope for our Country? Have mercy upon us we beseech Thee and arouse the energy of every man, that we may not become a by-word to all nations, a disgrace to the whole world. Some 2000 cattle have been captured besides great many horses, prisoners have also been brought in from Front Royal. We shall expect soon to see or hear that the entire Army in Virginia have been captured, or about to surrender. Some 30 pieces of cannon passed a short time ago, nearly all belonging to the U. States and nearly every man had on clothing taken from the Federal army. Have our leaders become a set of dunces or cowards, that such things are permitted. We feel like hiding our heads low in the dust & cry out shame, shame.

Laura Lee—June 25, 1863. Our whole army has crossed into Penn. The North is wild with fear. Large droves of cattle are passing through here everyday, sent back from Pa. Our army is to be subsisted entirely in the enemy's country. It is a time of intense anxiety and interest. We look eagerly each hour for reports of progress. It is said that we are to be deserted even by our Provost Guard. The stores are being sent from here, and the sick from the hospitals as fast as they are able.

Julia Chase—June 26, 1863. Provisions are very high. Butter selling for $1.00 a lb. Beef 50cts to $1.00 per lb. Onions 25cts a bunch, cherries 25cts. quart and everything else in proportion. The Richmond papers say that the Federals appeared in force at the White House, about 15 miles from Richmond. They also claim a glorious victory at Vicksburg, that Gen. Grant has lost 10,000 men but again has attacked them, whether he will be successful or not time only will determine. The rebels under Imboden are playing sad havoc on the Balt. & Ohio R. Road, having broken up the road from the Little Cacapon to the Grand [Tunnel] west of Cheat River. Great amount of property has been destroyed at Cumberland. The road also between Harper's Ferry and the Point of Rocks has been torn up, & one wagon burned. Is there no end to this. . . . Wagons and cattle are still being brought in from Pennsylvania.

Laura Lee—June 27, 1863. We have charming accounts from Pa. Thus far the progress of our army has been a perfect pleasure party. The men march through the country shouting and singing and telling the people how the war will soon be over, we have come back into the "Union." They live on the fat of the land, taking everything and paying in Confederate money. The merchants closed their stores, but they were re-opened and the soldiers proved rapid customers, paying always in Confederate money to the great disgust of the Yankees. Some of the Richmond papers complain that they pay at all, but Gen. Lee does not permit stealing in his army. They are lying around Chambersburg at the last accounts, the cavalry flying around the country in every direction bringing in horses, cattle, sheep, &c. The Pennsylvanians are frantic with rage and terror and Lincoln tells them they must defend themselves with militia.

Laura Lee—June 29, 1863. Willie Taliaffero came from Pa. yesterday with a train of ordnance stores captured and sent back. He said that when he left the whole army was at Chambersburg, but today it is said that Gen. Lee with Longstreet's Corps are moving toward Baltimore to meet Hooker and Ewell and Hill towards Harrisburg.

Julia Chase—July 1, 1863. It is rumored that Lee is within 15 miles of Baltimore, also that Harrisburg, the capital of Penn. is in possession of the rebels. Strange that this army should take whatever towns it may desire, without any opposition. . . . We expect to hear of very stirring times shortly. Baltimore & Washington menaced, should arouse in every man's heart, who is a true patriot, the desire and purpose to do all he can for the putting down of this rebellion. . . . The Richmond papers have nothing in regard to Vicksburg, so we are entirely in the dark.

Laura Lee—July 3, 1863. Our troops are at York, apparently crossing over towards Baltimore. The people are driving off the cattle, to try to secure them but not being very successful, as a full supply for the army is demanded and paid for in Confederate money, to the great disgust of the sellers.

Laura Lee—July 4, 1863. We did not remember that this was the 4th until dinnertime. Our old United States feelings have so entirely passed away.

Julia Chase—July 5, 1863. Gen. Hooker has been superceded by Gen. Meade.[10] A battle took place between him and Gen. Lee near Gettysburg on Friday, Gen. L having gained a victory, Meade falling back towards Baltimore, and is hard pressed by Lee, probably fighting may be going on today, unless the whole Federal army has been cut to pieces. Gen. Johnston, it is said has taken 5000 prisoners. Our hope is all gone and we cannot expect but that a few days will determine the fate of Baltimore & Washington, that our Government is not able to maintain itself. Oh God! Thou knowest what is best for us, help us submit to thy decrees, feeling that thou art just, that our wickedness is so great, that our Country's cause cannot be a just and righteous one & that thou art arrayed against us. If thou be not for us, who shall stand? Have mercy, we beseech thee, upon us. Gen. Grant it is said has also been defeated at Vicksburg. If our armies cannot succeed better, it would be far preferable that peace should follow than to sacrifice so many lives, and be considered a disgrace forever. . . . Can it be possible that we are a nation of cowards.

Laura Lee—July 6, 1863. We heard early yesterday morning that there had been a terrible battle at Gettysburg, and at night the reports which came in. . . have been very disastrous to us. Eight Generals killed, whole brigades cut to pieces, Gen. Lee retreating to re-cross the Potomac.[11] We find today that the reports are greatly exaggerated, but still they are far from what we could wish.

Julia Chase—July 7, 1863. It was said yesterday that the Federals had possession of Gettysburg, and Gen. Lee had fallen back to this side. We only hope that it may prove true, and that a victory might be gained by the National troops. The wounded have been coming since yesterday. . . . All unite in saying that it was an awful battle and great slaughter on both sides. Our town is alive with soldiers, and the secession ladies will have their hands full attending to the wants of the wounded. A very rainy day but quite warm. . . . There is a guard around Mr. A. Griffith's house and he is not permitted to leave his home. Mr. Besore was also arrested last week. It was said that when these troops first came in none of the Union people were to be disturbed, but they were not left in peace long. It will not be well for the Secessionists when the Federal army returns, if they molest those who do not, or have not disturbed them—but we will hope for the best.

Laura Lee—July 7, 1863. This has been an awful day. From daylight, crowds, hundreds of wounded men have been trooping by, all wounded in the hand, arm or head but able to walk. The commissary furnished rations for the citizens to cook, and the poor fellows had a good meal as soon as they arrived; some at the hospitals but hundreds at the doors as they pass through the streets. We hear nothing but rumors from the army but they are much more favorable than yesterday, but still vague and unreliable. . . . The fighting continued from Wednesday until Sunday and our loss is terrible. The ambulances of the badly wounded are still coming in at 9 o'clock, in a pouring rain, and everything is sad and dreary. To add to our other source of sadness, Mr. Barton, who has been failing for some time, about 12 o'clock began to sink, and was thought to be dying. He has revived somewhat, but will not probably survive long. About an hour ago an officer came to beg to be directed where to take two Lieut., each with a leg amputated. We could not send the poor fellows wandering about the town at such a time to seek lodgings and hastily prepared a bed in the back parlor and had them brought there. They have had supper and seem quite comfortable. . . . All the wounded who are able to walk are to go on tomorrow to Staunton to make way for others coming. It is heart-rending to live among such scenes. We have had no Richmond mail for three days and it is said that the Yankees have made another raid and have cut off communication.

Julia Chase—July 10, 1863. The clouds which have been heavy so long are disappearing and the light is breaking. The news comes to us today that Vicksburg, that stronghold, has fallen, with a complete surrender, also that Lee's army has been badly used up in Pennsylvania, it is thought his ammunition has given out, and he is making his escape through Frederick City. God be praised, if what we hear is correct. . . . About 10,000 wounded have been received here, all that are able to go on to Staunton. The loss has been very heavy on both sides, especially in regard to officers.

Julia Chase—July 12, 1863. The 4th of July, 1863 will be memorable as the surrender of Vicksburg. This is quite a blow to the South and there are many in our midst who will not credit it. We have no news from the Army of the Potomac & Gen. Lee, only that skirmishing is kept up every day. It has been a drawn game in Pennsylvania & Maryland, with heavy losses on both sides, would that our leaders & men would exert themselves, and that we might be gladdened with the sound of a great victory.

Julia Chase—July 15, 1983. Gen. Lee's main army is this side of the river, probably for the purpose of being nearer his supplies, it is said, however, his troops will pass through here tonight & tomorrow, falling back— we can only hope it may be true, and yet we would rather hear that they had been crushed in Maryland & Pennsylvania.

Julia Chase—July 18, 1863. Some 60 or more federal prisoners have been brought in this week. . . . The rebel wounded are still coming in a few each day. Port Hudson[12] is in possession of the Federals and an attack is being made upon Charleston. The papers speak of their having Morris' Island and preparing to shell the city.

Julia Chase—July 23, 1863. Ewell's Corps passed through town today, great many persons leaving and driving off their cattle, fearing the dreadful Yankees will get them. Very warm and dusty.

Julia Chase—July 24, 1863. We hear that the Federals are at one place and then another, but think there are none this side of Martinsburg. Several thousand cavalry passed through to Front Royal this morning and our town has been very quiet this afternoon, but few horsemen to enliven the streets, tho' there are cavalry still at Bunker Hill and they will be about until the

Federals make their appearance. The Secessionists are rather downcast, don't like the idea of their army leaving.

Laura Lee—July 29, 1863. Since my last entry just three weeks ago I have been confined to my bed, sick and suffering in mind and body, having to endure all the distressing and depressing influences of being left again to the enemy. The awful battle of Gettysburg disorganized both armies so seriously that neither made any attempt to follow up. Gen. Lee withdrew to Hagerstown, where he remained for three days offering battle to the Yankees, but they did not respond. In consequence of the wonderful torrents of rain which had fallen, the river became so high as to make it necessary to re-cross into Va. for fear of communication being cut off. . . . After lying quiet for a week watching what Meade would do, the army marched back through here to intercept him in his [march] on to Richmond through Eastern Va. We were left last Friday without a soldier except the wounded at the hospitals, and on Sunday afternoon had the pleasure of a call from about 150 Yankee cavalry. They adopted the courteous style. We were very polite to everybody. They went to the hospital and said they would wait until the next morning to parole the men, but that night a party of our cavalry came down the valley and drove them out. Since then our men have picketed below the town. Just as I am writing, the loud shouting on Main St. announces that the villains are in again, but in what numbers we cannot hear. Things have a very depressing appearance for us just now. The loss of Vicksburg and Port Hudson are serious calamities. We have driven off the enemy again at Charleston, and the serious riots through the North wherever they attempted to enforce the draft, are very favorable to us. . . . Mr. Barton died on Tuesday night, the 7th and Margaret Page, after a short illness, on Thursday, the 23rd. The usual stampede of citizens has taken place from here, but many more families have gone this time than usual.

Julia Chase—July 30, 1863. Again have we been agreeably surprised to find ourselves in the U. States. Our cavalry cam into town this afternoon at a flying rate, in pursuit of some Rebels, who were on the hill looking at them. . . . Have had the privilege of seeing the <u>Bal. American</u> of the 28th. Gen. Lee has eluded the pursuit of Gen. Meade (& we regret it so much) and is in his old position at Culpeper & Gordonsville. Morris' Island at Charleston, is in possession of the Federals & in a second attack on Fort Wagner in Charleston Harbor our troops have again been repulsed. . . . The Federals have evacuated Jackson, Mississippi. Rosecrans is organizing a force to attack Atlanta & to make raids on the N Western Georgia R. Road.

Julia Chase—August 5, 1863. Gen. Averill with his command left this morning at an early hour for Western Virginia as is supposed. We hear that Imboden has made a raid again upon the R. Road, whether correct or not cannot say. Our town is again in a state of quietude, we had expected to have found ourselves in Dixie today, but should judge there were few if any rebels near us. The N. York Cavalry were expected here but they have not made their appearance, tho' we don't look for troops here until the R. Road is in running order, which will be a few more days. Monday's papers says the attack upon Fort Wagner is to be abandoned and Fort Sumpter to be assailed. God grant it may fall and the Stars & Stripes soon floating upon it. . . . Mr. Sam Miller died today; a child of Mr. Dooley's buried yesterday of Dyptheria, several cases in town.

Laura Lee—August 5, 1863. Another week and I am still on the bed almost constantly, feeling very weak and languid. The weather is very hot and everything is sad and depressing. The Yankees who came in last Wednesday proved to be a brigade of cavalry under Gen. Averill. They have never really occupied the town, though they had guards at various points, but their head-quarters were several miles from town. There never has been such an easy time for us, no searching of houses and no troubling of the citizens in any way. They were rather tyrannical at the hospital at first, confining the surgeons to the house and forbidding the ladies to enter it, but it was only for a day or two and the restrictions were removed. Today we are again free, though for how long we can scarcely conjecture. They all went off last night, but it is reported that there is a force of infantry at Bunker's Hill on the way here. If so, we are booked for another occupation. We have at least the satisfaction today of sending letters up the Valley and of hearing of our friends.

Julia Chase—August 6, 1863. Today is appointed by the President of the U. States as a day of Thanksgiving, Praise and prayer to Almighty God for the successes given unto our National arms during the past month. Very warm weather we are having the past week. We hear that Mr. Phil Williams has written a paper signed by prominent secessionists in town to Imboden request-ing him to have the guerrillas removed from our midst, as they are committing so many depredations, stealing all the horses they can lay hands on.

Laura Lee—August 11, 1863. We are enjoying a blessed time of quiet and freedom. No Yankees anywhere near us and only Confederate scouts around all the time. We are able to live quite comfortably, as plenty of mar-keting is brought to town and vegetables are very abundant. Our wounded officers (Capt. Flower and Capt. Cameron) left us this morning. There are only 40 men left now in the hospitals here. . . . We have a mail down the Valley every few days, which is an immeasurable comfort to us all. We have great hope that this place will never be occupied by the Yankees again. . . . The weather has been intensely hot for a week past, and consequently I do not recover my strength but feel scarcely able to creep about. All we hear from our army is that Lee and Meade are both being reinforced from the West and are preparing for a fierce struggle.

Laura Lee—August 12, 1863. We had another visit from the Yankees today but they were only a small party of cavalry who stayed but a few hours and troubled no one except Capt. Shearer, who happened to be breakfasting in town and who was captured.

Julia Chase—August 13, 1863. Our troops, consisting of the 1st N York & 12th Penn. came into town this morning and succeeded in capturing the notorious guerrilla Captain Geo. Shearer. Several others were in town but effected their escape. The cavalry remained but two hours & left taking bedding from the hospital. Several of the Union refugees embraced the opportunity of coming home, tho' their stay was short. Went to Martinsburg this morning to see F[ather] who has been there a week. Excessively warm weather.

Julia Chase—August 17, 1863. We are again in the United States, the cavalry taking possession of our town this morning, brought provisions up for the rebel sick at the York Hospital, also at Jordan's. How different the treatment towards the rebel sick than is shown towards the Federal sick, when within reach, or under the rebels, the kindness seems confined to the one side. . . . North Carolina is getting heartily tired and sick of the war, dissatisfaction with the rebel rule, and we hope ere long to see her applying for admission again into the Union.

Laura Lee—August 18, 1863. We had quite a stir yesterday about our servants. Emily got into a passion and said she would get the Yankees to take her away with them. She went down the street to where they were to ask them. Sarah was very much distressed, but said that if Emily and Jim Will went, she must go too. However, Emily cooled off and came back home, and no one took the least notice of her blaze. She is in a very gracious humor today, but I have not the least doubt that she intends to go sooner or later. We thought for some time that things were tending that way. It will be very unpleasant, but only what everyone else has had to submit to. . . . We are so comfortable now that I fear it cannot last long, but we will be thankful for it and enjoy it as long as we can.

Julia Chase—August 20, 1863. It is said that Gov. Letcher has called for the Legislature to enforce the Conscription Act, calling for every male from 16 yrs. to 60 and the guerillas have commenced already to carry into effect here, several have been conscripted and some are already leaving town to get out of their clutches. Should this act be carried out, there would be a general skedaddling on the part of the citizens here and there would not be 100 men left in the place. Would for the sake of the Unionists, that Winchester could be held by the Federal troops. . . . It is said that Gen. Lee intends to enter Maryland again; we would suppose after his unsuccessful attempt so recently he would not be in a hurry. We have been looking for Imboden to make his appearance, as it was rumored he was but a short distance from Winchester, but as yet but few bushwhackers have been seen.

Julia Chase—August 21, 1863. Today's paper says that no change has been made in either Army of Meade or Lee's and there is no reason to believe the Army of the Potomac is to fall back towards Washington. . . . Mr. Kinzel was conscripted yesterday, and some have gone off post haste to Martinsburg.

Laura Lee—August 22, 1863. Rumors immeasurable. Meade retreating, Lee pursuing, Ewell advancing in this direction, Staunton again threatened & c., nothing certain.

Julia Chase—August 24, 1863. The news from Charleston, that the attack was commenced on Fort Sumpter on Monday last by Gen. Gilmore's land batteries. The Navy shortly after joined in the attack. The entire ironclad fleet with 7 wooden gunboats attacking Fort Wagner & Gregg silencing both & shelling the shore batteries to play upon Fort Sumpter. . . . Rosecrans army is near Chattanooga, where Bragg is strongly posted, and a battle may occur at any day. Two hundred citizens were killed by the Rebel guerrilla Quantrell & his men at Laurence City, Kansas.[13] Lee is supposed to be moving off upon the Va. Central R. Road to Richmond.

Julia Chase—August 25, 1863. The siege of Charleston is still progressing very favorably, Fort Sumpter to be surrendered or the city will be shelled by Gen. Gilmore. All non-combatants leaving the city very fast. Sumpter badly damaged. The fort said to be in ruin. It has been rumored here in town for a day past, that Fort Sumpter had fallen, the news coming from the Valley, whether this correct or not, we can't say. The <u>Richmond Sentinel</u> of the 24th says that the Yankees commenced shelling the city of Chattanooga yesterday, without giving notice. All quiet today. The rebel Quantrell was being closely pursued by Gen. Lane, the farmers flocking to him with their arms, determined to follow him into Missouri, & if Quantrall disbanded his gang they would hunt them down like wolves & shoot them. Later, it is said that Quantrell had been captured & 20 of his men killed.

Laura Lee—August 25, 1863. Fort Sumpter has fallen, and although that fact does not necessarily include the fall of the city, yet it is very distressing.

Julia Chase—August 28, 1863. The news from Charleston is gloriously encouraging. On Sat. night the Monitor fleet made a successful assault upon Fort Sumpter. The fire was directed upon the sea wall and was most effective, the balls & shells went through the wall, making huge holes. The Fort during the attack only firing a single gun but the other forts, Moultrie, Gregg & Beauregard rained shot & shell on the Monitors striking them frequently, but doing no damage. Only an immense pile of ruins remain of Fort Sumpter. . . . Preparations are being made by Gen. Gilmore for a grand attack by the army & navy upon Fort Wagner and Gregg.

Laura Lee—August 28, 1863. Milroy's trial is not over, neither has Fort Sumpter surrendered, though battered nearly to pieces. We walked this evening with the Bartons to the fortifications and it was very gratifying to see how much labor and expense the Yankees had expended on works which they had to abandon.

Julia Chase—September 1, 1863. The Federal cavalry came in this afternoon, between 5 & 6 o'clock, remained until 9 P.M., took one or two prisoners, also made a dash into town on the morning of the 29th, returning to Berryville.

Laura Lee—September 4, 1863. We are still living in peace and comfort. The Yankees were here on Wednesday evening but only for a little while, and they troubled no one. The weather is exquisite now, and except for the separation from so many friends and the constant anxiety we feel for them, we could almost fancy we were living in the good old times when war and all its attendant horrors were things we only read of. The Union people from here go to Martinsburg and get large supplies of everything. There is a good deal smuggled through for the "Secesh," though it requires great care and skill to accomplish it. There have been rumors for two days that Gen. Lee has moved on towards Maryland, but I can hear nothing to make me think the report true. There is nothing new from Charleston. The siege still going on.

Julia Chase—September 5, 1863. The papers are very barren of news this week, nothing from Charleston.

Julia Chase—September 6, 1863. The Federals entered town this morning between 1 & 2 o'clock, taking the Strasburg road, probably to break up the Provost Marshall's Office at Newtown & to capture if possible the conscript officer. Mr. Brannon Thatcher was arrested a few nights ago & carried off, it is said one of his neighbors was the cause of his arrest. The cavalry left at 6 P.M., taking some half dozen or more prisoners—quite a number from the army were in town, hidden away in the houses. The news from Charleston is that the shelling of that city was resumed from the Marsh Battery. . . & a few thrown into the city. It is said by deserters that the shells caused a great conflagration, one of them setting fire to a warehouse stored with cotton, a number of persons are said to be killed. . . . From Lexington (Ky.) Gen. Burnside had passed through the gaps in the Cumberland Mountains & was pushing on to Kingston, in Roane Co., some 40 miles from Knoxville. At Kingston he will have possession of the Va. & Tenn. R. Road, thus cutting off the retreat of the Rebels towards the west. Later, dispatches . . . say he has occupied Kingston, the rebs offering little serious opposition. All of E. Tenn. except the Chattanooga region has been evacuated by the rebs & is now free. Gen. Rosecrans's army is also successfully operating & will shortly surmount the difficulties opposing the advance on Chattanooga. No change in the armies of Meade & Lee.

Laura Lee—September 8, 1863. Quite an excitement today about some ladies from here who were allowed to go to Baltimore to shop and on their return were stopped in Martinsburg and their belongings confiscated. Anne Sherrard was among the number and has lost 2 or 300 dollars worth. She came home last night very indignant and disappointed after being detained several days in Martinsburg. We hope still that she will get her things as Gen. McReynolds promised to do what he could for her.

Julia Chase—September 10, 1863. The news from Charleston is glorious. Forts Wagner & Gregg fly the flag of the Union & the whole of Morris Island is ours. It took place on the 6th. Our troops now hold Cumming's Point in full view of the city. The evacuation, according to Richmond papers, was preceded by a heavy bombardment from our batteries & iron clad fleet, which was kept up all day without intermission & far into the night. . . . Chattanooga has also been captured by Gen. Rosecrans, fleet footed Bragg moving for some point further south. Our forces at Waxahatchee, Alabama & another force advancing upon Rome, Georgia . . . Knoxville is occupied by the Union troops, which will prove a heavy blow to the South. Peace meetings are being held in different portions of the State of North Carolina.

Laura Lee—September 10, 1863. The "good McReynolds" sent Anne's trunk to her last night with all her things safe and in good order. No news from Charleston since the great gun burst. Great excitement in the North about the ironclads which are coming for us.

Laura Lee—September 11, 1863. Last night about ten o'clock dear Bob arrived most unexpectedly to us. He has a furlough of 15 days, but will only stay in town one day at a time, for fear of the Yankee cavalry who are continually coming in. Strother Barton came too. They give good accounts of the army and say there is no prospect of a move. Many furloughs are granted now. Reports from Charleston and Tennessee are very unfavorable. We feel very anxious. Dr. Baldwin died last night.

Julia Chase—September 12, 1863. Mother & Mary went to Martinsburg. Very warm today.

Laura Lee—September 12, 1863. Attended the funeral this morning. It was very large and a great deal of feeling was manifested. Bob and Strother went into the country before daybreak this morning. They will come to town again in a day or two if it is safe. Bob seems so happy to be with us. It is hard that he cannot stay while he has leave, instead of having to come in and out of town in the dark and be shut up in the house while he is here, for fear the Union people should inform against him.

Julia Chase—September 14, 1863. Mother arrived home with sister Ellen & Willie, from the West. The Federal troops repulsed at Fort Sumpter a few days ago. . . . General Meade's army has advanced across the Rappahannock & that we hold Culpeper C. House, capturing a number of prisoners and guns. It is supposed that Lee's army has fallen back to Richmond, portions of the army being sent to Charleston & Southwest. We hope it may not be long before the glad tidings shall be wafted over the land that Charleston that nest egg of treason, is no more. The Union forces have captured Fort Smith & Western Arkansas & the Indian Country are now in our possession. Gov. Letcher of this state has issued a proclamation, that all persons from the ages of 16 up to 60 shall be conscripted.

Laura Lee—September 14, 1863. The boys came to town on Saturday night, but hearing a report that the Yankees would be in the next morning they went out again about eleven o'clock. Sure enough, a large body of cavalry came yesterday but stayed only a few hours. As soon as they were

fairly off, we notified the boys, who returned to town. . . . They stayed all
night and until after dinner today, when they took a final leave go back to
the army. It has been a great pleasure to see them, but it is too hazardous to
be altogether satisfactory. As usual, there are plenty of rumors, that the
whole army is in motion, part gone to Tennessee, part to S. Carolina.

Julia Chase—September 21, 1863. Went to Martinsburg with Ellen &
to Baltimore on the night train. A battle has taken place between Rosecrans
& Bragg & Gen. R has been compelled to fall back, after two days of hard
fighting.[14] If Gen. Burnside reinforces him in time all will be right, but we
fear as Bragg has been largely reinforced & from Lee's army, that Rosecrans
will not have sufficient force to fight him. The secessionists of course
are very joyful.

Julia Chase—September 23, 1863. Came from Baltimore today, arriving home at 6 this afternoon.

Laura Lee—September 24, 1863. Time passes on so quietly that there is
nothing to record of what is going on here. The Yankees come to town
every two or three days and generally steal some horses, but with that
exception do not molest anyone. We have news of a victory in Tennessee
but no particulars as yet.

Julia Chase—September 25, 1863. The Rebels are quite thick in town
today, and we fear all communication will be cut off between us &
Martinsburg.

Laura Lee—September 25, 1863. Imboden and Gilmer have come
down the Valley on an expedition against Martinsburg. I do not expect that
they will accomplish anything.

Julia Chase—September 28, 1863. We are in Dixie now, no one is
allowed to go out on the Martinsburg road and there is said to be from 1 to
3000 troops around us, we hope to see the Yankees soon driving them out.
The Richmond papers claim a great victory in the Southwest, that Rosecrans has been badly beaten & 50 pieces of artillery captured. We fear that
Burnside has been prevented from reinforcing Gen. R. and that nearly all
the Southern army has been brought to bear against him. When will this
sad war end & peace & happiness return. The secessionists in town are
rejoicing because they say France has recognized the Southern Confederacy. Tho' all the European powers should wage war against us, we will not
give up but trust that a wise Providence will still bring us safely through
all our troubles. The weather is very delightful, tho' cool. . . . The <u>Balt.
American</u> of today states that Rosecrans loss in the battle . . . was 1700

killed, 8000 wounded, 50 guns captured by the enemy—a heavy loss, tho' the papers state that the loss of rebel officers have been very great. . . . We have hopes that Rosecrans may in time be sufficiently reinforced to assume the offensive & the result end in a grand victory to the National arms.

Laura Lee—September 28, 1863. Sure enough, Imboden has gone back without firing a gun, saying the Yankees are too strongly fixed in blockhouses to make an attack prudent. The news from Tennessee is good. Rosecrans driven back, his army retreating in total confusion, 15,000 prisoners, and 89 guns taken and plunder in proportion. Lee and Meade are facing each other on the Rapidan. There must be a battle before many days. The cavalry has been skirmishing for a week past. I dread to hear this.

CHAPTER FIVE

October 1863–April 1864

"Is there no hope for us in Virginia?"

While events in Virginia for the most part remained quiet, both Julia and
Laura continued to follow as best they could the military operations
in Tennessee and at Charleston. In the aftermath of the summer campaigns,
the Valley in many ways had become a no-man's-land, with cavalry raids from
both sides now commonplace and accepted as a part of everyday life. Adding
to the hard times was the renewal of hostilities between Unionists and Confederates, and arrests of individuals from both sides increased considerably.
Laura summed up the situation perfectly when she stated that the retaliation
system had begun and there was no telling where it would end.

Julia Chase—October 3, 1863. A beautiful day after the storm—warm
and pleasant. The report that the Rebel lines extend to within 4 miles of
Chattanooga is false, the movements of the Rebels are looked upon as indi-
cating a siege, tho' Rosecrans will be able soon to resume the offensive.
Rebel reports from Charleston state that our forces were still vigorously
working away on Battery Wagner, making considerable changes & throwing up considerable sand works facing James Island.[1] There is said to be
great suffering in the city of Mobile, in consequence of the scarcity of food.
A riot took place in that city a short [time ago] in which the military were
overpowered by the women, wives of soldiers in the Confederate army,
clamoring for bread or peace.

Laura Lee—October 3, 1863. The Confederates have continued around
us this week, and the Yankees have kept closely in Martinsburg. They have
but a very small force there, most of the troops have been sent to Rosecrans.
Things have been quiet there since he retreated to Chattanooga. There will
be more fighting there very soon as both armies have been largely reinforced. We have had letters from the Rapidan which say that the prospect of

110

a battle there has passed away for the present, Meade apparently dreading to cross the river to attack. Things at Charleston are quiet on both sides.

Julia Chase—October 5, 1863. The news from the Army of the Cumberland is of the most satisfactory and cheering character. The army has been heavily reinforced & Gen. Rosecrans is expected to resume offensive operations shortly, his line of communication is unbroken. . . . At Charleston, Gen. Gilmore[2] is still constructing his heavy batteries on Cumming's Point, under strong rebel fire. . . . The active work of the siege was expected soon to recommence from the new batteries. . . . The rebel generals Imboden, Jackson, & others contemplate a movement on the western part of Virginia to lay waste, rob, murder & plunder the people in that section. The Gov. is putting forth strenuous efforts to put to nought the plans of these rebel generals & we hope every man will arise & do his duty.

Julia Chase—October 8, 1863. The news from Tennessee is very encouraging. It is said that Gen. Burnside has driven the enemy before him southward to the Hiawassee River and eastward as far as Greenville on the E Tennessee & Va. R. Road.[3] By this means we now hold all the passes to N Carolina & the right wing of Burnside's army is put in communication with the Army of the Cumberland. . . . Mr. James Mason, the Minister appointed by Jeff Davis to England, has withdrawn from that country to France, to act in concert probably with Slidell. The Southern Confederacy is not very well pleased with the conduct of England, hence the withdrawal. . . . Nothing new from the Army of the Potomac. Imboden[4] with 800 cavalry came down the Valley as far as Bunker Hill, but made no demonstration, he found probably the force at Martinsburg little too strong for him I imagine.

Julia Chase—October 9, 1863. Advises from Chattanooga represent the position of Rosecrans as impregnable & all his communication open. Dispatches from Bragg's army state on Monday the Rebels commenced shelling Chattanooga from Lookout Mountain, Gen. Rosecrans batteries replying briskly. . . . The withdrawal of Mr. Mason from England is still commented on by all the journals. . . . The guerillas who infest our neighborhood are robbing the people. One last night had a sack of salt taken from his wagon on his way up from Martinsburg, a gentleman in the country had 20 sheep stolen & as the country people bring their butter in those from the hospital take it from them. The Secesh must never complain about the Yankees (as they term them) stealing, for their own party are as bad if not worse.

Laura Lee—October 10, 1863. Another week of quiet. No Yankees here, and no news from anywhere. The weather very cold for the season, entirely too much so for comfort.

Julia Chase—October 12, 1863. The news from Chattanooga up to Friday are very encouraging to the national cause. . . . The damage to Rosecrans communication had all been repaired. Bragg's bombardment of Chattanooga from Lookout Mountain was a complete failure. . . . A party of Rebels on Tuesday were overtaken near Franklin by our cavalry, there they were again routed, 300 prisoners & 4 pieces of artillery being captured. Rosecrans is still receiving reinforcements & it is said that another division of Lee's army has been sent on to Bragg. . . . Jeff Davis' brother companion, A. H. Stephens,[5] has sailed for France with the intention of treating with Napoleon for recognition of the Confederacy. Poor Confederacy, it has had a hard time. England has given her the cold shoulder, but it is thought by the Rebels that France looks more kindly upon them & they hope soon to proclaim it far & wide that she has come to their relief. The rebel Quantrell has again made his appearance, upon an escort of Gen. Blunt near Ft. Scott. The rebs, 300 in number, dressed as Union soldiers, attacked his escort of 100. 78 of the Union forces were killed, it is said after they were captured. Gen. B. escaped & meeting reinforcements, started in pursuit of them. God grant they may be caught & meet their fate. Mrs. Wm. Henry Gold was buried a few days since, leaving a family of 7 children, the oldest not 15.

Julia Chase—October 14, 1863. Little excitement in town this morning, in consequence of the arrest of Mr. Trenary by the Rebels. They are determined he shall not run his stage from Winchester to Martinsburg, although they are aware of the fact that we are dependent on the <u>dreadful</u> <u>Yankees</u> for supplies. Nothing can be obtained from Richmond. Mr. T. was ordered by one of the Rebels to deliver up his horses & stage & tho' he had two pistols presented at him by these rascals, he did not flinch & would not yield, but was willing to go before Gilmore & have the matter decided. The result is that the stage cannot run until Gen. Lee is written to & heard from, so I suppose all communication will be cut off between us and Martinsburg. It is reported that fighting has been going on between Meade & Lee, and that Meade has fallen back towards Washington. We also hear that Rosecrans has surrendered, tho' we don't credit a word of the last.

Laura Lee—October 15, 1863. We are to have stirring times again. The town was full of our cavalry this morning and Imboden's whole command camped only 8 miles off. Meade has retired and Lee is following him. There has been fighting and we have taken 800 prisoners. This is all we know certainly, though there are many rumors. It is reported tonight that the Yankees have evacuated Martinsburg. It is rather unfortunate for us that communication with Baltimore is cut off just now as we heard only the day before yesterday of a large quantity of things for us, which were to be sent as soon as was possible.

Julia Chase—October 16, 1863. Still raining, with no prospect of clear weather. Yesterday's paper rec'd this morning, says that no general engagement has taken place between Meade & Lee, but pretty heavy cavalry fights, with severe loss in Gen. Gregg's division of the National Army. . . . The Army of the Potomac is on the north side of the Rappahannock, & it is said that Gen. Meade's position is such that any attempt to interrupt his communications by the Rebels will be fruitless. An attempt was made by the Rebels at Charleston to blow up the frigate Ironsides by a torpedo but has failed. But little if any damage been done to her. It is said the citizens of that city have offered a large sum in gold for the destruction of that vessel. The result of the elections in the states of Penn. & Ohio are very encouraging, showing the triumph of the loyal & the prostration of treason in those states by most decided majorities. The Copperheads will have to hang their heads low, and even the South were expecting much from these elections, hoping that that traitor Vallandighan would have succeeded in being Governor.[6]

Julia Chase—October 18, 1863. Another charming day, more like summer, sitting with open windows & doors. It was rumored a day or two ago, that the Federals had all evacuated Martinsburg, but the cavalry made their appearance in town this morning, also infantry & artillery passed out of the edge of town on the Berryville Road. Cannonading has been heard very distinctly all the forenoon, and it is said that Imboden & Gilmore passed through Berryville last evening, so that we fear that the Federals may perhaps have been captured, unless their force was sufficient to drive out the Rebels. A little fight also took place at Hedgesville yesterday. Out of the 35 Rebs who went down only 9 returned & nearly all of them without hats or horses. . . . The paper says that Rosecrans has shelled out nearly all those of Bragg's army who had possession of Lookout Mountain commanding the town of Chattanooga. We hope to hear some stirring news from that vicinity ere long.

Laura Lee—October 18, 1863. Yesterday we were roused by the passing of a company of Yankee cavalry. They just passed through the town and went down the Berryville Road. There was heavy cannonading during the day in that direction and at night we heard that Imboden had attacked

Charlestown and captured about 700 prisoners and all their stores. He sent them off at once and secured them. It was rumored last night, both from the North and South, that Rosecrans had surrendered, but it needs confirmation. Gen. Lee is reported at Bristow Station. A. P. Hill, who was sent round to Thoroughfare Gap to intercept Meade, failed in doing so, and some of those trifling North Carolinians ran and we lost about 600 men and Meade escaped us.

Julia Chase—October 20, 1863. Quite a large force of Federal cavalry came in town today, remaining some four hours—probably to ascertain the whereabouts of Imboden. It is believed he has crossed the river at Front Royal. . . . The soldiers did not conduct themselves very well today, and the officers do not appear to check or forbid such conduct. Stores were broken into & Mr. Atwell's about to be burned. They had made a fire under the counter. . . . If the Federal officers countenance such doings, we cannot as loyal people expect much, if any, protection. The soldiers say, that the Southern soldiers did so in Penn. but once ought to be sufficient for Winchester, as the cavalry coming so often & committing such depredations every time, there will be no safety in living here.

Laura Lee—October 20, 1863. We had a most disagreeable time with the Yankees yesterday. A large body of cavalry and artillery were sent here in pursuit of Imboden and were all the afternoon feeding their horses and themselves in the streets all around us. They were very rude and audacious in our yards and kitchens all the time. A party of them sent into the house demanding supper and saying if it was not given to them they would take it. There was no help but to let Sarah give them bread and butter. Mrs. Polk has returned from Martinsburg. She got permission from Gen. Pierce to have the box brought on from Baltimore and we hope it may come any day. Mrs. Polk's sister E. just from Clarkesburg with two trunks and a carpet bag, and protection from Gen. Kelly for her baggage. We hope she has some things for us amongst it.

Laura Lee—October 23, 1863. All is quiet around us and we have no news from a distance except that Rosecrans has been removed and Thomas[7] put in his place. Our new minister, Mr. Maury, arrived here on Wednesday. Yesterday afternoon we walked out to the furthest line of fortifications, where the Louisianians charged upon the Yankees and drove them out. It was a charming evening and very pleasant and interesting expedition. I brought home a small cannon ball, which I found lodged in a tree. I have just completed two new nightgowns, made out of three old curtains. Everything we have almost has been made over, and turned and twisted and made the most of.

Julia Chase—October 27, 1863. The intelligence comes to us that Lee has in force crossed the Rappahannock. A portion of his infantry made the transit of the river on two pontoon bridges, near Rappahannock Station, driving back Gregg's cavalry division, which suffered severely. What this movement of Lee means seems a mystery, like many other moves he has made. Whether he intends advancing on to Washington, time only will determine. Gen. Grant[8] has arrived at Chattanooga. The rebs were moving in large bodies to the left of that city & it was rumored that Atlanta & Rome had been attacked in their rear. . . . The Federal cavalry made a raid into town this morning, bringing with them 20 prisoners, 4 of whom were officers. Omar Gregg a prisoner. Chap Reilly was captured, but by representing himself a citizen of Strasburg he was released.

Laura Lee—October 28, 1863. These villainous Yankees have been tormenting us again. Yesterday morning before day about 300 passed through the town, and at night they returned and scattered all over the town to make the citizens give them supper. Mr. Maury, Mr. & Mrs. Baker, Mr. & Mrs. Meade and Mr. Clark were all taking tea with us, and just as we finished tea the Yankees began to come demanding supper. Five different parties came, some of them very rude and some asking quite humbly. We gave to some and refused others. This morning we heard . . . that they had seized and rifled Mr. Maury's trunk, which was being brought down the Valley, and which contained all his worldly possessions. . . . It has excited a great deal of sympathy for him and great efforts are being made to replace his loss.

Julia Chase—October 29, 1863. It is said cannonading has been heard in town today, and that Lee is driving Meade back. This is sorrowful news. Is there no hope for us in Virginia? Is it impossible for the Army of the Potomac to accomplish anything in this state? God have mercy upon us. Hear our cries & crown our Armies with success.

Julia Chase—October 30, 1863. An advance has been made by Gen. Thomas on Gen. Bragg, by a flank movement, against Lookout Mountain, driving him from his position. The enemy hope to drive Gen. Burnside out of East Tennessee, turn the flank of the Army at Chattanooga. The active siege of Charleston commenced on Monday last, Gen. Gilmore & Admiral Dahlgren engaging the Rebel batteries throughout the afternoon. Important arrests have been made in New York, facts of importance concerning the business of running the blockade, also throwing new light on the conduct & character of Vallandigham.

Laura Lee—November 2, 1863. We were very happy yesterday at being in our own dear old Church again. We like our new Pastor very much. Sister E. returned last Monday from her western journey. She had a great deal of trouble and annoyance, and at Martinsburg the Yankees took away from her 125 dollars worth of goods. . . . We have had many letters today. Those from the army say that the fall campaign in Va. is over, and that the army is lying quiet on the banks of the Rappahannock, where it will probably remain for the winter. So ends our hope of having them here.

Julia Chase—November 4, 1863. The Federals in again today, took 6 prisoners. One was shot so badly he could not be taken away. We hope they may be able to capture all these bushwhackers who are lurking about. There are indications that Gen. Meade is about to give battle to Gen. Lee. It would be a happy & glorious thing if Lee could be beaten soundly & our troops gain possession of Richmond, thereby releasing the Union prisoners who are suffering so in their prisons. God grant that deliverance may come to those poor creatures before it is too late. The accounts we have of their suffering is heart-rendering. Of over 100 released, 40 have died from exposure & starvation. We never want to hear talked of the chivalry of the South but we do hope to hear & see of an onward movement to Richmond, and that the efforts of the Federal army may be successful.

Laura Lee—November 4, 1863. The Yankees were in town this morning for a few hours. They picked up a few stray Confederates and arrested two of the hospital nurses and would have carried them off, but the Doctor . . . succeeded in getting them released for six days. The Yankees said they would be up in a few days to carry off all at the hospital, patients, doctors, nurses and all. This is a great outrage, as all have been paroled.

Julia Chase—November 5, 1863. The elections which have lately taken place in the Free States, including Maryland, are very cheering. The news from Charleston, in the late attack upon Fort Sumpter, is that the object of the attack was the prevention of the design of the Rebels to construct new batteries and covered ways in the Fort at the channel side by demolishing if possible the gorge wall & leveling the foundations to the water's edge. . . . The Rebel accounts say the cannonading was continued a whole week, day & night, directed principally against the sea wall, which fell with a terrible crash on Sat. last, crushing in its ruin a number of Rebel soldiers who were stationed inside to repel any assault which might have been made on the Fort. . . . There seems great scarcity of food in Richmond & the impossibility of obtaining bread at any price.

Laura Lee—November 5, 1863. Mary and I have just returned from a night expedition to the hospital. The surgeons have managed during the day to make every arrangement with the greatest secrecy and they will all go off as soon as the men can be placed in the wagons. We went down with the servants to bring away some of the things which were to be taken care of and to say good-bye to the poor fellows. . . . We have had many letters lately. All agree that there is no prospect of another battle this winter.

Julia Chase—November 7, 1863. At Martinsburg today, returning this afternoon. Today's paper speaks of an advance by Gen. Meade on the Rebels south of the Rappahannock & a battle was confidently expected. . . . A terrible riot has broken out among the miners in the vicinity of Mauch Chunk, Pa., growing out of enforcing the draft. Several murders have been committed, including the coal operator who was murdered in the presence of his family in his own house. Great change in the weather. Our Indian Summer has passed and winter is creeping on.

Laura Lee—November 7, 1863. We have heard that Dr. Dixon and his party reached Woodstock in safety last night, and have gone on today. They are now quite out of danger. They did not get off from here until ½ past 1 o'clock, as they could not begin to secure the wagons until after dark for fear of giving the alarm to these treacherous union people about here. . . . The Yankees have not been here since Wednesday, but a large body of them went through Millwood yesterday. They are in a panic at Martinsburg and have everything packed up.

Julia Chase—November 9, 1863. Very cold today—first fall of snow this afternoon. Good news from the Army of the Potomac. The enemy driven across the Rappahannock, 1200 prisoners with a number of officers and seven pieces of cannon captured. We hope to have further news of encouragement and that Gen. Lee may be badly whipped. The bombardment of Fort Sumpter still continues. Tho' the Rebel flag has been shot away a number of times, they still continue to hold out. Were the cause of the Rebels a righteous one, their perseverance & bravery in holding out so long would be an example worthy of imitation. The news from E Tennessee is still exciting, showing that the Rebels are making desultory attempts to maintain their position at some points. . . . The people of East Tennessee are reported as exhibiting very satisfactory signs of loyalty.

Laura Lee—November 9, 1863. We heard last night that the Yankees who were in Millwood on Saturday, had crossed to the Valley Road and were stealing and burning and behaving dreadfully. They went as far up as

Woodstock in pursuit of our hospital party, but they were safe having two days start. The Yankees returned through here, where arriving at dinnertime, scattered all over the town in search of provisions. Six different sets came here, but it being in the day we were brave enough to refuse to give them anything. They arrested Mr. Maury and his brother on the charge of having been in the army, but soon released them. To our great joy, they went off before dark.

Julia Chase—November 11, 1863. No fighting has taken place between Meade & Lee since Saturday last, excepting cavalry skirmishes. It is thought that Lee is falling back to Richmond, & within the fortifications they will attempt to check any advance of the Federal Army. . . . A great scarcity of food prevails in Richmond and fears are entertained of starvation there this winter. The Union prisoners in Libby Prison[9] have been cut off their rations of meat, there not being enough to supply the Southern soldiers. Measures are being taken by the Government to have provisions sent them. Very delightful day, the weather pleasant & warm.

Laura Lee—November 11, 1863. Rather gloomy news today. The Baltimore papers claim that Meade advanced and surprised our army, and captured the whole of Hay's La. brigade. Averill is threatening Staunton and all travel up the Valley is stopped.

Julia Chase—November 12, 1863. There has been no engagement between Meade & Lee, and Lee has fallen back to his strongly fortified position on the south bank of the Rapidan. It is thought by some that Gen. Lee has been sent South to supercede Bragg, & retrieve the character of that Army; that Longstreet is about to take command of the Army of Virginia. Refugees from Dixie are arriving at Newbern in large numbers, chiefly young men or boys, flying from the conscription.

Julia Chase—November 16, 1863. The bombardment of Sumpter is still slowly continued, but has already reached the utmost results as far as the demolition of the fort is concerned. It is now no longer a ruin but simply a heap of pulverized masonry. Great dissatisfaction prevails in Bragg's Army, it is not being altogether confined to the Kentucky & Tennessee troops. . . . The accounts still come to us of the severe treatment the Union prisoners have received from their confinement in Richmond, 53 out of the 180 having died.

Laura Lee—November 17, 1863. These horrid, abominable Yankees are back again, and will stay in town tonight. They drove back about 100 head of cattle and had wagons loaded with corn, chickens, yams & c. which they had stolen. As usual, they are going about to the houses in every direction for supper. We refuse them all the time now.

Laura Lee—November 18, 1863. We had a nice time last night. In the middle of the night we were roused by a noise, evidently some one trying a back lock downstairs. We got up and called out, and directly heard footsteps in the yard and the front gate slam. This morning we found that the robbers had broken into the inner cellar and had carried off milk, butter & besides tearing open various jars of pickles, tomatoes, & c. They were trying to get into the house by the cellar stairs, but were frightened off by the noise we made. They have all gone now, carrying off their plunder and some prisoners they brought in yesterday, also a few loungers they caught in town this morning.

Julia Chase—November 19, 1863. Very charming weather we are having, the air is quite balmy. The dedication of the National Cemetery at Gettysburg takes place today. A decisive and bloody struggle will take place for the possession of Chattanooga & East Tennessee. The Rebel batteries on Lookout Mt. played vigorously on Hooker's Camp Moccasin Pt. & Chattanooga. . . . Guerrillas are committing great depredations upon the Mississippi, Tenn. & Arkansas shores.

Julia Chase—November 21, 1863. Advises from Charleston up to the 17th say that our batteries on Morris Island had fired 24 shots into the city but doing no material damage. One of the Ironclads said to have been slightly injured during the recent bombardment of Fort Moultrie. Gen. Longstreet's forces met those of Gen. Burnside, having crossed the Tennessee when Gen. B. fell back to Lenoir, having inferior numbers. Gen. B fell back as far as Knoxville, and is determined to defend it to the last man.

Laura Lee—November 23, 1863. We have some important successes in Tennessee, but look with intense anxiety to the result of a great battle which must soon be fought there. All quiet on the Rappahannock. . . . Kate Conrad came today from Loudon, bringing us the money we were so anxious to get.

Julia Chase—November 24, 1863. Rain the forepart of the day. We had quite an exciting time & alarm in town today. 3 men dressed as soldiers came into town this morning, after robbing several persons on the Martinsburg Road of their money & horses, & demanding the horse of Mr. Ritters. He declined letting them have it, and while Mr. Geo. Baker tried to get him off, one of the soldiers presented his pistol at Mr. B causing him to retreat instantly into his house. Mr. Ritter in the meanwhile riding down to Mr. Legg's Mill. The soldiers followed him up & while some other persons in town who lived near attempted to get the soldiers away, they drew their pistols, with the purpose of shooting them down. Mr. Legg then interfered & the soldier's attention was drawn to him, when they fired at him, wounding him in the arm & struck their sabers across his head. Not satisfied with this, they then went across to Mr. Sidwell's, breaking in the door & taking fire out, took it across to the Mill & set it on fire. No one was permitted to approach for the purpose of putting out the fire, until the work of destruction went well on & the mill was burned to the ground, the ruffians making their escape. These men hail from Front Royal and it is said that one or two of them are known. May a swift vengeance overtake them. We have no safety whatever for our lives, that 3 men should come into town & keep all at bay. . . . What a life we lead! When will it all end? The news from Burnside is encouraging. After several days of heavy fighting at and around Knoxville, the Rebels have withdrawn from the south side of the town and re-crossed the river.

Laura Lee—November 24, 1863. Almost the greatest outrage of the war was perpetrated here today. Three men in gray clothes, but evidently Yankee scouts, came into town today from the Martinsburg Road about 10 o'clock. They had several horses which they had stolen, and when they came on this street, they attempted to take the horse of our butcher (Mr. Ritter) out of his wagon. He resisted, and one of them put his pistol to his ear and swore he would fire if he did not submit. Mr. Legg, who was near, interfered and remonstrated, trying to get the pistol away when the villain fired on him and cut him with a saber, wounding him each time though not severely. He escaped into a house. . . . They then swore they would burn his steam mill, a very fine building four stories high and nearly new. They were intoxicated and perfectly frantic. They fired incessantly at the people who were collecting on the street, and obliged them to disperse and hide behind the houses to escape the balls which were whipping by every time a man or boy showed himself. They deliberately took fire from a house opposite and fired the mill, and kept guard in front of it until it was full ablaze, firing all the time if a head appeared. At last they rode off with the stolen horses up the Staunton Road. . . . It does seem as if we were sadly subjugated when three armed men can keep a whole community at bay. Some persons declare that the men were not Yankees but a portion of a band of thieves who have been prowling and robbing in the mountains. . . . The mill was entirely consumed.

Laura Lee—November 25, 1863. Yankees in and out again today. To our great mortification it is almost certain that the villains of yesterday are deserters from our army. Mrs. Legg told Mary that their loss was certainly 40,000 dollars. There were large quantities of tobacco and bacon hidden away in the mill.

Julia Chase—November 26, 1863. Thanksgiving Day in the loyal states. Today's paper brings us good Thanksgiving news, dispatches from Gen. Thomas & Grant that they had gained a great victory over Bragg, capturing 2000 prisoners, and two of their important positions, Bragg being it is thought in full retreat.[10] Grant thinks he will be in Atlanta in 5 days. God grant us a great and decisive victory. Fort Sumpter is still being shelled by our batteries. The weather clear and cold. We hear that the three soldiers who set Mr. Legg's mill on fire had been captured. Am afraid it is not true.

Julia Chase—November 28, 1863. The Federals in town today, captured Charles Graves, who I imagine was a willing prisoner, and the son of Mr. Forney, who was in the Rebel army. We learn that he was hidden away in a hollow partition, which had been made between two of the rooms in his father's house. Rain commenced falling about 9 a.m. & continued until afternoon, with very heavy fog. We have the results of Gen. Grant's victory. About 60 pieces of cannon, from 5 to 7000 prisoners taken. Bragg & Breckenridge, thinking their position impregnable, & that the Yankees would not have the temerity to attempt an assault, came very near being captured also. Gen. Hooker is safe, Longstreet having withdrawn from before Knoxville to reinforce Gen. Bragg. It was thought, however, he will not succeed, being obliged to retreat into Virginia or cut up by the army of Grant.

Laura Lee—November 28, 1863. The news today from Tenn. is unfavorable. Our troops have been driven from Lookout Mountain, and Gen. Bragg will most probably have to fall back to the scene of the battle of Chickamauga. All quiet on the Rappahannock and nothing effected at Charleston.

Julia Chase—November 30, 1863. Fall is leaving us with very cold weather, today the coldest of the season, everything frozen up with considerable wind. Another battle has taken place in Va. After several skirmishes the Army of the Potomac engaged the rebel army on the south side of the Rapidan; after a severe fight the rebels retreated towards Orange Court House, leaving 900 prisoners in our hands.

Laura Lee—November 30, 1863. The Yankees claim a great victory in Tenn. They say that Bragg attempted to fall back and they pursued him and captured immensely of prisoners, guns, ammunition and stores. We can get no accounts from the South, but though all they claim is not true, it is evident that it has been a very bad affair for us. Some Yankees in town this evening and report that there has been fighting on the Rapidan for two days.

Julia Chase—December 2, 1863. It is said the rebels are making a stand & strongly entrenched at Mine Run Creek, 12 miles this side of Orange C House. Cannonading took place during Monday. One division of our army occupied Fredericksburg.

Julia Chase—December 4, 1863. A very charming day, more like spring than winter. The Army of the Potomac, after a very brief campaign[11] have re-crossed the Rapidan River back to their old camping ground, going in we suppose to their winter quarters. No hope now of our friends being able to return to their homes very shortly. Father has been an exile since the 12th of last June. Gen. Meade, I fear, is not the general for the place. His reasons assigned for not attacking Lee on last Monday . . . were that the enemy were in such entrenched positions, that an assault could not have been made on his part without great loss of life. . . . The loss sustained by him altogether amounts to about 1000. In regard to Gen. Grant's army we hope still to hear news of a cheering character. It is rumored that Johnston has reinforced Bragg. Longstreet has no doubt retreated into Virginia, tho' Gen. Foster it is hoped has been able to inflict some damage to him.

Laura Lee—December 4, 1863. We were shocked to hear that Strother Barton has lost a leg in the late fight. It was not a general battle, but quite severe as far as it extended. It was principally Johnson's Division on our side. Meade was entirely repulsed and has retired. Our loss was very small in killed and only about 300 wounded. The Southern accounts from Tenn. are not nearly so bad as we dreaded. Our troops were immensely outnumbered and flanked and had to retreat and in doing so lost a great many prisoners, but our loss in killed and wounded was less than 2,000 and theirs very great. . . . We hear that Bragg has been displaced and that Johnston is to succeed him.

Julia Chase—December 5, 1863. In the attack by Gen. Longstreet upon Gen. Burnside a week ago, the Rebels were repulsed with great slaughter, leaving their dead and wounded & between 2 & 300 prisoners in our hands. Gen. B. humanely offered a truce to the Rebels to enable them to bury their dead, which was accepted & the wounded of both armies exchanged. . . . Gen. Gilmore continues to throw shells into Charleston at the rate of 20 per diem & the bombardment of Fort Sumpter goes on slowly. All the inhabitants of C. have been removed to the rear of the city.

Julia Chase—December 8, 1863. Weather still cold, tho' it has moderated a little. President Lincoln yesterday issued a proclamation recommending that all loyal persons should assemble at their place of worship & render especial homage and gratitude to Almighty God for his great advancement of the National cause. Reliable information being rec'd that the insurgent force is retreating from East Tennessee under circumstances rendering it probable that the Union forces cannot hereafter be dislodged from that important position. Gen. Grant has captured during the war 472 cannon & 90,000 prisoners, having been more successful than any other of our generals. Would that they could follow his example, and have that military skill which is so necessary.

Julia Chase—December 9, 1863. Nothing has been heard in regard to the pursuit of Longstreet by the Federals. It is not known whether our troops will be able to overtake him or not, tho' dispatches say they are in full pursuit. Longstreet will, we think, retreat so rapidly, that the Union forces will hardly be able to get a glimpse of him. . . . The cavalry of the Army of the Potomac are kept busy looking after Mosby's Guerillas.[12] Would that every one might be captured. It is probable that both armies, Meade & Lee, are settling down into winter quarters.

Laura Lee—December 9, 1863. Yankees in nearly everyday. We received information ten days ago that preparations were being made at Harper's Ferry and Martinsburg for a grand raid up the Valley. We sent information of it, and hope they will be prepared. Longstreet has withdrawn from Knoxville into Va. in consequence of the large reinforcements sent to the former place. The Yankee papers call Meade's retreat a terrible disaster.

Julia Chase—December 10, 1863. The President's Message appears today, also a Proclamation of Amnesty to the rebel in arms. The document provides for the reconstruction of the Union, the enforcement of the Emancipation Proclamation & offers pardon to all in arms against the government on taking the oath of allegiance, except those holding positions in the army above the rank of Col. and in the Navy above the rank of Lieutenant & those who abandoned the service of the U States to join the Rebellion—restoring to them their rights of citizenship & property, except in slaves. It is thought by some that many will embrace the offer, the secessionists that it will only be something for the South to laugh over. Time will determine it.

Julia Chase—December 11, 1863. Today troops, infantry, artillery & cavalry passed through town en route for the Valley, probably to reinforce

Gen. Averill.[13] We don't know what object they wish to accomplish, but the secessionists say they will not be successful, and I do not wonder much at their want of success, being so indiscreet in communicating their plans to everyone, whereby the news is soon made known to the rebel officers. When will our people learn more prudence. The sight of the Stars & Stripes were very cheering, we only wish their stay might be a permanent one in the Valley.

Laura Lee—December 12, 1863. Yesterday the Yankees passed through on their way to Staunton they said. We were quite appalled at the extent of their preparations and fear very much that Imboden will not be prepared to resist. There were several regiments of cavalry, two infantry, a battery, and 75 wagons of provisions. At first we dreaded that they had come to stay here, as they have been threatening, but they told the people as they passed that it was a 15-day scout.

Laura Lee—December 14, 1863. The wagons are sent back as fast as they are emptied, and 15 or 20 full ones go up the Valley everyday with a large escort of cavalry, who are as audacious as they can be. Lincoln's message and proclamation are out. Beautiful documents both.

Julia Chase—December 16, 1863. The secessionists here report that 200 prisoners have been taken by the Rebels between Strasburg & Woodstock. It is also reported that Staunton is in possession of the Federals. . . . From Morris Island we learn that the rebels were working very hard on Sullivan's Island, increasing their works there & shelling Forts Wagner & Gregg. They seem determined to make a long & desperate resistance. We had hoped to hear of the fall of Charleston by Christmas, but we feel that the good news will be wafted over the breeze before very long.

Julia Chase—December 17, 1863. A very stormy day of rain & sleet, hard for the poor soldiers. The troops in the Valley have had some skirmishing with the rebels in the vicinity of Strasburg. On Monday last 30 were taken prisoners belonging to Gen. Ewell's Corps. Major Gen. John Buford, one of our most efficient cavalry officers of the Army of the Potomac, died yesterday in Washington. The news from Charleston through the Richmond papers is interesting. Fort Sumpter took fire on the 11th from some unknown cause, & 10 rebels killed & 20 wounded. Heard cannonading was kept up from our land batteries during the conflagration.

Julia Chase—December 19, 1863. Very cold indeed today, with the appearance of snow. . . . The rebels under Gen. Stuart attacked the Federal forces on the Orange & Alexandria R R and attempted to burn a bridge, but retreated before doing much damage. Richmond papers announce that Gen. Grant had evacuated Chattanooga, falling back upon Nashville, tearing up the railroad as he retreated. . . . Gen. Averill is threatening Staunton. It is said his object is to tear up the railroad. A fight had taken place in Greenbrier Co. in which the rebels were compelled to fall back through Lewisburg, which was occupied by Union forces.

Julia Chase—December 23, 1863. All quiet in the Army of the Potomac. Deserters represent Lee's army to be in very destitute condition. Many of the men of Meade's army have taken furloughs for a short time.

Laura Lee—December 23, 1863. We are so thankful that these wretched Yankees have returned from their raid up the Valley. They passed through town this afternoon, marching so rapidly that we hoped the report of their being pursued was true. They brought with them 40 prisoners and some contrabands. All went down the Berryville Road except one company of cavalry, who are now in the Market House, enjoying blazing fires made of the fences of the neighborhood. It is such a relief to us that they have gone back, for we dreaded their quartering themselves upon us. They were almost without food, and the weather is intensely cold. We feared they would come for Christmas, as they have been threatening. They accomplished nothing by their grand raid. They went to most houses for food, but fortunately for us none came here.

Julia Chase—December 24, 1863. The rumored damage to the Ironsides & 2 of the Monitors before Charleston is all false, a canard. No disaster has occurred to these vessels, and a fierce bombardment of Charleston City was progressing from the shore batteries. Shells had been thrown into the city day and night since the 17. . . . Gen. Averill's official report says that he succeeded in cutting the Va. & Tenn. R Road, a valuable line of communication to the Rebels, at Salem in Roanoke Co. & brought his command off in safety. He destroyed at Salem 3 depots containing large quantities of flour, corn, oats, meat, salt, leather, boots, shoes, & other supplies of immense value to the Rebels. The telegraph wires were cut, the R Road track torn up, several bridges & culverts destroyed.

Laura Lee—December 24, 1863. All the Yankees gone. We are so thankful to have our Christmas free from the sight of the odious bluecoats. We are to go to a Sunday school festival tonight at the Lutheran Church.

Julia Chase—December 25, 1863. Christmas. The weather continues very cold. Persons are filling their ice-houses. The boys have ushered in the day with the firing of their guns & c., and seem to enjoy it very much. The

children are crying out Christmas gift in all directions. They will not be
very numerous, I imagine.

Laura Lee—December 25, 1863. Clear but intensely cold. The celebra-
tion last night was very successful. A large crowd and all the children perfectly happy. Mrs. Tuley came in afterwards to get some chocolate and cake,
our X-mas Eve's entertainment Mr. Averitt furnished for us. The girls dined
at their fathers. . . . No Yankees about and no news stirring.

Julia Chase—December 28, 1863. A rainy day, the weather has moderated considerably. . . . The siege of Charleston is still progressing, the bombardment of the city & rebel forts being continued at intervals. It is supposed
that the rebels have erected a strong sand fort within the ruins of Sumpter.
We do not expect to hear of very active operations until Spring, tho' we
would liked to have heard of the fall of Charleston before this, but we must
be patience, feeling it will take place in good time. The Secessionists are
looking for their friends (the rebels) in Winchester every day, according to
their say. . . . The Richmond papers seem much excited in regard to the
recent raid of Gen. Averill. The accounts of the vast destruction of property
by him are fully confirmed. It was thought at one time he was endeavoring
to reach Danville, in order that the Union prisoners might be released.

Julia Chase—December 31, 1863. The last day of fall brings with it rain,
rain and also about 30 or more secesh cavalry. So many are dressed in Federal
clothing that we mistook them for our own troops. The Federals were in
town today also, some hours before the rebels made their appearance. . . .
The Richmond Inquirer is rather gloomy in regard to the losses sustained by
the rebel army in East Tenn., being deprived not only of their flour mills,
which previously supplied the whole army, but of vast machine shops, also
cut off from coal, iron and copper mines which were worth millions to them.

Laura Lee—December 31, 1863. Lal got off safely this morning on her
travels, to our great joy. The Yankees came into town before breakfast, and
we feared they would interfere, but they stayed only a few minutes and
went back. While we were at dinner Betty ran into the room delighted,
saying "our men are in." Some of them stopped and said the whole of
Imboden's command were coming on to night.

Julia Chase—January 1, 1864. The year has opened upon us, rather
unfavorably as regards our town, being in Dixie surely. A large body of rebel
cavalry have possession of Winchester, having entered during the night.
What their object is we cannot tell, whether to go on to Martinsburg & tear

up the R. Road, gobble up our troops at Charleston and play sad havoc everywhere. The rebels seem, however, undecided what to do, are riding up one street as if to go to Martinsburg, then in the direction of Berryville. The Secessionists are perfectly happy. . . . It is reported in town this morning that the rebels have Martinsburg . . . but we don't believe a word of it.

Afternoon—The Rebs seem somewhat uneasy, have all left town in considerable haste, afraid the Yankees are after them. Some of the soldiers have rode up to Fort Hill, also the boys and citizens, to see the Yankees come in, but as yet have not made their appearance. 5 P.M.—No Yankees yet, and not a rebel to be seen. Very cold and windy since dinner. Some of these poor soldiers will feel the biting wind through their thin clothing. Their horses look better than we expected. We don't know how long it will be before communication is opened with Martinsburg. Persons will be afraid to venture out while there are any rebs about.

Laura Lee—January 1, 1864. Imboden's men passed through town on several roads, but returned in the afternoon to their camp a few miles up the Valley Road. Gen. Early with three brigades is a few miles farther up. It is a scouting and foraging expedition, and also a feint against Martinsburg, while Fitz Lee[14] attacks the railroad in Hampshire. We are to have a little party for Mrs. Maury (the bride) tonight.

Laura Lee—January 2, 1864. Our party went off very well. Mary and Jennie Sherrard came last night, bringing us letters from the Masons and one from Lal, saying she had arrived safely in Woodstock. Our cavalry are picketing on all the roads below the town.

Julia Chase—January 3, 1864. It was rumored in town this morning that the Federals were advancing in large force this morning by the via of Front Royal, trying to get in the rear of the rebels now in the Valley. The Secesh soldiers hardly know which way to go, are riding up & down the street. 3 P.M.—The Federals are in town and have captured some 8 or 10 rebels. . . . Later—Our troops have left town, went some two or three miles out I suppose.

Julia Chase—January 4, 1864. This is a very stormy day. Snow commenced falling about 9 this morning & has continued on until afternoon. It will probably make some sleighing. The Federals were in town tonight, captured one or two rebel soldiers we understand. . . . It is thought that the rebels under Gen. Early are preparing for another move in the Shenandoah Valley. We have rumors of the rebel cavalry capturing cattle, wagon trains and Federal prisoners near Moorfield. They are anxious to redeem themselves from the disgrace attached to them during Gen. Averill's recent raid at Salem. . . . The weather continues very cold here indeed.

Laura Lee—January 4, 1864. Yesterday was a lively day. In the morning news came that the Yankees were advancing from Martinsburg, and were also crossing at Front Royal in the rear of our forces. All were ordered back except a few pickets, and at 12 o'clock they were also withdrawn. As usual, a few of the soldiers would not believe there was any danger, and when we went to S. School we saw six horses at Mr. Conrad's (most of the riders being in the house at dinner) and other soldiers coolly walking about the streets. In five minutes a large body of the enemy were in the town, and four of the men at Mr. C's were captured, one of them young Armstrong being severely wounded.

Laura Lee—January 8, 1864. We have been warned today that Col. Boyd said yesterday that the next time he came he intended to search here for blankets. Last Sunday Mr. Armstrong had come here for some just before he was captured. Those we had were so well secured that Mary sent him to Mrs. Cousad's and while waiting there he was caught. The blankets will go away tonight. Fitz Lee has captured a great many prisoners and a large amount of stores.

Laura Lee—January 9, 1864. We were warned again today, but the blankets are all safe. The villains are just coming into town and may be here any moment.

Julia Chase—January 10, 1864. A Lieutenant of the 3rd Arkansas rebel regiment has come into Fort Smith with a squad of the men of his regiment & delivered themselves up. We do not wonder at so many of the rebel soldiers giving themselves up, being deprived of their pay for so long a time & then their money is so depreciated that it will buy but a very small portion of food for their families, who in many instances are in a state of starvation. . . . The weather for the past two weeks has been the coldest for nearly 20 yrs.

Laura Lee—January 11, 1864. On Saturday night information was brought us that the 6th Army Corps (Sedgwick's) was to proceed through here about Tuesday to try to get to Staunton to destroy the Central R.R. This Corps has been at [Harpers Ferry] for a week, and there is evidently a move on foot. On Friday, Imboden's command was ordered down here, but when within 6 miles it was suddenly recalled by Gen. Early who had remained at Strasburg, and the whole force has fallen back to New Market.

Julia Chase—January 12, 1864. The plan of Gen. Early with the commands of Lee, Walker & Rosser, has resulted in a failure. His object was to proceed to Martinsburg, cut the R. Road at that point and capture what forces there might be between Martinsburg & New Creek. Being prevented from taking Martinsburg by Gen. Averill having a large force at that point, he endeavored the capture of the garrison at Petersburg. . . . The Baltimore & O R Road is now perfectly safe.

Julia Chase—January 13, 1864. Gen. Gilmore is throwing shells charged with Greek fire into Charleston. 20 shells were thrown a week or more ago, every one exploding. The result was that a fire was kindled in the southern part of the city, burning with considerable fury the balance of the day. . . . From N. Carolina we learn that 1100 people of Newbern have taken the oath annexed to the President's Amnesty Proclamation.

Julia Chase—January 15, 1864. Last night 4 rebel soldiers came into town and arrested Mr. Dooley,[15] a Union man who came home a day or two ago to visit his family. At the time of his arrest, Mr. D was attending Church and great excitement prevailed. It is said that it took 5 men to hold him. This is outrageous, and we fear that the Secessionists will be made to suffer. Mr. D's son went to Martinsburg to make the case known. It is thought that some of the secesh women have been the cause of Mr. D's arrest.

Julia Chase—January 16, 1864. Our cavalry have come up from Martinsburg with orders that if Mr. Dooley is not released in 2 weeks time, the Mayor and 50 secessionists will be held as hostages. This is just as it should be. . . . It is reported that Gen. Stuart with 5000 rebel cavalry have started on a raid towards Leesburg. We hope there may be no truth in this.

Laura Lee—January 16, 1864. On Thursday night Capt. Gilmore and a few of his men went into the Methodist lecture room, where a revival was going on and at the end of the services they took possession of Bill Dooley, and carried him off. . . . There was a great excitement. Some of the women screamed and one fainted. Dooley has been one of the most malignant of the Union men about here, giving information against all the Southern people here, and also assisting the Provost at Martinsburg. He was lingering at home because he expected the Yankees to come to stay here. We have had no letter from Lal yet, though we have heard through a letter from Mrs. Magill of their safety.

Julia Chase—January 18, 1864. Last night the rebels went to Mr. Griffith's house, broke his door open & threatened to blow his daughter's brains out. One of his daughters went to the chamber window & rung a bell to alarm the neighbors, which exasperated the soldiers, so they threatened her life. These guerillas are a great pest to society. No man's life scarcely seems secure. Mr. Haines, a Union man, was robbed of $40 in gold, besides other things. Mr. Swartz had his horse stolen, a blanket & his boots stolen by these same rascals. This is a dreadful way of living. We know not what an hour may bring forth. The troops from Martinsburg came up tonight & arrested Mr. Robt. Y. Conrad, but by his giving security & through the interference of some of the Union men he was released. The Union men are so fearful of being carried off to the dreadful prisons of the South that they seem obliged to do all in their power to prevent the arrests of Secessionists. Mr. Walter was also arrested & taken off. What the charges were against these two individuals, we have not been able to learn. A stormy day of rain, tho' not very cold.

Julia Chase—January 19, 1864. The weather is more propitious today, tho' a great change has taken place, being much colder with high winds. Father left for the West today. We shall be quite anxious until we hear of his safe arrival there.

Laura Lee—January 19, 1864. The Yankees came this evening with an order to arrest and carry to Martinsburg Dr. Huley and Mr. Conrad. The Dr. made his escape, and hid but Mr. C said he would never run from Yankees. He told the two officers who went to arrest him that he would not go with them unless they got a carriage to take him, that he would not risk his life by travelling on horseback at night at such a season as this. He said it was a great outrage that he should be held for such an infamous scoundrel as Dooley, who was taken by the Confederate military authorities and informer in the employ of the Yankee Government. The Yankees agreed to what he said and agreed to take his remonstrance back to Martinsburg and get further orders.

Julia Chase—January 22, 1864. The secessionists seem to be making no efforts to get Mr. Dooley released, so that they cannot but expect that the order given by the Colonel in Martinsburg will be carried in effect, that the Union men shall not be disturbed, but that it takes every man under his command Mr. Dooley shall be released. Later—This has been a very exciting day. Our troops from Martinsburg have come up to take what things Mr. Griffith may have in his factory to prevent them from falling into the hands of the rebels. wagons of wool was taken to Martinsburg. They arrested Mr. Boyd and have not permitted him to be paroled, but have taken him to Martinsburg. Now is the time for the secessionists to exert themselves. If they make no effort to get Mr. Dooley released, the Union men will be obliged to leave, fearing the rebels when they come in will arrest them. Oh what a dreadful state of affairs. Each man seems to be interested only in himself. Much selfishness is shown among the secessionists.

Julia Chase—January 23, 1864. A very mild morning. 3 of our Union men have left for Martinsburg, hoping to get Mr. Boyd paroled, that he may be permitted to do something for the release of Mr. Dooley. We do not know if the officer in command will grant their request. Should he not, all the Union men will probably leave town, then the secesh will have no one to interest themselves among our troops & will have to abide the consequences. We hear that the Rebels intend coming to the Methodist Church some night and arrest every man there—conscript them.

Laura Lee—January 23, 1864. This morning the Yankees came with a train of empty wagons to move Dooley's family and Griffith's down to Martinsburg. The Griffiths are going because a few nights ago some Confederates attacked his house, firing into it and breaking all the windows. The report is that one of Griffith's daughters rung the factory bell by a rope, which communicated from the dwelling house to give warning to hide the goods. The soldiers supposed it was a signal to the Yankees, and attacked the house in consequence, and the family are afraid to remain there. These villains today brought an order to arrest Dr. Fuller, Ed Moore and Dr. Boyd to be held for Dooley. The two first had gone up the Valley some days ago, but Dr. Boyd was carried off. The retaliation system has begun here, and there is no telling where it will end.

Laura Lee—January 25, 1864. The Yanks came today just at dark last night. They had been as far as Woodstock, and brought back 10 prisoners. They stayed in town all night but were quiet and did no harm except to take hay from everybody's stables. This morning most of the Union men went off with them, to stay away until the Dooley affair is settled, as they are afraid of being carried off by the Confederates.

Laura Lee—January 27, 1864. Dr. Boyd returned home last night. He is paroled to report to Martinsburg until the Dooley question is settled. Mrs. Polk goes tomorrow to get the box. We are all anxious to get our share.

Laura Lee—January 29, 1864. Mrs. Polk did not go. Mr. Conrad has received a letter from Gen. Kelly, containing a list of the papers found upon Dooley, who is now safe in Richmond. Among the papers is a pass from Gen. Sullivan (who had denied positively that Dooley was in employ of the U.S.) passing him through all pickets on secret service for the U.S., several letters addressed to Dooley the Detective, and a paper authorizing him to recruit Negroes. Enough, I should think to settle Mr. D's case. Gen. Early is receiving reinforcements for a move. He is now at New Market.

Julia Chase—January 30, 1864. The sad and distressing news of the death of our dear Father reached us last night. The dispatch says that he died very suddenly. Oh, to think we were not permitted to see his face again, or to hear his last dying words. We feel that the rebels have been the cause of our father's death, never having been the same person since he was taken prisoner by them.

Laura Lee—February 1, 1864. A large force of Yankees came in last night and kept the whole town in a ferment all night, shouting and tramping about the streets and tearing down fences for their fires. They broke into several houses and roused us up after 1 o'clock to inquire if this was a hotel and where they would find one and get whiskey. They are Averill's men and part of the 6th Corps.

Laura Lee—February 2, 1864. Mr. Burwell was allowed to come home today. He brought us charming letters from Lal, Lewis and others. The money all safe too. Mrs. Polk went to Martinsburg last Saturday, and is to be at home today.

Julia Chase—February 5, 1864. This has been a very exciting day. Bettie Ginn's wedding came off last night, and as the bridal party were leaving for Martinsburg, the carriage containing the Bride & Groom was stopped and Mr. Kemp ordered to get out. He did so. When the Rebels demanded his valise, he gave it to them and his money, watch & pistol was taken from him. He was then permitted to get into the carriage but was again stopped by another party of the rebels, and had to walk some distance with them. At last they permitted him to go back to the carriage and the whole party then drove off towards Martinsburg. A large force of rebels were in town, some 300. Their main object was . . . to rob the groom and capture the force of Federal cavalry which were expected up with the commanding officer at Martinsburg. Fortunately they (the rebs) were foiled in their object. . . . There is nothing scarcely done by the Unionists in Winchester or planned by the Federals but the secesh in town find out and convey the information to the rebels.

Laura Lee—February 5, 1864. We have had an exciting day. Last night we had a pleasant little party here. The Williams, Mrs. Pierce, the Baldwins, Maurys and Sherrards. Mr. Kelly arrived in time for the wedding to take place last night, and this morning by 7 o'clock the bride and groom packed in three carriages set out in fine spirits, but alas! When they reached Fort Hill they were stopped by the Confederates who had quietly taken possession in the night. Imboden's command is here again. They detained the party for half an hour and then let them go on. It is reported that they robbed the brides groom of his watch and 500 dollars. I hope it is not known he is a Yankee.

Julia Chase—February 10, 1864. Weather very cold today, but clear. An attempt was made by the Federals a few days ago to make a dash upon Richmond, release our men there confined as prisoners and burn the public stores. It failed because, as the Richmond papers state, the plan was betrayed by a deserter from our lines. It seems that every plan laid to take possession of Richmond, or even make a raid, has been very unsuccessful. . . . In the recent movement against Richmond, a plot was discovered for the assassination of Jeff Davis & the liberation of the Union prisoners. The Rebel raid into West Virginia within the past three weeks has proved very successful to them. There seems to be a great deal of bad management or misfortune in regards to military affairs on our part. We hope that these things will be looked into. The Rebs under Gen. Rosser, destroyed 2 bridges, one over Patterson's Creek & North branch of the Potomac Canal, capturing 40 prisoners. They also captured a train of 93 wagons loaded with commissary stores & forage. . . . In all 270 prisoners, 50 wagons & teams, 1200 cattle, 500 sheep.

Laura Lee—February 10, 1864. Two whole days without a Yankee. Reports tonight that a large force of Confederates are coming here. I doubt it amazingly. The <u>Baltimore American</u> gives accounts of the Yankees having been repulsed at three points during the past week. In Tenn., on the Rapidan, and in N.C. it is cheering to hear of even small successes, for the anticipation of the coming campaign and present troubles and anxieties keep my heart very, very heavy.

Laura Lee—February 12, 1864. A large force of Yankees have come in this afternoon. Artillery, infantry, cavalry and wagons. Many think they will remain permanently. Last night Harry Gilmore made a dash at Danfields, when the express train was passing, and captured money, goods, and some prisoners and got off safely.

Laura Lee—February 13, 1864. The Yankees have all gone back, to our great surprise. They stayed last night and began to move off by ten this morning. Mrs. Polk sets off this evening on another attempt to make purchases. Nellie brought the wonderful box at last, and almost everything in it was for Dr. Latimer and his sister. Mary's calico, a pound of tea for us, and scarcely a thing for the Polks, after all their trouble. We have had various successes lately in a small way along the sea coast and in Tenn. The army is being rapidly reorganized and we hope things look encouraging.

Julia Chase—February 14, 1864. A very high wind prevailing today. In the Valley there seems to be nothing but robbery & plunder continually going on. A Union man was robbed of $4000 in gold, also another man who was with him, by the rebel soldiers, and had their heads beaten considerably for resisting. No one is safe in passing up and down the Valley and we learn that throughout the South this state of things continues. Oh, the horrors of war and especially a civil war.

Julia Chase—February 17, 1864. The weather still continues very cold. . . . The rebels are conscripting to a great degree in West Virginia, thereby driving off a large portion of the citizens, being in a state of insurrection. 21 of the 110 Union prisoners escaped from Richmond have been recaptured—poor fellows, their fate will be a sad one.

Julia Chase—February 19, 1864. The weather has moderated considerably today. Quite a large scout of Federals passed through town tonight up the Valley.

Laura Lee—February 20, 1864. We have been very quiet all the week, owing to our troops having fallen back to Staunton to recruit. I had a letter from Lal on Thursday which ends the affair. She will stay some time longer. . . . Poor little Kate Tidball died a week ago of diphtheria at Mr. Whitehead's.

Julia Chase—February 22, 1864. A few guns fired off this morning in honor of Washington's birthday.

Laura Lee—February 24, 1864. Things are so quiet here now that nothing occurs worth recording. But we are warned that this comfortable time will not last much longer. All the reports from Martinsburg are that the Yankees will be here in a few days to remain permanently or at least until they are driven away. It is a dreary prospect, the only gleam of comfort it brings is that the Yankees being here will be certain to bring our army here. We hear many reports of another advance into Pa. I dare not hope it may be true. Many persons say it is the only way to end the war, but we have suffered awfully whenever we have attempted the invasion.

Laura Lee—February 27, 1864. All quiet here. The Yankees along the railroad are expecting a raid and stay to protect it, so we have had not one here since Wednesday. The news from our armies is truly inspiring. Almost universal re-enlistment, and more enthusiasm and ardent determination to resist to the end than has been exhibited since the beginning of the war.

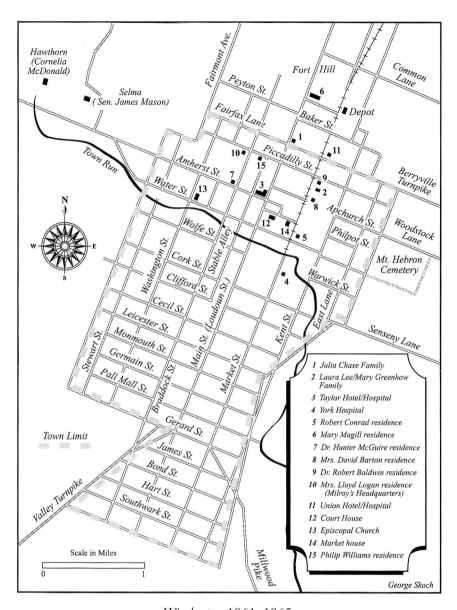

Hawthorn
(Cornelia
McDonald)

Selma
(Sen. James Mason)

Fairmont Ave.

Peyton St.

Fort Hill

Common Lane

Fairfax Lane

Baker St.

6

Depot

Town Run

Amherst St.

Piccadilly St.

1

11

10

15

Berryville Turnpike

Water St.

7

3

9

13

2

8

Wolfe St.

Apchurch St.

Woodstock Lane

12

Philpot St.

14   5

Washington St.

Cork St.

Stable Alley

Mt. Hebron Cemetery

Clifford St.

Main St. (Loudoun St.)

Cecil St.

4

Warwick St.

Leicester St.

Kent St.

East Lane

Senseny Lane

Stewart St.

Monmouth St.

Germain St.

Pall Mall St.

Braddock St.

Market St.

Gerard St.

Town Limit

James St.

Bond St.

Hart St.

Valley Turnpike

Southwark St.

Scale in Miles

0   1

Millwood Pike

1   Julia Chase Family
2   Laura Lee/Mary Greenhow
    Family
3   Taylor Hotel/Hospital
4   York Hospital
5   Robert Conrad residence
6   Mary Magill residence
7   Dr. Hunter McGuire residence
8   Mrs. David Barton residence
9   Dr. Robert Baldwin residence
10 Mrs. Lloyd Logan residence
    (Milroy's Headquarters)
11 Union Hotel/Hospital
12 Court House
13 Episcopal Church
14 Market house
15 Philip Williams residence

George Skoch

Winchester, 1861–1865.

Union general
Philip H. Sheridan.

Confederate
general Thomas J.
"Stonewall" Jackson.

Confederate general
Jubal A. Early.

Union general
Robert H. Milroy.

Mrs. Mary Lee.

Mary Tucker Magill.

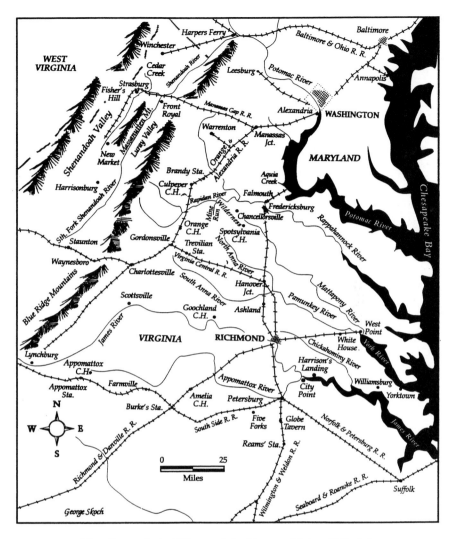

The Shenandoah Valley and the Eastern Plain of Virginia.

Laura Lee Headstone,
Mt. Hebron Cemetery.

The Lee residence, 132 North Cameron Street.

Julia Chase Headstone,
Mt. Hebron Cemetery.

The Taylor Hotel, 125 North Loudoun Street.

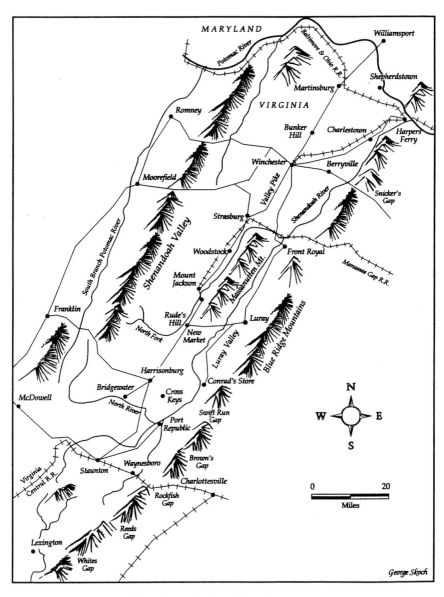

The Shenandoah Valley of Virginia.

Julia Chase—February 29, 1864. Selma (Ala) is occupied by Gen. Sherman's[16] forces—the city of Montgomery is in danger also, being threatened by the Federal troops. The Housatome [Housatonic] was blown up by a Rebel torpedo in Charleston Harbor—2 officers and 3 men lost. A battle has taken place in Florida. $1,500,000 worth of property destroyed. Great excitement exists throughout the state and we learn that the Gov. has called for all her citizens to defend their state. The people of that state have seen or felt but little of the horrors of war, tho' there now seems to be a scarcity of provisions, 1 sack of coffee costing $2800 in Confederate money. . . . We hear that in Richmond a dreadful state of things exists. Every man is being conscripted, not excepting those who have furnished substitutes.

Laura Lee—February 29, 1864. Mr. Davis and Mrs. Magill brought us half a dozen letters yesterday, two from Lal. Mr. Jones has gone for Mrs. J. and Lal will return with them, probably the last of this week.

Laura Lee—March 1, 1864. We have heard what seems to be very strange. That Gen. Bragg has been made Commander in Chief of all our armies, even over Gen. Lee. It is said too that Gen. Ewell is forced by bad health to retire, and that Gen. J. E. B. Stuart is put in his place. We have had a heavy fall of snow today, the second this winter. How very different from last year!

Julia Chase—March 2, 1864. Dispatches from Vicksburg continue to assert the occupation of Selma by Gen. Sherman, after a severe fight. Rebel papers admit that Polk had been badly outgeneraled by Gen. Sherman. . . . Gen. Longstreet is stated to be falling back to Atlanta, Ga., part of his forces having reached there, but it needs confirmation.

Laura Lee—March 3, 1864. The Yankees were in yesterday. There is a great deal of talk again of their coming here to occupy. The 10th of this month is the time fixed on. We have another considerable victory in Florida. Grant is in motion and the spring is already opening. The greatest anxiety prevails in every department throughout the Confederacy and all seems bright and hopeful.

Julia Chase—March 4, 1864. The late movement of the cavalry of the Army of the Potomac is said to have been directed toward Richmond, Gen. Kilpatrick[17] in his progress was to destroy telegraph lines, railroads, bridges, & c. Whether he has met with success is not known.

Laura Lee—March 5, 1864. We have had some very pleasant successes lately in Tenn., in Florida and in Miss. There has been a raid from Meade's army towards Richmond and an advance on the Rapidan, but have as yet heard nothing certain as to the results.

Julia Chase—March 7, 1864. It was talked in town yesterday among the secessionists that Richmond had been taken, the women and children leaving as fast as possible, but we give no truth to it. . . . Later—it seems that our hearts are never to be cheered with the news of Richmond being in our possession. Reports say that Gen. Kilpatrick has been driven back from that point, with considerable loss. . . .

Laura Lee—March 7, 1864. Kilpatrick's raid has been a failure. He had over 5,000 cavalry and many infantry, and was within 6 miles of Richmond. He destroyed several miles of both the railroads and Hanover Junction and was driven back by the Home Guard of the city. . . . Our communication with Richmond is cut off by the tearing up of the R.R. Lal could not have left before the attack.

Laura Lee—March 8, 1864. A merciful Providence has averted what would have been an awful calamity to us. On the body of Col. Dahlgren[18] was found a copy of their orders and plans. They were to make a rush into Richmond, hang the president and Cabinet in the streets and then burn the city. They were met by the Home Guard, had a terrific fight, and were driven off into the swamps where our cavalry were still pursuing them. . . . Gen. Custer made a raid on the R.R. at Charlottesville at the same time that K. advanced on Richmond and thus our cavalry was drawn off at first, but they soon drove Custer back in the rear of Kilpatrick.

Julia Chase—March 11, 1864. Lieutenant Gen. Grant has taken Gen. Halleck's place, tho' it is thought he will not confine himself to Washington but remain in the field. The treatment by the Rebels to Col. Dalgren's body, who was killed in the late raid to Richmond is awful. No one knows where he is buried, and the editor of one of the Richmond papers says that nobody cares. . . . The editor remarks that documents were found upon his person, in regard to the plan adopted by Federal officers should they succeed in reaching Richmond, that the city was to be sacked, ravages committed, Jeff Davis & cabinet to be killed, one word of which we do not believe for a moment, a lie gotten up by these same editors or other rebels.

Laura Lee—March 11, 1864. The Yankee papers say very little about the raid. It is evident they are ashamed of the whole affair. The Herald calls it a miserable failure. Everything has been quiet since they were driven off. The Yankees made an advance in Tenn. but were driven back. Great preparations are being made there on both sides and there must be severe fighting before long. . . . We think Lal will certainly be here tomorrow. Bob has gone back to his regiment, but our Fitz Lee has promised to get him transferred to his cavalry.

Julia Chase—March 14, 1864. It is said that Imboden is about making a demonstration on Charlestown or Martinsburg, some 700 rebels having passed through Berryville. We hope the Union troops will be prepared for them. Suffolk was taken possession of a few days since by Gen. Butler, but it is reported that the rebels have recaptured it. We don't know that this is correct.

Laura Lee—March 16, 1864. The Yankees were in town this morning and the rebels this afternoon, but they did not meet. There is a report again that Meade is moving to make an attack. There is a strict blockade between here and Martinsburg.

Laura Lee—March 21, 1864. Mrs. Coutee and Miss Waring went down to Martinsburg yesterday but were sent back without being permitted to enter the town. Grant has been placed in command of the Army of the Potomac and another "on to Richmond" is the program. This is just the lull before the worst of the storm. All accounts from our army are very encouraging.

Julia Chase—March 22, 1864. The weather has been quite cold for several days past. A slight fall of snow last evening. Moderated considerably today. The Federals were in a short time yesterday, capturing a few prisoners. A few days ago a bridal party were captured by our men, being the fourth captured within a few weeks—rather dangerous getting married, the rebels think. . . . Military orders are and have been very strict with Martinsburg the past week or two. No one is permitted to go in or come out, unless they are refugees. It makes it very bad for the loyal people of Frederick to be thus cut off so. Gen. Grant is now with the Army of the Potomac. We hope that he may be able to impart some activity into the troops and officers and that they may for once gain a victory in Virginia. The rebel guerrillas have been committing great depredations throughout the country, going from house to house, stealing horses, threatening persons lives, so that there seems no safety whatever.

Laura Lee—March 24, 1864. Lal arrived this evening, to our great delight. She reports all thing quiet and none of our troops in the Valley except a picket force at Woodstock. Strict blockade still with Martinsburg.

Laura Lee—March 26, 1864. A heavy snow last night. Some Yankees in town with a report that they were rebuilding the R.R. between H. Ferry and this place, to come here very soon to stay.

Laura Lee—March 29, 1864. Report today . . . that a large force of Yankees will pass through here tomorrow to occupy the Valley above us. We will be cut off from the South, but hope at least to have the alleviation of being able to get some clothes. There is no confirmation of the report of Gen. Lee's advance.

Julia Chase—March 30, 1864. We are having winter weather in good earnest. Snow fell last night quite deep and is still continuing. No prospect of fair weather. The blockade still continues at Martinsburg. We hear that the R Road from Harper's Ferry is being rebuilt & that it is finished as far as Charlestown. Gen. Grant is with the Army of the Potomac. We shall expect to have stirring times as soon as the weather permits. Gen. Lee is said to have large accessions to his army, every available man almost being conscripted into the army.

Laura Lee—April 2, 1864. We have had a whole week of rain and snow, and have been kept indoors all the time. We have received several letters lately. One from Bob saying that he feared his transfer to the cavalry could not be accomplished, but still he wrote cheerfully and said the life of a private was not so unpleasant as it appeared to a looker on. A letter from Lewis[19] written from Richmond, said that he had been ill and his health was so delicate that his surgeon had warned him to be very careful. He had resigned his captain commission and was trying to get some indoor duty. There has been no advance anywhere, but the Yankees are making great preparations to move against Gen. Lee and up the Peninsula simultaneously. My heart sinks at the thought of the awful struggle which must come.

Julia Chase—April 3, 1864. We have witnessed a sight today that I never expected to see. A Negro regiment came into town this noon, have just passed by. Their object in coming we learn is to conscript all the able bodied Negroes/men in the county.[20] This causes great excitement among the whites as well as blacks. I don't know how we are to get along, shall have no one to do anything for us in the way of cutting wood, tilling the ground, & c. We shall expect most anything after this. . . . The blockade still continues at Martinsburg, so that we have no chance of knowing what is going on in the world.

Laura Lee—April 4, 1864. We were fared yesterday to have a sight which we had been for some time dreading, that of Negro soldiers. A regiment marched in from Berryville just after we returned from Church. Feeling as we must, it was a most revolting spectacle, but divested of that idea it was perfectly grotesque and equal to any caricature of such a set of real black niggers . . . we ever saw, such rambling, shambling, tumbling for marching, such grinning and grimacing. There is nothing which so clearly exhibits, to me, the madness and folly of the Yankee Government, as the idea of expecting such creatures to fight. There were white officers riding down each side of the column, and they looked as if they were driving a flock of black sheep. They halted at the market square, where they cooked dinner and about 4 o'clock they all marched down the Martinsburg Road where they halted about 6 miles from town. This morning there is considerable excitement. Some cavalry who were here yesterday have returned and arrested Dr. Boyd, Mr. Williams, and Mr. Conrad as hostages for Judge Kennedy and some other employees of the bogus Wheeling Government, who were captured at Bath by our men two weeks ago. They say the Negro reg't is to be in again today to conscript all the Negro men here, and in view of such a thing they are all hiding.

Julia Chase—April 5, 1864. We are having winter weather in good earnest, more like midwinter than April. Snow commenced falling yesterday afternoon, and still continues with some hail this morning. Dr. Boyd was arrested by our troops yesterday and taken to Martinsburg, whether on the same charge, as hostage for Mr. Dooley, we have not been able to learn. We hear that about a week ago the Rebels captured Union men in Bath. It may be in retaliation that Mr. B has been taken. As he has some influential friends and relatives in Martinsburg, I do not apprehend his treatment will be very severe or his imprisonment of long duration. Such a marked difference in regard to the two parties. One, the Unionists, see nothing but misery and starvation before them, the other, an abundance of everything that money can procure.

Laura Lee—April 6, 1864. The gentlemen who were taken from here on Monday are paroled in Martinsburg for the present. The blockade between there and here is still very strict. Nothing is permitted to come. . . . We had letters from the boys today. Bob hopes to get his transfer soon. Lewis is staying at Mrs. Mason's and Lee Powell's waiting orders.

Julia Chase—April 9, 1864. The 1st & 21st N York troops in this morn., advanced as far as Newtown but no Rebels to be found. About 270 other New Yorkers came in again this afternoon but without accomplishing anything so far as we could see. Never in time, always behind, after the Rebels have accomplished their plans.

Laura Lee—April 12, 1864. Yankees in today for a little while. There is a large force collecting in Hampshire to advance on Staunton. There must be a move on the Rapidan before many days.

Laura Lee—April 18, 1864. We have had a considerable victory in Kentucky [Tennessee]. Forrest has made a great raid, capturing large numbers of horses, stores & c. and has ended by storming and taking Fort Pillow[21] and afterwards Paducah. He took 14,000 prisoners at the former place.

Julia Chase—April 20, 1864. The news through Rebel papers that our troops have been defeated at Fort Pillow, that Gen. Banks has lost 14,000 of his men as prisoners, besides several hundred Negro troops who have been burned. We don't believe much of it, tho' probably our troops have been repulsed. The Government seems to be working backwards this Spring.

Laura Lee—April 23, 1864. Mr. Conrad arrived this evening from the penitentiary in Wheeling, where he and the other hostages have been confined for a week past. He and Mr. Dandridge are paroled and sent to Richmond to try to arrange an exchange with those miserable scamps for whom they are held. The six gentlemen are confined in a large room with 180 criminals of every grade and subjected to outrageous treatment.

Julia Chase—April 24, 1864. Mr. Conrad returned last night, has been paroled for 60 days, as to take measures for the release of the Union men who were taken from Bath. He says that Dr. Boyd & Mr. Williams are in prison at Wheeling, receiving prison fare, have not been sent to Ohio as we heard.

Julia Chase—April 28, 1864. The Rebel account of the Fort Pillow massacre say that Forrest attacked the Fort, the garrison consisting of 300 white & 400 Negro troops. The fort refusing to surrendered, it was carried by storm. 100 prisoners taken, the balance were slain. The fort ran with blood, many jumped into the water and were drowned or shot. Over $100,000 worth of stores were taken, 6 guns captured.

Laura Lee—April 30, 1864. Reports from various sources today make it no longer doubtful that the Yankees are coming here again, not to occupy with a large force, but to pass through with a heavy column, through Staunton, "on to Richmond." This place to be the base of their supplies. Some men from Martinsburg are here securing houses for stores.

May 1864–September 1864

"For the first time we have seen a glorious victory"

Like two years before, the Shenandoah Valley once again became the scene of major military activity during the summer and fall of 1864, as the Federals made repeated attempts to gain control of the region. And as events unfolded, Julia and Laura followed the actions of the two armies with keen interest. The Federal efforts thwarted early on, Julia continued to express her anguish over their inability to gain a victory in the region. In September, when the situation was reversed, Laura became disheartened after the Confederate defeat at the third battle of Winchester. Her dismay was heightened when she learned that her nephew, Robert, was seriously wounded during the engagement.

Julia and Laura followed the military events taking place in the rest of the country with equal attention. They understood completely that the fate of both their causes hinged on the outcome of the brutal fighting before Richmond and Atlanta. When the Federals captured Atlanta in September, Laura readily admitted that it was a severe blow to the Confederate cause and would have an adverse effect on the North's upcoming presidential election.

Julia Chase—May 1, 1864. We are once more under the protection of the Stars and Stripes. Our troops entered and took possession of our town today, causing much joy among the Unionists but sadness to Secesh. Quite a large force of cavalry and infantry are here. Whether their stay will be long or short, we are unable to say. The <u>Bal. American</u> says that Gen. Lee is being very heavily reinforced from Longstreet & Johnson's armies, so that his numbers swell pretty largely. We almost dread to hear of a battle in Virginia. There will probably be heavy slaughter on both sides. God grant success to the right.

Laura Lee—May 2, 1864. Here we are again in Yankee hands. This is the explanation of the strict blockade between Martinsburg and this place for the past six weeks. They have been massing troops and immense quantities of stores at the former place. Yesterday while we were in church they began to arrive, and before night 7,000 had passed through camping at Hollingsworth's a mile from town. They say there will be 30,000 here in a day or two. Seigel is in command. They were tolerably quiet last night, but this morning about 7 o'clock a cry of fire was raised which proved to be in the fine storeroom of Miller, just opposite the Taylor Hotel. It was unoccupied and two soldiers were seen coming out of it just before the fire broke out. . . . Some of the Yankees worked very hard to extinguish the fires, but others said, "Let them burn, Let them burn." More Yankees have passed through today, but the column will not move until all are collected here. Some of the sutlers have opened stores today. Almost everyone is out of groceries and will buy all that is possible. We were fortunate enough to receive a letter yesterday, just before the Yankees came in, from Lewis. He has been put on Gen. Ewell's staff, which is a very fine appointment.

Laura Lee—May 3, 1864. The 30,000 was, as usual, only a boast, but 7,000 have come. They are quiet as yet and seem to be under strict discipline. Very few are allowed to come to town except the Provost Guard. No doubt they will be audacious enough when they are fairly settled. . . . They have brought in a great many men arrested in the neighborhood, as being liable to military duty. The country people who had come to church on Sunday are still detained. The sutlers are not permitted to open their goods in town, so our only alleviation in having them here is denied us.

Julia Chase—May 5, 1864. The Federals, a few days since, burned Orange C. House, whether according to orders we know not. The weather has moderated very much and it is very warm and Spring like. Our town is very much enlivened by the army being here. Trains of wagons, & c. are continually passing by, so different from the long quiet and dullness which has existed here for so many months.

Laura Lee—May 5, 1864. These miserable Yankees are searching all rebel houses today. We have just finished our preparations for their reception, which are quite elaborate and very troublesome. There is a great excitement. The news has just come that Mosby dashed into Martinsburg last night where there were only 500 Yankees left. We cannot learn exactly what he did, but two reg'ts of cavalry were sent down from here at once. There is a most singular order out today. No citizen is allowed to go on the street on any pretense. . . . I was interrupted by a squad arriving to search the house. They were civil and good natured and we had no trouble. Every house is to be searched. They go from one to the other in regular succession. . . . We are expecting each day with the most intense anxiety the tidings from the Rapidan.

Julia Chase—May 7, 1864. The Army of the Potomac have made a forward movement, crossed the Rapidan some days since, and Gen. Lee is said to have left his entrenchments, falling back to Richmond.

Laura Lee—May 7, 1864. The searching is ended and the embargo on outgoing removed, but we are nearly in a state of starvation. Not a particle of marketing has been brought in for a week, and the people not expecting the Yankees had no extra supplies. There is a report that they are moving tonight. Some officers came from Martinsburg this evening and report that Grant has crossed the river, surprised Lee, and captured 17,000 prisoners. Rather absurd.

Julia Chase—May 9, 1864. The army which have been here a week have struck tents, and are leaving up the Valley, to join in all probability Gen. Grant's army. The Baltimore American of today says that heavy battles took place on Thursday and Friday,[1] our troops (the Federals) occupying Petersburg, but heavy loss on both sides. It is also rumored that Gen. Longstreet, has been killed, but it is not credited here in town. In all probability it is incorrect. . . . We hear that Mosby and 500 of his guerrillas are lurking about, ready to pounce down on the wagon train or any soldiers that may be passing along. The weather continues very warm and dusty, a little rain would be very acceptable. The news from the Army of the Potomac is that very heavy fighting had taken place on Thursday and Friday last, and that though no victory could be claimed, yet the result was rather favorable to the Union cause. From 6 to 8000 wounded had been sent to Washington, while showing the desperate nature of the fight, also shows that order and confidence still prevailed. The Rebels, however, claim a victory, and Gen. Lee in his dispatch says, under the kind Providence of God, we are once more successful, having repulsed the enemy at all points, capturing over 1000 prisoners besides some 4 pieces of artillery.

Laura Lee—May 9, 1864. We are again blessed in being free from our tyrants. Yesterday . . . all things were quiet until late in the afternoon when there were rumors that they had heard something unpleasant. In a little while the trains began to move . . . and early in the morning the main body moved off in the direction of Front Royal, it is supposed to join Grant, if they are permitted to do so. They have left in great haste evidently, as besides burning a good deal, they have abandoned an immense quantity of things in the camps, which the people have been securing all day. It is reported in every direction that Grant has been driven back, but thus far no one has come down the Valley with Southern accounts. It is a time of intense anxiety.

Julia Chase—May 12, 1864. Fighting has still been going on between the 2 armies in Virginia. Gen. Grant said to have his headquarters below Spottsylvania C[ourt] House,[2] showing that Lee has fallen back. Heavy loss on both sides, and we regret great loss among our officers. Gens. Sedgwick, Wadsworth and Hays are killed, Gen. Seymour a prisoner, and Gen. Wadsworth's body is probably in the hands of the enemy. Many other officers have fallen, sorrow and mourning still over the land. . . . Gen. Longstreet is said to be severely wounded, also Gen. Stafford mortally wounded, and the Gen. Jones killed, no mention made of the Rebel loss otherwise. From Gen. Sherman, we hear that the attack on Dalton had not commenced, Gen. McPherson finding the Rebel position at Reseca strongly fortified. From N. Carolina, our gunboats had an encounter with the Rebel ram in Albemarle Sound, but that the latter succeeded in escaping, probably in a damaged condition.

Laura Lee—May 12, 1864. Our suspense as to the battle has ended. We have had a glorious victory. If we could only hear of the safety of our dear boys, I should be completely happy. Two of Rosser's scouts were here today to get information as to Seigel's numbers and movements. They say that Grant's army has been defeated and routed, his pontoons destroyed and his retreat cut off. Their reports of numbers, prisoners & c. seem so fabulous that I will not write them down until I hear more certainly.

Laura Lee—May 13, 1864. We are still in misery and suspense about the boys. A report has reached town today that either John or Clayton Williams has been killed. No other name belonging about here is mentioned. The rumor is so vague that Mrs. Williams has not been told of it. Seigel is at Woodstock, and we hear no communication in that direction. . . . The Balt. American today says that Grant ordered another advance of all his forces for 5 o'clock last Tuesday. There has been no doubt another battle. . . . Banks has been superceded in La. He has practiced the lessons of running which Jackson taught him, to such good purpose that he has finished his course. This is a time of great misery. Each morning I dread what we may have to hear. I tremble every time the bell rings.

Julia Chase—May 14, 1864. The news from the Army of the Potomac is most encouraging and cheering. Gen. Hancock engaged the enemy, capturing some 25 guns, the whole of Stonewall Jackson's old brigade as prisoners, besides Gen. Ed Johnston and Gen. Stewart. Gen. Grant, in his official dispatch says, after 8 days heavy fighting I have captured between 30 & 40 guns, and 4 or 5000 prisoners.

Laura Lee—Sunday night—May 15, 1864. I hope I may not be called on to spend many such miserable days as this has been. This morning yesterday's <u>Balt. American</u> came with the most flaming accounts of their success on last Wednesday. It said that Gen. Johnson and a great part of his division had been captured, the Stonewall Brigade entire, and Brig. Johnson and Stuart. Also that Gen. Lee had been wounded and sent to Richmond. The last item we know to be false, unless it is Gen. Fitz, but the particulars of the capture are so minute, that it is evident there is foundation for the report. . . . The trains have been passing through the town for several hours, with cavalry. The infantry will be down tomorrow. There will be one blessing attending his return. Our dreadful state of suspense will be ended. We will at least know the worst or best.

Laura Lee—May 15, 1864. Seigel has moved higher up the Valley, instead of returning here. The trains of last night were empty, with some wounded in skirmishes. We have had a week of rain, but it has cleared off brightly at last. Mr. Conrad and Mr. Dandridge returned today. They have been detained ten days in Woodstock, but have heard constantly from the army the last four days, when Seigel moved up. Their reports are all we could wish. A soldier just from the army. . . has sent word that none of the men from Winchester have been hurt. This gives us hope.

Julia Chase—May 16, 1864. Another mishap to our troops in the Valley. Gen. Siegel was attacked by the rebels, and as usual with superior numbers, fighting on Saturday and Sunday, with considerable loss to our troops, Gen. Siegel falling back to Cedar Creek.[3] The wounded came in this evening, over 200 in number, and several officers of the 34th Mass. were killed. Col. Boyd of the 1st N. York, ran into a Rebel camp and had 200 of his men captured, the whole thing ending in our troops being pretty badly handled & whipped. . . . It seems that we are doomed to disaster in the Valley, not one victory has ever been gained over the Rebels since the Federals entered Virginia . . . and even now we expect nothing else but to see our troops falling still further back, the Rebs pursuing.

Laura Lee—May 17, 1864. Everything is perfectly quiet today. . . . About 8 o'clock the wagons began to pass through town, but not more than ten wagons had passed when an order came to stop them and turn them out of the way of a train of ambulances and wagons, which proved to be filled with the dead and wounded from a terrible fight on Sunday at Brock's Gap, 2 miles above Mt. Jackson. They were attended by only a few cavalry and there were numbers of poor wounded creatures on foot. They hurried through without a moments pause and seemed thoroughly disheartened and frightened and only anxious to get on. The stragglers talked very freely to the people and said they had been terribly whipped, had lost 2,000, leaving most of their dead and wounded on the field, and only escaped the capture of the whole force by retreating rapidly by burning the bridges behind them. Seigel's whole command is at Cedar Creek tonight, and we suppose they will be through here in the morning.

Julia Chase—May 19, 1864. From the Army of the Potomac—There has been no fighting since Friday last, necessarily a lull in the progress of the campaign, Gen. Grant resting his men, receiving heavy reinforcements, while the dreadful condition of the roads from the late storm render army movements almost impossible. . . . Both armies are now concentrated on the direct road to Richmond. . . . From Georgia, we hear news of the success of our arms under Gen. Sherman. He, after a hard fight had forced Gen. Johnston to fall back first from Dalton and now from Resaca. . . . The Richmond papers speak of the death of Gen. J. E. B. Stuart, his funeral having taken place on the 13th. All the telegraph lines leading to Lee's army have also been cut by the Federals.

Laura Lee—May 20, 1864. A long train went up today with a heavy guard, and an empty one came before Seigel passed through here last night on his way to Washington. A Richmond paper of last Monday containing four official dispatches, one from Gen. Lee, one from Beauregard, one from Johnston, and one from Breckenridge, all announcing decisive victories for us. . . . It is true that J. E. B. Stuart is dead.[4] He suffered himself to be surprised and was mortally wounded in trying to get off.

Laura Lee—May 21, 1864. Seigel has been superceded by that villain Hunter, who passed through here today with his staff to take command up the Valley. They report that they are fighting again on the Rapidan. More misery and suspense for us. Mary Jackson returned from Washington, after an absence of nine months. Her reports are very favorable to our cause. The papers of Thursday report a massed attack on Gen. Lee's left wing, but without any decisive result.

Julia Chase—May 24, 1864. This has been the warmest day we have had, a fine rain, however, tonight has cooled the atmosphere, besides laying the dust. By order of Gen. Hunter, several houses in Newtown have been destroyed, in consequence of guerrillas firing from these houses upon the train as it passed down. We think it exactly right. If persons will harbor these outlaws, they must expect the consequences. . . . Official dispatches from Gen. Sherman report his continued success. At Rome he captured considerable amount of provision & 7 iron works with their machinery. The rebels in speaking of this, say that it is of more importance by far that Georgia should be held than Richmond, tho' the capture of Richmond would prove of greater importance in a political point of view to the Federals than any other sense.

Laura Lee—May 24, 1864. Seigel and his staff passed through today. He did not know he was to be superceded until Hunter arrived. Tonight a long train of 300 wagons, nearly all loaded, came through going back to Martinsburg. It seems strange as two went up only today.

Laura Lee—May 25, 1864. This is the second anniversary of Bank's run [retreat] from here. The explanation of the return of the loaded wagons is that Hunter sent them back intending to live on the country entirely, until everything is exhausted. Our troubles are beginning again. Hunter sent a squad down to Newtown yesterday to burn four houses, from which some soldiers declared they had been fired upon the day before. It was perfectly untrue, but they burned the houses. . . . There has been no fighting on the Rapidan and Butler has been driven back.

Laura Lee—May 27, 1864. The <u>American</u> says today that Lee is falling back on Richmond, and though they have as yet had no decisive victory, Grant's skillful and masterly maneuvering is certain to accomplish it in the end. We hear nothing from Southern sources for several days. This is certainly the most agonizing time of all this horrible war.

Laura Lee—May 28, 1864. Hunter is moving up the Valley, burning and destroying everything his men do not use, so as to leave "nothing for the rebels, if they ever come here again."

Julia Chase—May 30, 1864. Gen. Grant has crossed the Pamunkey with his whole army, found Lee's army strongly entrenched between the N. Anna & South Anna rivers and executed another flank movement by which the rebel position was rendered strategically useless. Our army consequently being some miles nearer to Richmond. From Gen. Sherman, we learn that having flanked Alatoona in Alabama, threatening Atlanta, Gen. Johnston moved out to meet him. The armies met at Vine Creek, the battle resulting in favor of the Federals.

Laura Lee—May 30, 1864. A provision train which passed up through here on Sunday afternoon, has been attacked two miles above Newtown, the guard captured, and the wagons rifled and burned by a company of

Gilmore's men. . . . The people living on the road are in great anxiety expecting to be burned out as fulfillment of Hunter's threat. . . . Major Mosby sent this morning to Hunter to say that he should hang ten Yankee prisoners for every house that was burned.

Julia Chase—June 1, 1864. The siege of Richmond may said to have begun. The Rebel army has been forced from its last entrenched position this side of the Chickahominy & Gen. Grant's forward movement places him within seven miles of the Rebel Capitol. Out cavalry were sent out to destroy the bridges over Little & South Anna Rivers & tear up the railroad. While preparations for battle were going on, the rebels attempted to turn our left, but were repulsed with considerable slaughter.

Laura Lee—June 1, 1864. There is quite a panic here tonight. It is said that Hunter has fallen back this side of Middletown, and that he sent down orders this evening to burn Newtown and all the houses between here and Washington. It seems too bad to believe.

Julia Chase—June 2, 1864. From Georgia, reports say that Gen. Sherman was attacked on Tuesday morning & after several hours hard fighting repulsed him—our line being advanced to the railroad near Marietta, which is 20 miles from Atlanta. The main portion of the army occupied Marietta, capturing 400 prisoners & a railroad train with sick & wounded. From the Shenandoah Valley, Gen. Hunter found the Rebels 4000 strong in his front. Nothing but skirmishing occurred. Gen. Hunter issued an order holding the inhabitants of the county responsible for the depredations committed by the guerrillas.

Laura Lee—June 2, 1864. Major Stearns and a party of cavalry were really sent down to burn Newtown last night, but the prayers and tears of the women and the proposal of a good many of the men to take the Yankee oath, moved him to forbear until they consulted again with Hunter. It is a cruel fate for the poor people. They have been earnest and active in their devotion to our cause from the beginning of the war.

Laura Lee—June 7, 1864. Major Gilmore was in town last night. He says there was severe fighting around Richmond last Wednesday, Thursday and Friday, and that the Yankees were repulsed at all points. Hunter was still at Harrisonburg, and the Confederates were entrenched at Mt. Jackson, at the latest reports.

Julia Chase—June 9, 1864. We have news today, coming from Rebel papers of Richmond, that Gen. Hunter has defeated the rebels in the Valley, our troops occupying Staunton & the Rebel Gen. Jones was killed. The fight occurred about 12 miles from Staunton. The secessionists in town, however, will not give credence but say it is all a fabrication. Rumors are afloat in Washington that Gen. Grant had fallen back 15 miles, changing his base. We don't like to hear of these rumors & hope there is no foundation for them, tho' there has been no fighting for the past several days.

Laura Lee—June 10, 1864. The most contradictory reports prevail with regard to Staunton. One story is that the Yankees are certainly there. The other is equally positive that they have never been there. There is not a word about it in the <u>American</u>, which gives us hope that the latter report is true.

Laura Lee—June 11, 1864. Still doubts about Staunton. The very last account comes from Woodstock today, asserting that a body of Yankee cavalry flanked around and entered Staunton on Monday. They left again on Tuesday morning, having first burned all the public buildings and paroled 800 home guards who were there. Whether this is true or false remains to be proved. The <u>American</u> of yesterday hints at rumors which prevail of Grant's having fallen back 10 miles to change his base. A report comes from Baltimore that he has retreated to Harrison's Landing. Lincoln has been nominated unanimously by the Baltimore convention.

Julia Chase—June 12, 1864. Today's paper . . . confirms the fact of Gen. [Hunter's] victory, that our troops destroyed nearly all the public buildings in Staunton & that the Federals under Averill had destroyed the Military Institute at Lexington, some 40 or 50 miles south of Staunton. As the Rebel P.M. [postmaster] and another secesh citizen from our town returned home today, bringing the same news, they cannot doubt the truth. . . . Poor Richmond! It has had a hard time, scarcity of food, & then scarcity of water. The poor prisoners in Libby Prison & elsewhere will feel it very sensibly. Would to God that our troops under Gen. Grant could have possession of that city & release those in confinement. We heard a few days since that Mr. Dooley was dead.

Laura Lee—June 13, 1864. This is the anniversary of Milroy's retreat. The truth about Staunton has reached us at last. Gen. Lee telegraphed to Imboden to hold out until Monday if possible, when his reinforcements would reach him. Hunter attacked him on Sunday with four times his numbers, and he was forced to fall back to Waynesboro. On Monday Hunter sent 600 cavalry into Staunton, who burned the government workshops and then returned to the main body the next morning. . . . The <u>American</u> of Saturday claims that some cavalry had gone on to Lexington and burned the Institute. Nothing new from Richmond.

Laura Lee—June 14, 1864. It is true that they have burned the Institute at Lexington. Hunter is moving from Staunton, but which way is not known. Grant is also moving, it is supposed to the south side of James River to unite with Butler.

Julia Chase—June 16, 1864. Dispatches from Gen. Hunter state that Gen. Averill & Crook's forces moved from Staunton. An expedition sent to Waynesboro returned after destroying several R. Road bridges & tearing up the track. The Rebel troops under Imboden are said to be thoroughly demoralized. Gen. Sheridan, it is rumored, has arrived at Gordonsville on his way to join Hunter.

Laura Lee—June 16, 1864. The sad news reached here today of Lenny Swartzwelder's death. He was wounded last Saturday, died on Sunday, and was buried on Monday, his eighteenth birthday. The fight was near Louisa C.H. with Sheridan, who was fighting to get through to join Hunter at Lynchburg. He was defeated and routed by Hampton and Fitz Lee. Hunter is moving on Lynchburg, but Pickett is in front and Breckenridge in the rear.

Laura Lee—June 20, 1864. The American of Saturday claims that they have taken Petersburg. A dispatch came from Mr. Conrad this morning from Woodstock, claiming a great victory for us on the south side of the James River, but we are afraid to trust it yet. Night. The news is confirmed in various ways from both North and South. Even the American admits that the announcement of taking Petersburg was premature and there was a rumor that Butler was defeated. . . . Several reports say that Ewell is advancing in this direction and has reached Gordonsville, but this I doubt entirely.

Julia Chase—June 22, 1864. The fighting which occurred on Saturday between Gen. Grant & Lee was very severe and our loss heavy. We have no account of the rebel loss. . . . Our loss in the fighting of Friday & Sat. of Gen. Grant's army is put down at 8000. What a large number of our countrymen at this time suffering. It costs a vast expenditure of blood & means to put down this cursed rebellion. . . . Gen. Hunter, so the Richmond papers say, is within a few miles of Lynchburg.

Laura Lee—June 23, 1864. Hunter was within eight miles of Lynchburg last Friday when he was attacked by Breckenridge and driven back with the loss of 3,000 prisoners, 12 guns and a train of wagons. On Saturday Early arrived, and as soon as Hunter learned it, he commenced to retreat, closely pursued of course.

Julia Chase—June 27, 1864. The Secesh were very jubilant over a dispatch that was received this morning, that Gen. Hunter's army had been captured, his artillery destroyed & only 3000 men left, but before night the Federals coming in, they pulled down their circulars in great haste, fearing the Yankees might see them. We feel as if there might be some truth in the rumor, as it was supposed that probably Gen. Hunter had fallen back to Staunton and supplies were being sent on to him, but when we were expecting to see the troops pass through town, word came that they had been ordered back again to Martinsburg, so we know not what to think.

Laura Lee—June 27, 1864. We have constant communication now with the South and frequently see Richmond papers, which give the brightest and most cheering accounts. Dr. Reed came to town yesterday and he says he saw Bob just a week ago in Lynchburg and was quite well. The last reports of Hunter are that he had abandoned his artillery and trains and that all of his men but 3,000 had been caught.

Laura Lee—June 29, 1864. The Yankees admit that they were repulsed with heavy loss before Petersburg last week. Grant is making another swing around to the Weldon R. Road. Hunter says he retired from want of ammunition and got out safely with slight loss. The Southern accounts of him are still conflicting. Mosby made a raid to Duffield's Depot last night and captured 200 prisoners.

Laura Lee—June 30, 1864. Some Confederates in town today. Hunter did escape with nearly all his men. Night. Great News!! Quite a large army will be here tomorrow or next day on to Penn. We were spending the evening at Mr. Sherrard's and heard at first a report that Early was as near as Woodstock, but I did not believe it. . . . But soon after tea some soldiers passed and said it was all true and Bob Munson said that our Bob had come with them to town. We all rushed home, but found that Bob had not come, nor did he come until Saturday, having been stopped by the pickets. . . . At ½ past six this morning Bob came to our great delight, quite well and as bright as a bird, though worn to a shadow by this dreadful two months campaign. After he had bathed and dressed we were having prayers when there was a sudden clatter of horses, which I knew at once to be Yankees and Lute jumped up and carried Bob off to hide him. Our scare soon was over as the Yankees did not dismount and were gone again in ten minutes. After breakfast two brigades of cavalry passed through and Gen. Early came about 12 o'clock. We had some happiness of Lewis at home once night fell but the infantry will not pass through until tomorrow. This is an Army of the Valley with two corps of infantry and one of cavalry, all under Early. Some of the staff are coming here to tea this evening.

Julia Chase—July 2, 1864. What a change 24 hours or even less than that has brought about. We understand that the whole of Ewell's Division is very near town, and as proof of it Imboden's Cavalry has come in & are marching on to Martinsburg. Who would have thought it, tho' we understand the Secessionists remarked yesterday that their troops would be in today. A few of the Federal cavalry came in this morning early, but seeing signs of a strong force of Rebels, they soon left. Some 7 pieces of cannon has also passed through town and our streets are filled with Rebel soldiers, the secessionists being in high glee. We are only too much afraid that our leaders are not aware of this move, and the next thing we shall hear is that the rebs have entered Maryland, or torn up the R. Road. The same party of rebs who disturbed the company last evening, went about 1 o'clock to a Union gentleman's house (Mr. Milloy) to arrest Mr. M. by orders as they said of Major Gilmore. The lady did not see proper to let them in, as her husband had been quite ill and she would not have him disturbed. These rascals told her if they did not come in they would destroy her property, but she dared them to do it, telling them if they did, that the Federals would make the Secessionists suffer for it. They talked a long time in a very insulting manner & said they would carry her answer to Major Gilmore. She told them they could do it, but as for taking her husband off, they should not do that, & that they left but before morning they returned again & demanded entrance or they burst the door open. Mrs. M. thought it best to let them in, but with the full determination that Mr. M. should not be disturbed. They searched through the house for Mr. M. and when they came where he was, tho' suffering so much, these scamps insisted upon arresting him as a spy & said if they thought he would live to get to their colonel they would take him at all hazards, but they left at last without carrying out their threats. Mrs. M's Secession neighbors are the cause again of all this trouble, and there are some such despicable creatures in our town that they do not care what becomes of the Union people. If they could have their way, should all be shot or hung, & yet these Southern people call themselves such praying people, that they are more righteous & holy than the Northern people. . . . Just one year ago the battle of Gettsyburg was being fought. What will the coming anniversary of our Nation's independence bring forth—shall the news be favorable or unfavorable. . . . Oh God! May thy right hand lead us, and if it please thee give success to our National Arms.

Julia Chase—July 3, 1864. Early's division [Corps] is now passing through this town. I have noted some 4 or more colors and 33 pieces of cannon with those that passed through yesterday. It is said between 25 to 30,000 troops, & their object to destroy the Bal. & Ohio Railroad, probably also to enter Maryland & Pennsylvania. We shall expect to hear of much destruction of property in retaliation of the property destroyed by our generals in recent raids. We only hope that our troops may be somewhat prepared for them. Would that this war was at an end, and Peace declared, but in a conversation Gen. Early had with Mr. M., the Union gentleman, he asked him how he expected to live here[,] that the South would never be subjugated, but he was sure of the South's Independence being declared. Time alone will determine these things. . . . Gen. Hunter's loss while operating against Lynchburg is put down to 600 in killed, wounded & missing. Finding that the rebels had been reinforced by Gen. Early, Gen. Hunter withdrew. It is said that he inflicted serious injury & damage upon the railroad lines over which he passed, also destroyed the house of Gov. Letcher at Lexington, and now we shall feel the retaliation which the rebels will carry out in their progress. We expect to hear before many days of the Bal. & Ohio R. Road being destroyed, Martinsburg & Harper's Ferry taken. . . .

Laura Lee—July 4, 1864. Gen. Early and half a dozen of his staff came to tea on Saturday, and afterwards Gen. Elzey, Major Snowdon, Major Rogers, Major Myers, Capt. Clay and various other standing officers. . . . At ½ past four on Sunday morning we were roused by the music of bands and found the troops were beginning to move through the town. We dressed and went to the corner. They were in the finest spirits, though very shabby after their incessant marching and fighting for two months. Gen. Early and his staff at the head of his old division passed on this street. We had a good many in to breakfast . . . and by ten all had gone except a few who had leave for the day. Lewis went after dinner, but Bob had leave until today. In the afternoon news came that the cavalry which went through town on Saturday had captured Martinsburg and all the stores in the night.

Laura Lee—July 5, 1864. The army are crossing today into Maryland, some at Shepherdstown, some at Harper's Ferry. Already people are talking of their returning in a few days and leaving us again to the Yankees. I suppose it must be so. . . . We hear very little which is reliable from either side of us now. The official communication is by signal, as there is no telegraph nearer than New Market.

Julia Chase—July 9, 1864. There seems some commotion and uneasiness in town today. The Federals are said to be about, and the sick are being sent off. We only hope it may prove true and every reb be out of town before many days. The Federals are said to have been to Martinsburg last night, capturing the Rebel pickets, also recapturing 100 of their own wagons. It is said also that Shepherdstown is full of Yankees, and they are at Halltown too. Later—The uneasiness seems to have passed off, and we fear there is no such good news as these chaps leaving. The weather still continues very warm & dusty, having had no rain for 5 or 6 weeks. Should we not have some soon, there will be every prospect of a drought. The gardens are all drying up & the corn is suffering for want of it. We hear that the rebel army is near Baltimore, expect soon to hear of that city & Washington being taken. Can't find out anything of the movements of the federal army. Everything is gloomy and sad. We hear that Gen. Sherman in Georgia has been whipped by Johnston.

Julia Chase—July 10, 1864. This has been a very noisy day, great many wagons are passing up & down. Cavalry going on to Martinsburg, which looks like the whole of Lee's army pushing this way, more troops about than we had any idea of, and we fear the report of the Federals being at Martinsburg and other points is incorrect.

Laura Lee—July 11, 1864. We had an alarm yesterday about Mary. She has exhausted herself by incessant exertion at the hospital for the past week, and when she came home from Church yesterday she fainted and remained insensible nearly two hours. She is much better today. We hear nothing but rumors from Md. All communication is cut off. . . . Hunter is said to be following Early rapidly. This suspense is almost as terrible as what we endured a few weeks ago. . . . There is a report that Gen. Early re-crossed the river at Leesburg.

Laura Lee—July 12, 1864. This morning the stage drove up and Col. Ned Lee came to the door and said Mrs. Gen. Gordon[5] was there and that we must take her in. We were extremely unwilling but could not refuse to let her come in until she could make other arrangements. We have applied everywhere, but no one can take her, so here she must remain. She is extremely pretty and very pleasant, but we did not wish to have any lady in the house. She has a little son with her. There is not a word from Md., but some report that Yankees are coming here from Martinsburg. The men who are here are organized and kept on duty. They consist principally of stragglers and invalids returning to duty who arrived here after the army crossed into Md.

Julia Chase—July 13, 1864. The troops are still here; quite a force of cavalry went out on the Martinsburg Road. We hear that their pickets were again captured by the Federals. The secessionists are rather downcast, the news today is that Petersburg, the key to Richmond, is in our possession, and instead of Gen. Sherman being whipped by Johnston in Ga., he has been doing well, capturing Atlanta. We can't get any papers, but learn that one Richmond paper was in town yesterday, but no Union person could get a peep at it. This is just as good, we know that if things were going well with the Rebels, we should hear enough of it. It is very hard for them to believe they can be whipped & the soldiers probably get to see so few papers that they are ready to believe whatever is told them, but that is the program with the Rebels, keep the greater portion of the people in ignorance.

Laura Lee—July 13, 1864. A report has come that Early has taken Baltimore, but it is not much credited. Gen. Imboden has taken command here, as he cannot get to his own command in Md. The Yankees are said to be in Martinsburg and Charlestown.

Laura Lee—July 15, 1864. We hear that the army is re-crossing the river at Leesburg, bringing off all their captured stores. Wild stories are afloat that we have Baltimore and the outer defenses of Washington, but the truth is that after fighting and routing the 6th Corps on Saturday at Frederick, instead of pursuing them to Baltimore, as they expected, Gen. Early suddenly turned upon Washington and on Monday evening attacked their entrenchments within four miles of the city.[6] There was only skirmishing, as he found their fortifications so formidable that he would not risk his comparatively small force, so he withdrew to the river, bring off 600 prisoners, 4,000 horses, more than 2,000 cattle, valuable medical stores & c.

Julia Chase—July 16, 1864. Another of our citizens has died. Mr. Milloy, a Union gentleman, who has been persecuted by his enemies, and would in all probability have been arrested and carried off by these troops, were it not that sickness prevented. His neighbors have been very bitter towards him and have done all they could to annoy him. We had heard that Early's troops were falling back and would be in town today, but the day is past and there is no appearance of them. Instead of it, we fear that they are still fighting with the Federals, some say at Leesburg, others this side. Some 200 wounded were brought in this morning, from the late fight. . . . They are said to have gone within 4 miles of Washington City, and we learn have burned the house of Postmaster Gen. Blair, also Gov. Bradford's in Maryland, in retaliation, I suppose, of Gov. Letcher's house & the Military Institute in this state. Ammunition & guns have been brought in town today, so we fear that the Rebels have no idea of leaving very soon.

Laura Lee—July 16, 1864. The army crossed on Thursday, and they are now resting around Leesburg. We have heard that our boys are safe and Gen. Gordon,[7] too. Mrs. Gordon has been utterly wretched. . . . The expedition has been a perfect success, and has produced the greatest panic throughout the North. Two corps have been sent from Grant's army.

Julia Chase—July 17, 1864. A very warm morning, and no appearance whatever of rain. Our gardens are yielding us nothing, on account of the drought.

Laura Lee—July 18, 1864. The army moved up on Saturday to the Shenandoah, yesterday crossed and went into camp around Berryville. Bob came while we were at church and in the evening Gen. Gordon sent up for Mrs. G. to come to meet him at Mr. McCormick's, as to stay a few days. It is all mystery as to the future. Many think they are going into Penn. in a few days.

Julia Chase—July 19, 1864. Great excitement in town this afternoon. The Federals are advancing upon the Martinsburg Road, being only 6 or 7 miles from town. Skirmishing has been going on all day, the rebs falling back, their wagons are being packed up and sent off. We hope to see the Federals in town tomorrow.

Laura Lee—July 19, 1864. There is quite a panic this evening as the enemy has appeared on the Martinsburg Road and our cavalry have fallen back to town. The Yankees have gone into camp about 6 miles off. The refugees are going off in haste, and couriers have been sent to Gen. Early to ask for more men here. Prisoners taken yesterday say that Hunter has been removed from his command, which is good news to us. Last Sunday he sent a party of soldiers to Charlestown with orders to seize Mr. Andrew Hunter and burn his house, which order they obliged to the letter, allowing the family to save only a change of clothing. Mr. Hunter is his first cousin and there was no charge against him except that he was a "rebel" and had left his home whenever it was in Yankee lines.

Julia Chase—July 20, 1864. The Federals have not made their appearance yet. Gen. Early's wagon train passed through town quite early this morning and there is great stir with the soldiers. Wagons, artillery, ambulances, & c. are coming in from the Martinsburg Road. It may be that a battle will be fought today between the 2 forces. It would have been a very easy matter for the Federals to have dashed in last week, or even yesterday, as the troops in town were broken down, many without arms, but the Federals never come just in the right time. The weather still continues very warm & dusty, no appearance of rain. There will be a great scarcity of corn this season, and the army have taken a large quantity of wheat, have had the mills all pressed in Clarke & the adjoining counties, for the army, so that another winter will probably produce much suffering in this part of the country.

Laura Lee—July 20, 1864. Here we are left again to the enemy. All last night there was bustle and movement, and at 5 this morning Mrs. Gordon arrived on her way back, which is a sure indication. She said the Yankees were discovered moving up the river yesterday evening towards Berry's Ferry and our troops were at once put in motion and went in the same direction this side of the river. The trains are all sent through here up the Staunton Road, and all the sick and wounded who can be moved are gone and stores are all sent off and nothing remains but Ramseur's division left to protect trains. Mrs. Gordon and Bob will go this evening.

Julia Chase—July 21, 1864. Since 4 o'clock this morning we have passed from Dixie into the U. States, and now the Stars & Stripes are waving over our town, and may the time never come when we shall not rejoice to see them. Gen. Averill commands the forces here. . . . What a difference in regard to the treatment between the Federals & Rebs. When the Federals were brought in as prisoners, & when some had to return on account of sickness, after leaving town, the Union girls were not allowed to take the least thing.

Laura Lee—July 21, 1864. We have had a sharp fight here, and have been worsted. Gen. Ramseur had orders not to fight but he was misled by a false report of the numbers of the Yankees and thought he would make a brilliant affair of it. Mrs. Gordon and Bob went off soon after dinner, and about 4 o'clock we heard sharp cannonading and in a little while stragglers came running in saying that our men were driven back and had lost a whole battery. The wounded soon began to pass and it was perfectly heartrending to see them. . . . There was some blunder in the arrangements of the line of battle and some negligence in sending the orders and one or two regt's got into a hot place and soon ran back creating confusion, but they were soon rallied and a new line formed, but the fighting was not renewed. . . . The Yankees came in this morning, about 2,500, and are at the fortifications. Averill is in command and things are very quiet. He is always disposed to act kindly. The Yankees who have gone up the Valley are Hunter's men, under the command of Crook. A great many persons went to the battlefield today carrying off provisions.

Julia Chase—July 23, 1864. What a life we are leading & how uncertain war is. Yesterday thousands of troops came in & we were in hopes the Rebels would be held in check. This morning—how different. Every street is filled with wagons, moving off with a very heavy guard. The rebs have been reinforced and in all probability we shall see them driving our troops before them. Skirmishing has been going on, and we expect to hear of very heavy fighting ere many hours. We learn from the papers of the 20th, that Gen. Sherman's operations in Georgia continue to be good & full of promise. The army has crossed the Chattahoochie, and our army was only 10 miles from Atlanta. . . . Nothing but skirmishing & picket firing is going on in the Army of the Potomac. Siege preparations continue. . . . The excitement this morning has passed away and all is quiet. The rebels, thinking only a small force of Gen. Averill was here, advanced very rapidly and near town, thinking they would make a complete rout and capture all of the little force. . . . Our troops drove the rebels back, and we learn are advancing. We have some 20,000 troops at this place. . . . The weather is rather cooler than for several weeks past but extremely dry and dusty. The prospect of a corn crop is very unpromising, and the coming winter will cause considerable anxiety and distress.

Laura Lee—July 23, 1864. This has been a most exciting and anxious day. At 8 o'clock this morning the wagon trains began to pass back through all the streets attended by large bodies of infantry, marching rapidly. Soon as the trains were stopped and at 1 o'clock all returned to where the Yankees were in line of battle, about 1½ miles from town. They said our men were drawn up about 2 miles farther up the road and that a battle was expected every minute. There was skirmishing all last night and pretty sharp early this morning in which our men captured four guns and 150 wagons. This afternoon they reported that the rebels were retreating, but since 8 o'clock the wagons have been passing incessantly down the Martinsburg Road. . . . We have been suffering for weeks from the most distressing drought. Everything is parched up and the dust perfectly stifling.

Julia Chase—July 24, 1864. This has been a day of excitement, with some fighting, the Federal army retreating, the Rebs advancing. We are completely discouraged, disheartened and provoked. It seems impossible for our army to show any fight, and this same thing has occurred so often in our midst that we begin to think the Federal soldiers do not know how to fight, or that our officers understand but little in managing affairs. 2 o'clock—Every street is filled with wagons, ambulances, horses and men.

Secessionists looking on with glad and joyful countenances. Are we never to have better days? Is this state of things to continue much longer? God forbid! . . . Later—The cavalry and artillery are passing out of town in good order, but the infantry will probably move on each side of the town. Some of the soldiers think the army will fall into their fortifications, but it is more than likely they will not stop short of Bunker Hill. The artillery have been taken to the fort, and they are throwing their cannon balls from that point. A bullet has struck one of our windows, shattering & breaking 4 panes of glass, entered into the woodwork and glanced off. We go downstairs, not knowing what will come next—perhaps a shell—but we are in the hands of the Almighty. He can protect us. 4 o'clock—The Rebels are coming into town slowly. I asked one if Gen. Early had been reinforced, he says only with one brigade. Oh, we had hoped and expected better things from Gen. Crook, but we are always disappointed in our officers. Our hearts are sad & heavy enough. . . . The rebel cavalry are coming in pretty fast, and within the past two hours we have passed from the U. States into Rebeldom.

Laura Lee—July 24, 1864. Here we are safe again in Dixie. Yesterday was fought the second battle of Kernstown, and we witnessed a repetition of the Banks races. On Saturday night the Yankee wagons returned to the camps and all was quiet until about 12 o'clock, when cannonading commenced. An officer came to the church door and beckoned out all the soldiers and . . . said there was a general engagement at Kernstown. At 2 o'clock we went out to go to Sunday school, but finding the streets were filled with returning wagons and stragglers, we dismissed the school and hurried home. We recognized the indications of a retreat and went to the top of Mr. Brown's house to watch it. The hills were covered with columns and batteries and though the dust and haze of the wagons was very great we could easily distinguish every movement. The firing had gradually appeared nearer, and the musketry was very sharp. About ½ past 4 o'clock the columns began to move back steadily on the hills, and the artillery soon came through the streets with large bodies of cavalry. The road over Fort Hill was a perfect jam of wagons, ambulances, guns, caissons, cavalry and stragglers. The signal flags were working furiously, and the whole force continued to fall back steadily. Soon we saw our first skirmish line stepping up over the farthest hill and then we came home. The streets were filled with soldiers moving steadily back. . . . Some of them said, ladies you had better go in, you will get shot, and we took their advice, but kept the door open to look out. They had scarcely reached the corner when we heard bang! Bang! And the bullets whipped past. The men began to run in every direction and the skirmishing sounded all over the town. We looked out again and Lute shrieked out "here are the rebels" and out we ran, and there were Bob and Ranny Barton and a few others who had been firing on this street. I seized on Bob overjoyed and thankful to have him safe. . . . Our infantry had marched 22 miles that day and were so exhausted that they were halted a few miles from town and only the cavalry continued the pursuit. Lewis did not come through but went around with Gen. Johnson to try get ahead of them. They burned their trains and caissons and we captured but very little.

Julia Chase—July 25, 1864. This has been a sad day, to see our poor wounded who have been brought in lying on the floor without any comfort or attention at all, the Confederates occupying all the beds, bedsteads & everything belonging to the Federal army. . . . 62 prisoners have been brought in today, making the number between 1 and 200. They all seem very hungry, having had nothing to eat since yesterday morning, and it is the same with the Rebels, as usual they are half starved. We have had a great many calls today for something to eat, but it is impossible to feed a whole army, and they must go to their friends, but they often turn them away empty-handed.

Julia Chase—July 29, 1864. It is said that Early's army crossed into Maryland this morning—this may be true tho' many do not believe it. We also heard that the 6th Army Corps from Gen. Grant's army was at Charlestown, but this cannot be correct. Some 12 threshing machines stolen from a Union man of Martinsburg were brought up today, but the rebs never steal, oh no. What then, only taken. . . . The Union ladies again visited the prisoners today—as it seems to rest with them whether these men shall starve or not. It is horrid to think of. Some 8 or 10 of the prisoners made their escape last night, which made the guard doubly strict, and the ladies were not permitted to hand the food to our soldiers, or have any conversation with them. . . . This afternoon they have all been removed farther out of town, to prevent the ladies, it is thought, from taking them anything.

Laura Lee—July 29, 1864. A note from Lewis today says that they have moved down toward Williamsport, but as Mrs. Gordon has not come back, we feel sure they do not intend to cross the river. We are looking anxiously for more tidings from Georgia. Atlanta is in very critical condition. The Yankees are near enough to shell it and have done so without giving warning.

Julia Chase—July 30, 1864. The weather has been very warm for several days past, today excessively so. A <u>Bal. American</u> was in town today, saying that the Rebs had been terribly whipped at Shepherdstown, and that Gen. Sherman was doing finely at Atlanta. God grant that while everything has been so terrible dark and gloomy to us this week, there may still have been many bright places in our National skies.

Julia Chase—August 2, 1864. Today we have been subjected to a humiliating sight, seeing Federal prisoners under guard cleaning up the streets in town—Rebel dirt. Why do not their own men do it, or get the colored people. We have never seen Rebel prisoners set to work at this thing, but we hope the time is not far distant when we shall be permitted to see rebels put to the same thing and treated exactly as they treat Federal prisoners.

Laura Lee—August 2, 1864. Lewis came to town to spend last evening with us but returned to the camp at Bunker Hill at 10 o'clock. Gen. Early keeps them strictly at their posts. Mrs. Gordon returned here on Monday but now regrets very much that she did not stay where she was, since everything continues so quiet. News comes today that some of Grant's mines exploded without any damage to us. . . . He is moving over again to the north side of the river to make another attack.

Julia Chase—August 3, 1864. The rebels say that their cavalry have destroyed a portion of Chambersburg—burning 270 houses because the citizens refused complying with their demand of paying $170,000 in gold, giving a week's time to pay it in.[8] The rebs want to enrich themselves greatly off the North, and we hope this thing every few months will tend to cause a more united North, and a more determined effort on the part of our best people to do all they can in putting down this Rebellion.

Laura Lee—August 3, 1864. News has just come that the army is moving down again to the border, and Mrs. Gordon has gone down to the camp to say good-bye to the General. The Baltimore Sun states that Chambersburg has been burned by "the rebels." It is very likely, for our cavalry went there last Friday with orders to levy a tax of $100,000 in gold as reparation for the late burning in Va., and in default of payment to burn the town. The affair at Petersburg last Saturday is called in the Balt. papers "a terrible disaster." They admit a loss of 5,000 men. They say they have more mines ready. Nothing to report from Geo.

Laura Lee—August 5, 1864. Gen. McCausland has returned safely from Pa. by the way of Romney, with the loss of only 40 men. He levied the tax in Chambersburg and the people only laughed at him. He told them the alternative and named an hour for their decision. They still refused and he burned 257 houses in the heart <u>of the town</u>. It is dreadful, and seals our fate when the Yankees come back here.

Julia Chase—August 9, 1864. There is every appearance of the army falling back. Wagons, ambulances, & c. passed through on the 7th. Today, Pegram's brigade of infantry, with Cutshaw's battery, march through, with their wagons, cattle, & c. The 18th Ga. Cavalry have passed through town, droves of sheep, young cattle also. It is said the whole army will pass through town today. . . . The weather still continues exceedingly warm. This has been undoubtedly the warmest summer for a number of years.

Julia Chase—August 10, 1864. What a night and morning we have had. The Federals advancing & it is said in large force. The rebels commenced falling back. Such a commotion with horses, wagons, ambulances, infantry & artillery passing, it seemed as if the whole world was let loose. The Federals are advancing upon the Berryville Road and fighting was going on at the Opequon yesterday. This morning cannonading has been heard and it is said the armies are but 2 or 3 miles from town. Noon.— Everything is quiet in town now, but few soldiers are to be seen and the cannonading ceased—the lull may only be portentous of the storm.

Laura Lee—August 10, 1864. Gen. Early is camping today at Jordan's Springs. The Yankees are moving up slowly. . . . Anderson's division is reported at Culpeper coming here. There is a report that Grant is moving back to Washington, and also that we succeeded in undermining and blowing up another mine which he was preparing. Night. 12 o'clock. We are to be left again to our fate. The Yankees are sending a flanking force around by Millwood toward the Valley Road. Our troops are in line of battle all around the town. Gen. Gordon has just left here for his camp. He is a splendid looking man. Gen. Johnson of N.C. and a good many others were here this evening. Troops were passing through and there was much excitement. Many think they will fight tomorrow. The Yankees only 5 miles from town.

Julia Chase—August 11, 1864. The rebel army are retreating up the Valley as fast as possible. Wagons, horses, artillery, cattle & everything that could be taken has passed on, and but few cavalrymen are to be seen. Cannonading has been heard very distinctly all the morning—the two armies probably skirmishing. We shall probably see the Federals making their appearance soon. 2 P.M.—The Federal cavalry have made a dash into town, some 150 or more. A few rebs remained until they had gotten into town, called upon them to come on but took pretty good care to keep far enough ahead to escape the shots & bullets. A very large army of the Union troops are pressing after Early's army. Whether Gen. E. will take a stand & fight is very doubtful, he will doubtless hurry on as fast as possible.

Laura Lee—August 11, 1864. All gone and everything quiet in the town, but brisk cannonading going on a few miles off. The Yankees moved on early this morning trying to cut Gen. Early off. . . . As soon as all was quiet we began to pack up our clothes to provide for the contingency of the town being burned. The soldiers we have seen are about equally divided in regard to their opinion as to whether or not we will be burned out. We had the silver buried. The report of Anderson's division coming is universally believed, though no one knows how near A. is. Night. At 2 o'clock our last pickets came in and ten minutes later several hundred Yankees dashed through with drawn pistols. They only went to the edge of the town and in a little while returned, and remained in town until 5 o'clock but very few dismounted. We felt considerable trepidation at first, and had our trunks ready to carry into the garden and hide them in the weeds on the first alarm. Some of the soldiers told the servants that they were not the burning party, but that they would be in tomorrow. It is all perfectly quiet now.

Julia Chase—August 12, 1864. The 37th Massachusetts Infantry are doing provost duty in town. Everything is very quiet about us. They will probably remain here but a short time, when they will be relieved by other troops. Deserters from the Rebel army report the capture of Mobile by the Union forces, but no official report having been received, it needs confirmation. Gen. Sheridan, from the Army of the Potomac, has command of the Middle Division, including this portion of Virginia.[9] He has a large body of his men with him. Atlanta is being bombarded with heavy shell. We hope soon to hear of its capture.

Laura Lee—August 13, 1864. A train of 400 wagons passed through town this morning. There were 100 more but last night. Mosby carried off 75 and burned 25 more. On Thursday evening Ramseur caught the Yankees in an ambush and captured nearly 1,000. He has retrieved his disaster here. Early established himself at Strasburg and the Yankees are very near. There are certainly three Corps of them. We scarcely dare to hope that they will leave us so entirely unmolested as we have been in the past three days. . . . There is every reason to expect a battle tomorrow.

Julia Chase—August 15, 1864. The army, we learn, has fallen back two miles. The next thing there will be a backward movement by the entire army.

Laura Lee—August 16, 1864. There has been a great commotion all
day among the Yankees. Hundreds of wagons, both full and empty, and
large bodies of soldiers have gone down the Berryville Road. It is believed
that the whole force of 30,000 men is just outside of town, but whether to
retreat or to fight is still a mystery. The soldiers say that Longstreet is crossing the river at Snickersville and also that Fitz Lee burned 300 wagons
which went down in that direction last night. These men all look depressed
and discouraged.

Julia Chase—August 17, 1864. The same thing has taken place today
that we always see. Our army never advances in the Shenandoah Valley, but
to take a backward move. Gen. Sheridan with staff came into town last
evening, and the inference was easily drawn. The army have been passing
through town up to 2 P.M. Gen. Talbot covering the retreat. The Rebels
still pushing forward and sometime this afternoon fighting between the
opposing parties commenced, continuing until after dark. The Federals
commenced falling back into town about 7. . . . About 9 P.M. the enemy
made their appearance into town. The Rebel army is pouring into town,
Gen. Early having been reinforced by Gen. Longstreet. A battle of course
will be fought in Maryland. There will be no peace and quietness in this
section of country for some months, unless the Federals are very successful.

Laura Lee—August 17, 1864. Since 4 o'clock this morning the Yankees have been swarming through the town down the Berryville Road.
The 6th and 19th Corps, numbering they say over 50,000 men, all under
the command of Sheridan. I can readily believe that the numbers are not
exaggerated, for such swarms of men, such trains of wagons, such thousands
of horses I never have seen. They were generally quiet and well behaved,
but some were very rude when we tried to prevent them from taking all the
peaches on the trees. . . . There is a great deal of talk about burning the
town. The soldiers told the servants that they had burned half of Kernstown
and that the cavalry were burning and destroying everything as they come.
We will soon know, as all have passed through except the cavalry. We have
our trunks packed and tubs of water ready. It is still a perfect mystery to us
why this immense army should have fallen back in such haste. . . . There is
no evidence of there having been anything more than skirmishing with
Early, which makes it so surprising that they should run from certainly less
than half their numbers. Night. The rebels are in again! About 2 o'clock we
heard that there was fighting near Kernstown. . . . The skirmishing continued all the afternoon and about 6 o'clock a brisk cannonading was opened
which continued for two hours, but toward the end of it we found the

Yankees were running. They moved off quietly at first, but at last it was a
real run. After all had passed through the town there was perfect stillness for
ten minutes and then the firing in the streets commenced. Fortunately there
was none on this street, and we stayed on the porch watching eagerly for
the first sight of our blessed graycoats. . . . They say the Yankees have
burned all the barns and crops wherever they have passed, from Front Royal
and from Strasburg, to this place.

Laura Lee—August 18, 1864. The army passed through this morning
and are resting for the day a mile below the town. Gen. Anderson has
joined Gen. Early with Kershaw's division of infantry and Fitz Lee's of cavalry. We have had a house full all day. Gen. Fitz and Gen. Lomax, Major
Mason, Major Ferguson to breakfast, and Gen. Gordon, Gen. Breckenridge, Major Kyle and some small fry to dinner. . . . The Yankees behaved
outrageously yesterday as they fell back burning and destroying everything.
They burned 150 bushels of wheat at Mrs. Barton's, took every particle of
stock off the farm, all the meat out of the house, in fact everything. Betty
went off last night with the Yankees.

Laura Lee—August 19, 1864. There has been another severe fight at
Richmond, on the north side of the river. The Yankees got through our
lines at first, but were driven back seven miles with terrible slaughter. It is
said that the other divisions from Longstreet which were on the march here
have been recalled to Richmond. Things look very dismal there. There is
great talk of starvation both for the soldiers and citizens, and much is said of
the army being forced to fall back for want of provisions. We have had a spell
of damp, dark weather, which adds to the depressing influence of the time.

Laura Lee—August 20, 1864. Things remain quiet yesterday. Bob is at
home again, his reg't being left here on guard duty. Gen. Fitz Lee called this
morning and said he would come with his staff to spend the evening. They
did come, bringing a band, a violin player, and Gen. Thomas to dance. We
had a very merry evening and about 11 o'clock a courier came with dispatches, which Gen. Lee said as they were going that they would move in
the morning.

Julia Chase—August 22, 1864. Rain for several hours today. Our
neighbors, Mrs. Wright and Gibbons, had their houses searched at a very
unusual hour (10 o'clock) last night. The soldiers had no authority whatever, but were probably sent by malicious persons.

Julia Chase—August 23, 1864. A severe fight occurred on Sunday
between Gen. Early & Sheridan at Smithfield. The Secessionists in town say
the Federals were whipped, their dead & wounded having fallen into their

hands. There have been no prisoners brought through town, neither any Federal wounded, excepting 4 or 5, but some 33 ambulances containing Rebel wounded came in last evening.

Laura Lee—August 24, 1864. Everything is quiet around Charlestown as far as we can learn. The Yankees made an attack on the Weldon R.R. last Friday, which was finely repulsed. We took 2500 prisoners. Nothing from Atlanta, but the people begin to look very anxious when it is spoken of. Mobile too is in a very critical position.

Julia Chase—August 26, 1864. Another fight took place yesterday between the Federals and Rebels at Leetown and it is reported the Rebels were terribly whipped, one of their regiments being badly cut to pieces. 6 ambulances have just passed by containing Rebel wounded. There are a great many in town. The McDonald house is used as a hospital.

Laura Lee—August 29, 1864. Gen. Gordon sent horses up yesterday morning for Mrs. Gordon to go to Bunker Hill, which is a sure indication that things are quiet for the present. . . . There was a large fire last night, said to be part of Smithfield burning. The news from Petersburg is confirmed. Gen. Lee's official report is in the paper today. We took 2,000 prisoners, 9 guns, and seven stands of colors. Our loss very small.

Julia Chase—September 3, 1864. The Richmond paper says their troops on the 26th recaptured the Weldon Railroad from the Federals, capturing great many prisoners, also artillery. We are sorry to hear this, and as it was said the Federals were so strongly fortified, we were not expecting to hear it. The weather for a week past has been much cooler, but very dusty, have had no rain for two weeks. It is said that fighting has been going on today . . . on the Front Royal Road to the right of Newtown. The noted Harry Gilmore was badly wounded in the skirmish at that point.

Laura Lee—September 5, 1864. No advance of the enemy occurred yesterday, though they appeared on three different roads, but later in the evening it was found that they had gone back in consequence of the fight at Berryville the evening before. . . . Bad news! The Balt. papers of the second claim that they have possession of Atlanta. Richmond papers of the same date speak of a battle, the result of which is not known.[10]

Julia Chase—September 6, 1864. The Richmond papers speak of the fall of Atlanta, the Federals taking quiet possession of that city on the 2nd. They say now its fall is of but little consequence, when for more than a year past, their papers have spoken of the importance of holding it & if Georgia is given up, that the Confederacy was gone. (Sour grapes we think) The rebel Gen. John Morgan at Greenville, Tenn. on the 4th & his staff captured with the exception of one—thus has another of their bad men been called away. We shall hear no more now of Morgan's raid.

Laura Lee—September 6, 1864. Still raining and cold. No movements today. No papers today, and therefore no particulars of the fall of Atlanta. The Yankees are very triumphant of course. This will have an unfavorable effect on the election. McClellan and Pendleton are the nominees. Many persons think the nomination put an end to our hopes of peace, for the present, even if the Democrats are successful.

Laura Lee—September 13, 1864. The Yankees advanced to within 3 miles of town on the Berryville Road. Kershaw was ordered to stay until the result of the skirmish on that road was known. He has marched down to the front. McClellan has accepted the nomination as a war candidate of the Democratic Party.

Julia Chase—September 15, 1864. Judging from appearances this morning, the army is moving off. In the fight which occurred near town on Tuesday the Federals we learn captured a regiment of rebels. The rebel cavalry have not acted bravely since they have been here.

Laura Lee—September 17, 1864. Gen. Lomax[11] called this morning. He said there was to be a forward move at 2 o'clock. The Yankees burned all the mills along the Opequon last night. There is a perfect quiet at present at all points, as regards to fighting. The whole energy of the Yankees is directed toward reinforcing Grant.

Julia Chase—September 19, 1864. The army is falling back. Fighting commenced quite early this morning & cannonading has been going on all day to the east of us on the Berryville Road, but a mile or two from town.[12] It was said that Gen. Bradley Johnson was wounded & brought into town early this morning. Great many wounded have come in—loaded wagons, ambulances containing sick and wounded, horsemen & footmen have been passing through town for several hours. We hope to see no rebels in town by tomorrow, tho' we do not know what the result might be. 5 o'clock—The Federals have gained the victory over Gen. Early and are now coming into town. Heavy fighting continued up to that time and probably heavy loss on both sides. Great many Rebel wounded have been brought in. Gen. Rodes, we understand, has been killed.

Laura Lee—September 19, 1864. This is the end of the most dreadful day we have ever spent. . . . This morning at 5 o'clock we were roused by the firing on the Berryville Road where Ramseur[13] was posted. Bob and

Ranny mounted their horses and went down to the front. At 7 Bob came riding in with a serious wound in his leg. He volunteered as aide to Gen. Ramseur and in carrying a message he was shot . . . the wound is 14 inches long. We fixed him comfortably in the office and thought we had him there safely for weeks, but in a few hours we were only too glad to send him off safely up the Valley. Gen. Ramseur held his own finely until 10 o'clock when his men began to give way.. . . . It was soon found that they were too many for us. They outnumbered us two or three times, and the attack was along the whole line of 8 miles. By 2 there was no doubt that our men were giving back and at 3 there was a terrible panic caused by a cavalry stampede back upon a number of ambulances. . . . The stampede of the cavalry let the Yankees get on the flank of Gordon's division and the men, when they found it out, got into a panic and ran back. The officers tried in vain to rally them . . . but it was of no avail. They were thoroughly disheartened and they were allowed to go back quietly. The other divisions had gone. Mrs. Gordon and Mrs. Breckenridge, who arrived only last night, got off among the last, while the shells were whistling over the town every moment and the Yankee skirmishing drawing very near. In ten or fifteen minutes they were in the town firing through the streets. They came in in scattered small parties and quietly, with no apparent intention of pursuing at once. No large force has yet passed through and it is perfectly quiet now. What it will be tomorrow is a serious question. Our loss is severe, and we do not yet know the full extent. Gen. Rodes was mortally wounded. . . . All of our friends called to say good-bye. They seemed disheartened and troubled in every way.

Julia Chase—September 20, 1864. The Federal wounded are being brought in from the battlefield, as well as others. The Rebel loss was between 4 & 5000 prisoners, 2 batteries, besides 5 general officers killed. Considerable of a stampede occurred before the army retreated, and for a short time there was a great commotion of ambulances, wagons, horsemen, wounded walking, with others flying in all directions. Such an afternoon— oh, the horrors of war. The Taylor House has been taken for a hospital, receiving the Federal wounded. 5 other hospitals are established, and the ladies will have their hands full. God grant that this war may soon come to an end, and a peace honorable to the whole country be established.

Laura Lee—September 20, 1864. Again our town is one vast hospital. . . . All day the streets have been filled with ambulances and wagons of their wounded. They have taken the Taylor Hotel and six churches besides other houses. They brought in 4,000 [wounded] without doubt, and over. . . . The citizens are indefatigable in attending to our wounded, but of course there must be a terrible amount of suffering in the confusion of such a time, and many must die for want of proper attendance. . . . The Yankees moved up the Valley early this morning and there has been skirmishing.

Julia Chase—September 21, 1864. Some 2000 prisoners have been brought in. . . . Our troops are driving the Rebels at a rapid rate and do not give Early scarcely a chance to take a stand. For the first time we have seen a glorious victory in the Valley of the Shenandoah on the part of our troops. May they continue to be successful.

Laura Lee—September 21, 1864. They are still bringing in numbers of wounded Yankees, and they say they have sent as many back to Berryville. It is awful. Things are getting into more order at our hospitals and the men are more comfortable, but the prisoners are nearly starved. The Yankees have not given them a crumb. . . . The citizens have very little in their houses . . . but all classes give liberally to both wounded and prisoners. Mr. Hardy has just brought us a note . . . saying that Bob and Ranny are getting on very comfortably. . . . We are going all the time from one hospital to another. We have plenty of surgeons and the Yankees seem inclined to do all that is possible for the comfort of our men. They are even disposed in arranging for the crowds of their wounded, that the citizens are left unmolested, except that the soldiers take everything that is left in the gardens and rob the cellars at night.

Laura Lee—September 23, 1864. The Yankees are sending off their slightly wounded today, but hundreds are being brought in from the army above us. They claim to have driven Early from Fisher's Hill.[14] They say Averill flanked our army and that they have captured 3,000 prisoners, 19 guns and many wagons, and that Early is retreating as fast as he can in the greatest confusion. I am afraid there is no doubt that they have Fisher's Hill, however, the other part may be exaggerated.

Julia Chase—September 25, 1864. About 2 or 300 prisoners were sent off today, who were captured a day or two since, and about 17 pieces of cannon. Mosby's men attacked the ambulance train containing the wounded who were being sent to Harper's Ferry, wounding two & killing one. Our troops captured some of these guerrillas & shot 8 and hung 2. This will be the only way to prevent & put a stop to this horrid warfare. The notorious guerilla Quantrell has been captured. The building occupied as the Post Office & the house adjacent, was burned yesterday afternoon. Whether it was set on fire purposely by the soldiers we have not heard, but whatever thing is done will be in retaliation for Chambersburg, which was destroyed by the rebels this summer. The weather very cool today.

Laura Lee—September 27, 1864. We know nothing in these dreadful days but Yankees rumors of their progress up the valley. Everybody attends at the hospitals with everything nice that can be procured. . . . The number of deaths is unusually small.

Laura Lee—September 30, 1864. Rumors today claim that Sheridan has been repulsed and driven back at Harrisonburg, though the Yankees still say that they have possession of Staunton. There is a report also coming through the Yankees that after two days of severe fighting at Richmond, Grant had gained no advantage owing to the overflowing numbers of rebels. We hear so many conflicting reports that we never know what to believe. Dr. Cromwell, who has charge of over 300 patients, has refused to let his men be moved to the Camp Hospital, and the Yankees, strange to say, permit him to decide about it. They certainly are wonderfully indulgent and considerate about our wounded. They supply them abundantly with everything they have for their own men.

CHAPTER SEVEN

October 1864–April 1865

"I have not the heart to write more"

Because Julia's diary concluded with her entry for September 25, 1864, the closing months for the war are seen only through the eyes of Laura. Although she never wavered in her dedication to the cause, it was clear by events that the future of the Confederacy was in doubt. In October, Gen. Philip Sheridan routed the Confederates at the battle of Cedar Creek, which gave control of the region to the Federals. Two months later the Confederates were defeated in Tennessee at the battles of Franklin and Nashville, thereby ending all hopes of victory in the West. And in January, the Federals captured Fort Fisher, the last remaining seaport to the outside world.

Laura also had to contend with the Federals disrupting the lives of her and the other members of her family in a much more direct way. Having endured her hostile attitude and defiant manner for months, in February 1865, Sheridan finally banished Laura and the other members of the Lee household from Winchester. On February 21, he had Laura and her family put in wagons and sent south through the Federal lines. In the weeks following, the Lees lived like nomads, making their way as best they could up the Valley in the hope of reaching Staunton and eventually Richmond.

Laura Lee—October 3, 1864. The Yankee papers claim that they have taken some of the outer fortifications of Richmond, but the soldiers say that Grant has been again repulsed. Father Sharron says they have taken only some of the outposts at Chapin's Bluff, which were not thought worth defending.

Laura Lee—October 4, 1864. A bright, warm sunshine makes everything look brighter today. The country people are permitted to come into town with supplies for the hospitals and are doing nobly. The Yankees are wonderfully indulgent about our men and they have made them quite comfortable by giving supplies of bed, blankets, & c. There is a report of a fight on Sunday at New Market in which the Yankees were badly whipped, but we cannot yet learn the truth of it.

Laura Lee—October 8, 1864. Sheridan is certainly falling back this way.[1] It is generally believed that Longstreet is in command in the Valley, and if so his Corps is here too. It is certain that Grant has been defeated at Richmond.

Laura Lee—October 11, 1864. I was in bed Sunday and yesterday with a chill and fever, but I am up today. The weather has moderated. For three days it was really very cold and we feared the patients at the hospitals would suffer terribly, but it was not the case. The Yankees have supplied them pretty well with blankets, and the surgeons have been able to close up the open windows and doors sufficiently to make it bearable. The <u>New York Herald</u> speaks of the disaster at Richmond and the reported death of Gen. Butler. Sheridan is said to be at Fisher's Hill. There has been a great stir and bustle among the Yankees for the past two or three days, but they say they are to remain here this winter. Col. Thomas, commanding the post here, yesterday turned Mrs. Polk out of Mr. Logan's house and took it for his headquarters.

Laura Lee—October 12, 1864. It is reported that Sheridan has taken a fresh start up the Valley. Mr. Meade told me today that Longstreet is certainly <u>not</u> in command in the Valley, but Early still in command with reinforcements. Things here go on as usual. The hospitals are quite well supplied with delicacies by the people from the neighboring counties, many of whom come every day. There are no restrictions on those who come for that purpose. The sutlers have groceries, etc. and we could get what we want from them though there is an order against it, but their prices are so enormous that few are able to buy.

Laura Lee—October 15, 1864. We fought the Yankees yesterday near Cedar Creek and captured 1,500 prisoners and some guns. Early's position today is between Strasburg and Cedar Creek, and Sheridan's between the latter place and Middletown. His trains are at Newtown. Everything has been quiet here today and no appearance of moving. Groceries and provisions were taken from a good many people today. They had bought them from a man who they supposed was a sutler, but who proved to be a commissary, selling for his own advantage. Information was given, and the houses were searched and the goods confiscated. Mrs. Tuley lost about 160 dollars worth.

Laura Lee—October 18, 1864. There is much talk everyday of the Yankees leaving here, but as yet there is no evidence that such an event is contemplated by them. They say that Early has received more reinforcements and that another great battle will be fought near here in a day or two. Persons from the North say that Lincoln's re-election is considered certain.

Laura Lee—October 19, 1864. Heavy cannonading was heard here from daylight this morning. It was distant but very distinct. By 10 o'clock news came that Early had made the attack at Middletown and had been very successful, cutting up the 6th and 19th Corps badly and capturing a large number of guns and prisoners. . . . Everything was packed up and the streets all full of wagons ready to move if necessary. At dinner time they reported that the 6th Corps had moved up and succeeded in capturing all that had been lost in the morning.[2] This is not believed here though it is thought probably they may have checked Early for the time. There was fighting again this afternoon and much nearer than in the morning. The trains have all gone out to Kueffstown and are waiting there. At 11 P.M. all is quiet. Many persons suppose that Early does not intend to come here but is only making a demonstration.

Laura Lee—October 20, 1864. This morning early the returning trains warned us that our prospect of freedom was over for the present. Gen. Early has retired to his former position at Fisher's Hill. The Yankees say they have retrieved their losses of yesterday morning and have captured many guns and prisoners. They say Gen. Ramseur is mortally wounded and in their hands. . . . We can learn nothing except from Yankee sources.

Laura Lee—October 21, 1864. Some of our wounded have been brought down today, and from them we learn particulars of the fight of Wednesday. They report that Gen. Gordon attacked the camp of the 6th Corps and captured everything, keeping possession of it for six hours, and all that time sending off immense quantities of supplies and many prisoners. In the afternoon Early came up with the remainder of the army and allowed the men to scatter for plunder. The 6th Corps attacked them at that time and they were obliged to fall back. We had taken 40 guns but were compelled to abandon them for want of horses. We sent off several thousand prisoners and immensely valuable stores. . . . Gen. Ramseur is the only one of our generals reported injured. . . . He died yesterday in Newtown.[3] Major G. his Adj. Gen. says that our success in the morning was one of the most brilliant things of the war, but in the afternoon the 6th Corps came up and the fight was renewed in our men being scattered, thinking it was over. We lost all the guns we had captured (over 40) and a good many of the wagons. The prisoners were sent off safely, but the Yankees captured nearly 1,000 of our men.

Laura Lee—October 25, 1864. A new excitement today. All the men in town have been arrested and shut up in the guardhouse. No reason is assigned. This afternoon a few have been released (who were very old or sick) to report tomorrow, but more than 200 are detained. Early has received some reinforcements.

Laura Lee—October 27, 1864. The gentlemen are still in prison and are warned that they will be sent to Fort McHenry tomorrow. No charges are brought and no reason assigned except that it is done to weaken the southern army. Things above here are quiet and we hear nothing from Richmond.

Laura Lee—October 28, 1864. The Yankees sent off today between 70 and 80 citizens of all classes. A good many were released from the guardhouse paroled, to report everyday to the Provost. Mr. Burwell was among those sent. We were all shocked today to hear that Florence Miller is certainly to marry a Yankee surgeon in a day or two. She has always been vehemently Southern and says she is so, but is perfectly infatuated and insists in marrying him in spite of the bitter opposition of her friends. We received a letter today from Lewis, who gives cheering accounts. Bob is moving about on crutches. Early is at New Market. I fear there is a hope of a move down this way. Florence Miller is to be married tonight. She has known the wretched little Yankee exactly one month. A great many new arrests were made today, who are to be sent off tomorrow.

Laura Lee—October 29, 1864. More arrests of citizens today. The Yankees are pulling down numbers of houses, stables and barns to burn, all the fences around the outskirts of town are already destroyed and the only fuel they bring to town for their numerous hospitals and offices is rails, and this has been the case ever since they came here five weeks ago. They will not take the trouble to cut wood, but send out long trains of wagons which return filled with rails. Mr. Conrad is arrested again.

Laura Lee—October 31, 1864. Our Church was closed yesterday as Mr. Maury is hiding for fear of being arrested. Florence Miller was married on Saturday night, and went off this morning in an ambulance. It is too disrespectful. Mr. Conrad was carried off this morning. They tried to make him walk, but he positively refused and at last they permitted him to get into a wagon. We have heard that the gentlemen who were sent off last Friday are at Fort Delaware. Sheridan has been in town for several days inspecting the hospitals.

Laura Lee—November 3, 1864. I am afraid we are in Yankee hands for the winter. They are rebuilding the railroad from Harper's Ferry to this place, which proves that it is their intention to stay if they can, and it is too late in the season for Early to drive them out.

Laura Lee—November 4, 1864. We have heard from the gentlemen who were carried off last week. They were taken at once to Fort McHenry. The weather is very cold and we have scarcely any wood, and scarcely any money to buy more. Wood is 8 dollars a cord and flour 20 a barrel in greenbacks.

Laura Lee—November 10, 1864. Our pleasant party will soon be broken up, I fear. So many of the men have been sent away from the Union [Hotel] that it will soon be closed as a hospital and our friends sent off, and then we will begin to realize that we are again in Yankee hands. They have been very outrageous at many places, but have not molested us at all. Today they took possession of all the upstairs rooms at Dr. McGuire's, avowedly for the purpose of punishing Mrs. McGuire. Sheridan has fallen back to this place to make his winter quarters here. The R.R. from Harper's Ferry is more than half-finished and I am much afraid there is no hope of our being released this winter. Lincoln is certainly elected as I always was sure he would be. I believe it will be best for us in the end.[4]

Laura Lee—November 15, 1864. They are putting up a telegraph to the depot today and the cars are to come in a few days. They are settled on us for the winter. There is great talk everywhere about Mr. Davis' message, in which he alludes to the possible necessity of putting negroes into our army. Everything looks dark and depressing.

Laura Lee—November 19, 1864. Mosby captured 65 out of a party of 80 Yankees on the Martinsburg Road yesterday. The Union hospital is to be broken up, we hear on Monday, and our friends will have to go directly after, to the distress of all of us.

Laura Lee—November 22, 1864. Sheridan is to come here in a few days to settle for the winter. The R.R. is almost finished. Sherman has burned Atlanta and is moving on Macon and Augusta, according to the Balt. papers.

Laura Lee—November 23, 1864. We hear nothing from the South except Yankee rumors, and not many of them. They say that Early has fallen back to Harrisonburg or Staunton, and that nothing more will be done in the Valley this winter.

Laura Lee—November 24, 1864. Today it is said that in consequence of Early's making a move toward Western Va., Sheridan will fall back from here. Leaving only some cavalry and a Provost Guard, but we never know what to believe, there are always so many stories afloat. This is the Yankee's National Thanksgiving Day and there is a great holiday among them. Sheridan has had 100,000 pounds of poultry brought on for their dinner.

Laura Lee—November 28, 1864. Dr. Cromwell and Brevard have been notified to be ready to go tomorrow morning. We all feel very blue at the prospect. Sherman is rushing through Geo. [Georgia] at a wild rate.

Laura Lee—November 29, 1864. We were up at daylight to give the gentlemen their breakfast. They were off at 8 o'clock in an ambulance to Stephenson to take the cars. There were six others of our surgeons who went at the same time. Mr. Williams went to Dr. Lawson's hospital as soon as they were off, but I fancy he will not remain there very long. He came back in the evening to dinner and then said a final good-bye. He and Mr. Foster are going to try a venture tonight. We feel very anxious.

Laura Lee—November 30, 1864. Mr. Williams and Foster got off safely last night to our great delight and Dr. Lawson's intense indignation. Sherman's cavalry has been repulsed in Geo. It is said that Early has gone with part of his force to Richmond.

Laura Lee—December 5, 1864. The last of the 6th Corps has gone. We hear nothing from Geo. but that Sherman is floundering through the state, destroying everything in his path. Hood has had a fight with Thomas in Tenn., in which the Yankees claim to have been successful. . . .

Laura Lee—December 9, 1864. Mr. Burwell reached home today. 65 of the citizen prisoners from here are released. About 25 are still retained in Fort McHenry. A great many of our convalescents were sent off today. The Enders and Baker hospitals are to be broken up on Monday and Dr. Lawson soon after, leaving only the York with between 50 and 60 patients who will not be able to move for some months.

Laura Lee—December 10, 1864. These vile traitorous Yankees have taken our surgeons to Fort Delaware instead of sending them straight through [the lines] as they promised to do. We are so distressed and indignant. The Balt. papers claim that Sherman has almost reached Savannah.

Laura Lee—December 14, 1864. The Yankees are quartering themselves everywhere. At some places they take only two or three rooms. At others the whole house except one or two rooms, where the family have to live whether they like it or not. They use all the furniture, house linen, kitchen utensils and everything as if all was their own property. They are at Sherrard's, William's, Averill's, Parker's, Graham's, and twenty other places. Four officers went to Mrs. Tuley's and told her they were coming to take five rooms in her house, that they had the authority to take it all, but would leave her enough rooms to make her comfortable. We have escaped thus far. Luty Swain heard them say Mrs. Lee's house is too small.

Laura Lee—December 16, 1864. The Yankees claim a victory over Hood in Tenn. They fired a salute today in honor of it. The old Union hospital fell down this evening burying a number of Yankees in the ruins. They had been pulling it to pieces ever since the hospital was broken up. The roof and almost all the woodwork had been removed, and a party of soldiers had made fires within the walls, when they fell upon them.

Laura Lee—December 19, 1864. There is no doubt but that Hood has been terribly defeated in Tenn., and has been driven back 40 miles. The news from Geo. too is very depressing. Sherman has reached Savannah, and has invested it after forming a junction with the fleet. There is but little hope that it can be successfully defended. This is the darkest and most trying time we have ever seen. Everything seems depressing and almost hopeless, the more so perhaps come its being the usually bright and happy season of Christmas. The 6th Corps passed through here this morning en route for Petersburg. They are going to make another attack there.

Laura Lee—December 20, 1864. There is a great deal of talk of the Yankees leaving here, but I do not credit it at all. They have sent off all the men from our hospitals who could possibly be moved, many indeed who ought not to have been. Dr. Lawson's will be closed tomorrow, which will leave only the York with about 40 cases who cannot be moved this winter. We are going to have a nice dinner for them on Christmas day, which will be our only attempt at festivity. Mr. Maury insists on having the church dressed though no one is in the spirits to take much interest in doing it.

Laura Lee—December 24, 1864. We have been busy all day with preparations for our hospital's party tomorrow, the only festivity in which we expect to partake this X-mas. The sutlers stores are crowded with delicacies and luxuries, but we have no money to waste on them.

Laura Lee—December 26, 1864. Our feast yesterday passed off finally. The men were very happy and enjoyed everything. Our church in the morning was crowded with Yankees, both male and female. Gen. Sheridan and Custer were there displaying themselves. There were many splendid entertainments and great feasting. Our Christmas dinner was a small piece of beef and a dish of tomatoes, with a plate of cake later, but we were very content. . . . Savannah is in the hands of the Yankees. Our forces evacuated it. I am very glad it was given up without a battle. Sherman has there 50,000 and we but 15,000. Yesterday Sheridan mercifully distributed to a number of citizens black and white a small piece of beef each. Dr. Baldwin was one of the favored. I wonder he could allow it to come into his house.

Laura Lee—December 30, 1864. Our hearts are rejoicing this morning by seeing the streets filled with the trains of the 19th Corps. The whole corps has now passed, and immense quantities of cavalry. They say they are only going to Stephenson's Depot 4 miles from town for the winter, but we know the whole corps is to go over into Md. They have nearly finished a R.R. from Frederick to Cumberland on the Md. side, and the one on this side is to be given up. There is only one brigade of cavalry above us now.

Laura Lee—December 31, 1864. I fear we were rather premature in our rejoicing yesterday. The 19th Corps has stopped at Stephenson's Depot and the men are putting up winter quarters there. Sheridan and all his belongings are apparently fixtures here. Everything looks as if they were settled for the winter. This afternoon two surgeons came to take the two office rooms for the medical director, but Mary succeeded in preventing it.

Laura Lee—January 4, 1865. The last of our surgeons sent off today except Dr. Love, who is to be sent tomorrow up the Valley and through the lines at once as a special favor. Another letter came today from Dr. Cromwell in which he said the flag of truce boat was waiting for them and he would leave his letter to be sent after their departure. We conclude they were really sent through the day before New Year. Hood has safely crossed the Tenn. River. The 33,000 bales of cotton which the Yankees claimed to have captured at Savannah has dwindled down to 5,000 in their new accounts. We have captured a whole line of pickets with all their wagons a few days ago at Petersburg.

Laura Lee—January 6, 1865. This morning the wagon camp which was all over our garden . . . was gone, and we thought we were to be rid of Yankees, but in an hour a new set came with a quantity of timber to build an additional stable. The first set left a cow, which we captured at once and the new ones have promised to feed her and furnish us with wood. We shall see. They say they are a new brigade under Gen. Pleasanton, who is to command the post.

Laura Lee—January 7, 1865. Gen. Fessenden is the new commandant. There is no news today except the accounts of resolution of submission from the Mayor and many citizens of Savannah, to the eternal disgrace of all concerned in it.

Laura Lee—January 11, 1865. Everything is quiet about here. A great many persons have been allowed to go to Baltimore with permits to buy a moderate quantity of goods for their own use.

Laura Lee—January 16, 1865. We went this evening to the hospital to tell the men good-bye. All except three are to go off in the morning. Many of them are totally unfit to be moved, but the Yankees want the hospital for their own men. There are Peace Commissioners in Richmond, but no one expects that anything will come of it.[5]

Laura Lee—January 17, 1865. The York hospital broken up and the only two men left were taken to the Taylor Hotel hospital. We went to see them and found them very comfortably situated.

Laura Lee—January 18, 1865. Terrible news today! Fort Fisher is taken and Wilmington must be given up.[6] We hope it will be evacuated and the army saved. It is a great shock to us, for since Butler's repulse, we had thought it impregnable.

Laura Lee—January 19, 1865. No more news from Wilmington. The Yankee loss very heavy, they say. . . . Susan Jouls came to consult us about resisting the encroachments of the Yankees who are occupying part of her house. Mrs. Burwell went to Balt. today with permission to purchase and bring home 300 dollars worth of goods.

Laura Lee—January 21, 1865. Anne Sherrard came down today in a terrible storm of snow and sleet to consult us about the outrageous behavior of the Yankees at their house. We advised her to go at once to Gen. Emory, who is in command now in Sheridan's absence. She went to him and he promised to redress her grievances, but Yankee promises generally amount to nothing. We have cause to be very thankful that we have been so little molested. Our garden is a wagon camp and they have just put up sheds for their horses half way down to the house, but thus far our house is free from the pollution of sheltering our enemies.

Laura Lee—January 23, 1865. A day of constant rain, snow and hail, and no news from anywhere. The papers are full of extracts from Richmond papers of the quarreling in our Congress about the overtures of peace from Lincoln.

Laura Lee—January 25, 1865. Since Fort Fisher has fallen . . . it is said that Wilmington is being evacuated. The weather is extremely cold. . . . These Yankees are living in the greatest luxury, with roaring fires day and night, sleighing all day . . . and drinking every night. Sheridan has been away for a week and has just returned. It is reported that Thomas' army has been brought in from Tenn., part to go to Grant and part to come here for the campaign against Lynchburg in the spring.

Laura Lee—January 28, 1865. The greatest number of Yankee women have come here. Mrs. Gen. Emory, Mrs. Gen. Fessenden, Gen. Merritt's daughters, and Col. and Capt's wives innumerable. The officers gave a ball last Thursday night at Merritt's Hd. Qtrs. and actually sent invitations to a good many Southern ladies. When they found that their invitations were instantly refused, they sent up to town and countermanded the oysters which had been ordered. It is reported that great preparations are being made for immediate attacks on Wilmington, Charleston, and Mobile. Gen. Lee has been made Commander-in-Chief of all the Confederate armies. The bill for arming a certain number of negroes has passed.

Laura Lee—January 30, 1865. Mrs. Burwell came on Sat. night and brought everything she intended to get except the summer dresses which could not be purchased at this season. The weather has moderated at last after a whole week of the coldest weather we have ever known here. For the past three days we have been without wood, except a few old knots and a few shocks borrowed from the neighbors. We could not buy any and the Yankee wagon master who occupies our garden, true to his nature, after promising solemnly that we should not suffer for wood, never sent us a particle though we sent to him time after time.

Laura Lee—January 31, 1865. Sheridan giving a grand ball tonight at his Hd. Qtrs. . . . More than 200 letters from the South were brought in today. We had six from Lewis, Bob, Mrs. Gordon and others. Gen. Early's Hd. Qtrs. are at Staunton, Gen. Gordon's 8 miles from Petersburg. Sheridan indulged himself in one of his amusing little farces today. He arrested Mrs. Sophia Cohen . . . and sent her to Mrs. Sherrard's to stay till further orders. Her offense is coming into his lines without permission. She tells them a Capt. gave her a pass, which she has lost since she came to town, but the truth is that a Yankee scout, who she knew, smuggled her in. She has been at her mother's for three weeks and some malicious person informed on her. It is intended as an insult to the Sherrard's sending her to stay with them and it is extremely unpleasant.

Laura Lee—February 1, 1865. Old Mr. Blair has returned to Washington from his second sham embassy to Richmond. Sherman is advancing on Charleston. There was a grand review of all the troops here today, preparatory to another raid on Gordonsville.

Laura Lee—February 4, 1865. There is a great talk about the Peace commissioners from Richmond. Lincoln himself has gone to meet them, but it is all bosh. . . . A grand raid against Gordonsville started today.

Laura Lee—February 6, 1865. The Peace Conference has ended, as I was sure it would, in nothing. Lincoln, after inviting it, refused to listen to any terms except on the foundation of restoration. We, of course, would listen to nothing which did not begin with acknowledging our independence. So after an interview of four hours our Commissioners returned home. . . . The paper today says that Lincoln, in his late conference with our commissioners, made arrangements for a general exchange of prisoners at once. There are about 60,000 on each side, and the exchange is to be conducted at the rate of 1,000 a day.

Laura Lee—February 9, 1865. Another letter today from Lewis . . . in which he says that Bob has been transferred into the Ordnance dept. It is an inexpressible relief, as he had been pronounced unfit for the infantry service, and now this coming campaign has lost at least one of its terrors.

Laura Lee—February 10, 1865. The Yankees say that we are now evacuating both Charleston and Mobile. The U.S. Congress has called on Lincoln to give a report of his interview with the Rebel Commissioners. There is much talk everywhere of European interference after the 4th of March. Sheridan's staff went out this morning on a fox hunt. We do wish Mosby was where he could take a part in it.

Laura Lee—February 14, 1865. Lucy P. went today with our last letters for some time. Mr. Parsons told Mary Jackson today that he is perfectly aware of the passing of letters and intends to stop it, and that the first fine day he shall send several parties of ladies who have been engaged in it through the lines and mentioned the names of the Lees and Sherrards particularly. This is coming rather near home.

Laura Lee—February 17, 1865. Another heavy snow. The weather is mild and the streets almost impassible. We are kept in the house, but are pleasantly occupied with our sewing. Our diet for some weeks past is simple to say the least of it. Mess pork and bread, and coffee, three parts rye, without sugar.

Laura Lee—February 20, 1865. Gen. Sheridan returned last night and brought the news of the evacuation of Columbia and Charleston, and this afternoon a salute of 100 guns was fired in honor of their having gotten possession of the hot bed of Secession. It was very hard to have to listen to their triumphing, though indeed, they got nothing at Charleston but a mass of battered houses.

Laura Lee—February 28, 1865, Mt. Jackson. Since my last entry a week ago, we have passed through a severe experience. Last Thursday morning in the midst of a torrent of rain a messenger came from Gen. Sheridan to notify us that we, with the Sherrard's family, were to be sent through the lines as soon as the weather became good. Of course it was a great shock to us. Mary went at once to him to ask what charges he had against us. He said he had plenty of charges, but did not choose to tell what they were, but that we should have sufficient time to make arrangements and might put someone in the house to protect it. The rain ceased in the evening and after another order came to the effect that "Mrs. Lee, Miss Lee and the Miss Burwells, having been placed by the fortunes of war within the lines of the army, have given constant annoyance, either from a wish of notoriety, or want of reflection, or from not being true to themselves, they are therefore ordered beyond the lines, and Maj. Parsons, Quartermaster, will have them conveyed to Newtown on Saturday morning." The Sherrards received the same order. There was no help for us, so we began to make arrangements that night. We packed the silver and carried it away and went in various directions to try to get a tenant for the house, but were unsuccessful. Then we collected our clothes and were busy until ½ past two packing, that we might have our last day free for securing our furniture if possible. There was the greatest sympathy felt for us and expressed in every possible way. All the smaller and more valuable articles were taken away and secured, but the heavy furniture we had no hope of removing. . . . The servants were in the greatest distress. We promised to arrange that they should remain in the kitchen and left them some provisions, knowing that they could easily support themselves. We prepared provisions to last until we could reach Staunton, and packed up the groceries and other supplies to leave behind. But it was but little we could save of the things we valued most. We concluded all our arrangements late at night and by 8 o'clock the next morning many persons arrived to see us off though we were not to go until 9. Many efforts had been made to induce Gen. Sheridan to retract the order, but in vain. I applied at first to be allowed to go to Clarkesburg, but it was refused. Mr. Burwell was almost crazy about the girls and tried in every way to get them released from the order. We would not allow anyone to ask the Union people to intercede for us, as we knew it would be of no avail and we did not choose to be so humiliated. It was a most cruel outrage and perfectly undeserved. The only thing we have ever done against their orders was to receive and send letters, and that is done by three-fourths of the people in the town, and the Yankees are perfectly aware of it and know also that they cannot prevent it. They have proved it on several persons but have never punished them. The true reason is that we kept entirely aloof from them, asking no favors, making no acquaintances, and in fact perfectly ignoring their existence. We were among the few people who were able to do it and Sheridan determined to punish us and humble our pride if possible. Our departure was a perfect triumph. Large numbers of our friends crowded around the ambulance and many ran through the streets, following us to the Provost's Office where we were to join the Sherrards. We were all excited enough to have a very cheerful parting and the Yankees saw no tears except from our servants and other colored friends. Mrs. Cutter had petitioned Sheridan to send us as far as Woodstock, reminding him of the impossibility of our procuring transportation at any nearer point. He promised it should be as far as Middletown, 12 miles, but when we reached the edge of Newtown, only 7 miles, the officer in charge of the party said he had orders to search us and then leave us. It was so perfectly inhuman, a heavy rain was falling, everything covered with snow and ice. We argued the cruelty of opening our trunks in such a place. At last he agreed that if we would give our word that we had no letters about us, he would not search and would take us to a house in Newtown. We assured him we had none and then moved on. As we were unloading our baggage, Mr. & Mrs. Jones drove to the town. As soon as the Yankees were gone they came to see us and proved their affection and sympathy for us by trying to make arrangements for our going on at once. After much difficulty we hired a wagon for the trunks, a little carriage for four of our party, and Mr. Jones lent us his carriage for the other three. They were to take us as far as Woodstock, 30 miles from Winchester, but it was too late to start until the next morning. Mr. Jones carried Lizzie, Lal, and myself to Vancluse for the night. They did everything that kindness and hospitality could prompt to give us pleasure and comfort. Mrs. McCloud in Newtown was equally kind and refused to take a cent of pay for the nights lodging, supper and breakfast. This kindness at the outset was very reassuring, as we had been told that everybody in the Valley was so ruined that we must expect nothing. Sunday morning was clear and quite cold. . . . After traveling at a walk for ten hours, we reached Woodstock at 5 o'clock. The hotel is kept by Mrs. Hollingsworth, from near Winchester, and here again we received the greatest kindness. They entertained us most hospitably, and would not receive any pay. On Monday morning after incredible exertions, we procured a wagon for the trunks and two spring wagons for the party, to bring us on to this place twelve miles further. The prices were enormous but we were determined to get on as fast as possible as information had been given us the day we left home of an immense raid up the Valley, which was to leave W [Winchester] on Monday. We found our pickets at Edinburg and told the officer, and when we arrived here a soldier was sent at once to New Market to telegraph Gen. Early in Staunton of the raid and of our being banished from our house and asking for army transportation from this point. The river at the edge of the town was so swollen . . . as to be past fording, and Mr. John Miller from Newtown, who has the reputation of being the kindest man in the world, immediately adopted us and did everything possible for our comfort. He and Betsy were really distressed that they could not take us all to stay with them, but we secured two very nice rooms in the hotel here with fires furnished, but nothing else. Fortunately our provisions hold out well and we lead a very pleasant picnic life. We found we should be obliged to remain here several days, from being unable to cross the river even if the raid should not come as we expected. Some persons thought it was going to Gordonsville through Luray Valley. Last night Col. Moore came from Edinburg to see us, and we were all taking a nice little supper in the room, when Phil Boyd rushed in to say that the Yankees were coming. The Col. ran off to hide, and in a little while all the soldiers about here were swimming their horses across the river or hiding in the mountains. We had warned all the soldiers about Woodstock and Edinburg to get out of the way. This morning early our last pickets passed through here with those vile Jesse scouts at their heels and in five minutes the advance of the Yankees began to pass. Sheridan himself is in command, with from 12 to 14,000 cavalry, four pieces of artillery, pontoons, wagons, etc.[7] They were detained until nearly dark at the river, the current being so strong as to prevent the laying of the pontoons. . . . We felt a little uneasy at finding them stopped so near us, fearing they might trouble us. While the troops were passing we recognized several of the servants who have been so much in our kitchen, belonging to Sheridan's staff officers, among them George, who . . . .said he had hired himself to Gen. Forsyth in order to get to Staunton. He said too that directly after we left Gen. Sheridan had an order posted on the house forbidding anyone to trouble anything in it. . . . Mrs. Cochran moved in on Saturday and has a Col. staying with her, who will protect the house.

Laura Lee—March 1, 1865. Mr. Miller came to see us this morning and said that Maj. Bailey, Provost-Marshall, dined at his house yesterday and inquired very particularly about some ladies who had been banished from Winchester, and who they heard in Woodstock had given warning of the raid. Mr. Miller declined to know anything about us, except that he had heard we said we did not know whether the raid was coming. They went off with the idea that we are ahead, and will no doubt look out for us. I feel very anxious about the result of this advance. We have evidently very few troops of any kind near, and I fear they will do terrible damage. We must remain here until something is decided about these Yankees. There is a report that infantry went by Front Royal and that Gordonsville is the destination of both parties, but as yet it is uncertain. We have persuaded the Sherrards to go to Mr. Miller's today as the prices here are fearful.

Laura Lee—March 2, 1865. No news from above us except that the raiders are pushing on rapidly for Lynchburg, through Staunton. . . . We will be forced to remain here until they return or are driven back some other way. Our life here is quiet but will be very pleasant for a little while, except for anxieties. We cannot buy a morsel of food and are living on the provisions we brought for the journey, with occasional additions from our kind friends, the Millers.

Laura Lee—March 4, 1865. Lincoln's inauguration today. The reports from above us are mere rumors that Sheridan passed through Staunton yesterday, part of his force going towards Waynesboro and the remainder towards Gordonsville. We are settled here for an indefinite time as no one will venture out with horses while the Yankees are above. . . . We receive a plentiful supply of nice things everyday, though nothing like provisions can be bought.

Laura Lee—March 8, 1865. This morning the report was that Sheridan was returning through here, but this evening it is said that he has gone to Farmville, after making a feint on Lynchburg. He is aiming to burn the long bridge, which will be a terrible blow to us, if he succeeds. We had made all our arrangements to go on tomorrow to Staunton, but now it is raining in torrents and the river will be so high in the morning that it will be impossible to cross it.

Laura Lee—March 9, 1865. The river is past fording again, and we must wait patiently until it is the will of Providence to permit us to continue our journey. The people here have been extremely kind, but we are anxious to get on. We shall have much trouble even after we reach Staunton, for the railroad is torn up and the canal beyond Lexington too. No certain report of Sheridan, still.

Laura Lee—March 11, 1865. Our hopes of getting on were again disappointed. The wagons were being packed when a man rode into town calling out "the Yankees were coming." The wagons were driven across the river instantly, and the drivers refused to make another attempt to go today. . . . Some of our scouts up today say there is no truth in the report of Winchester being evacuated.

Laura Lee—March 12, 1865, Harrisonburg. Sunday though it was, we had to begin our journey today, the baggage in one wagon and our party of seven with Mr. Long in the other. Mr. Miller and Park Miller on horseback. We crossed the river safely, though it was still very dark, and reached this place before dark. We made ourselves comfortable, had tea and coffee made, and gave the gentlemen a nice supper in one of our rooms. Here there is a report that Sherman has been defeated, but it is not confirmed. Bettie Effinger and Mrs. Clapp came to see us. Mrs. E. said that one of Custer's staff told her that the reason we were sent out was that we were detected sending out military information. Of course it is the merest pretext.

Laura Lee—March 13, 1865, Staunton. We reached here tonight, after a safe and not very uncomfortable journey. We had been warned on the road that all communication was cut off beyond here. We find that the railroad to Charlottesville is destroyed, the canal, too, below Lynchburg, and the road from here to Lexington almost impassable. So here we must stay for at least a week or ten days. The gentlemen here tell us, too, that things about Richmond are so uncertain, that it is best not to attempt to go there at present. Sheridan is still at large on the north side of the James River. Fitz Lee is keeping up with him on the south side, and Lomax with infantry is in his front. . . . We have received the most hospitable welcome here. Col. Nadenbush begged us to take as many rooms, call for everything we please, and stay as long as is convenient to us, without any charge. This is very generous in these times. We have had many visitors tonight, and numberless invitations.

Laura Lee—March 14, 1865. Our party scatters today. Mary is to stay at Dr. Stribling's, Jennie and Lizzie L. at Mr. Taylor's, Anne S. and Lal at Mr. Stuart's, and Lute and I to Mr. Jones'. I have been comforted by hearing that Lewis saved all of his clothes. He is the only one of Early's staff who saved anything.

Laura Lee—March 15, 1865. The people here are very kind, but very gloomy. They seem perfectly hopeless about the future because Sheridan has not yet been defeated. Most of our cavalry was disbanded to recruit the horses and there is only infantry to oppose him, and he avoids meeting the forces we send out. It is reported that another force of 10,000 from

Fredericksburg have united with him. Mary dined with us today, and in the afternoon it cleared and we all walked out.

Laura Lee—March 16, 1865. Still nothing but rumors. The Central road is being repaired, but it will be three or four weeks before the trains will run. For the meantime we must stay here, for things in Richmond are very uncertain, and there must be something decisive before many weeks are past.

Laura Lee—March 17, 1865. We have a great many visitors and every one is extremely kind. Sheridan is still afloat near the R.R.

Laura Lee—March 20, 1865. I enjoyed the services yesterday, extremely. Dr. Sparrow is a fine preacher. Johnny Williams walked home with me to hear about home. William Allen was here and says that a battle at Richmond is imminent, and that it would be madness to attempt to go there now, as the departments and valuables are being removed preparatory to a fight.

Laura Lee—March 27, 1865. Lewis came last night. He was captured by Custer's men near Richmond while returning from carrying dispatches, but escaped. Gen. Gordon had a fight last Saturday near Hatcher's Run and drove the enemy finely, taking 500 prisoners.

Laura Lee—March 31, 1865. Mr. Mason and Kate write urging us to come to them, and Mr. and Mrs. Maury invite Mary to come with one of the girls to them. I am afraid to go to Richmond, and that is the truth, unless some very decided change takes place in the aspect of affairs. News from Winchester tells us that the blockade there is very strict, and no chance of our being allowed to return, even if wished it, which we do not.

Laura Lee—April 3, 1865. Richmond was evacuated by Gen. Lee last night, and this morning at ½ past 9 the Yankees marched in.[8] I have not the heart to write more.

Laura Lee—April 4, 1865. The evacuation of Richmond was made necessary by Grant's having sent a flanking party of 30,000 around to break the South Side Road, at the same time that he made a violent attack on our front at Richmond. We repulsed Grant very successfully, but the danger to the only R.R. left to Gen. Lee made it absolutely necessary that he should withdraw his army while he could. As yet we have heard no particulars. There is a report that Sheridan has returned to Winchester, and is again advancing up the Valley with a large body of infantry.

Laura Lee—April 5, 1865. Still no particulars from our army except that it was at Amelia C.H. yesterday.

EPILOGUE

When the Civil War was over, both Julia Chase and Laura Lee lived a peaceful, quiet existence. Julia never married and continued to live with her mother in Winchester until her mother's death in 1879. She then lived with her nephew, G. Clarence Miller, of Winchester until her death on March 15, 1906. She was buried two days later in Mount Hebron Cemetery.

Laura, too, never married and lived in quiet obscurity for the remainder of her life. After the war, Laura and her sister-in-law, Mary Lee, moved to Baltimore, where in 1895 they both helped found the Baltimore Chapter of the United Daughters of the Confederacy. She died from apoplexy on June 24, 1902, at her home at 714 Park Avenue. The next day her remains were taken by train to Winchester and she was interred in Mount Hebron Cemetery the following day.

NOTES

CHAPTER 1: JULY 1861–FEBRUARY 1862

1. Valley farmers throughout the summer complained repeatedly about the militia being called into service. What angered them most was that the men were called up at the height of the summer harvest and their departure left many families with no one to work the fields. Sarah McKown of Gerrardstown in Berkeley County commented on the farmers' plight: "The wheat fields will soon be ready for the scythes, but where are the reapers. . . . It is a sad tale to tell but they have gone to war." For more on this subject, see Michael G. Mahon, *The Shenandoah Valley, 1861–1865: The Destruction of the Granary of the Confederacy* (Mechanicsburg, PA: Stackpole Books, 1999), 30–32, 144–45.

2. Gen. Joseph E. Johnston, Confederate commander of the forces at Harpers Ferry. Soon after the outbreak of the conflict, the Confederate government sent Johnston to Harpers Ferry to organize and train the troops assembling there and to defend the region from attack. Realizing that Harpers Ferry could not be defended, Johnston retired to Winchester in June, where his command remained until the middle of July. The Confederate forces were then transferred to Manassas, where they took part in First Bull Run. A biography of Johnston's military career can be found in Richard N. Current, ed., *The Encyclopedia of the Confederacy* (New York: Simon & Schuster, 1993), vol. 2, 859–61.

3. After the Confederate forces occupied Winchester, a considerable number of families, not wanting to be around when the fighting broke out, elected to pack up their belongings and leave for safer surroundings. This exodus also took place throughout the other regions of the Lower Valley and continued periodically for the rest of the war. For more on this subject, see Mahon, *Shenandoah Valley*, 32–33, 145.

4. Former Virginia Governor Henry A. Wise served as governor of Virginia from 1856 to 1860. When the Civil War broke out, Wise was appointed brigadier general in June 1861 and soon after saw action in West Virginia. See Current, *Encyclopedia of the Confederacy,* vol. 4, 1736.

5. Maj. Gen. George B. McClellan. A month after the war started, McClellan was appointed a major general and commanded the Department of the Ohio and soon after directed the Federal campaign in West Virginia, where he was successful in defeating the Confederates in several small engagements. In the wake of the Federal defeat at First Bull Run, McClellan in late July was appointed commander of the Army of the Potomac. For more on his career, see Stephen W. Sears, *Landscape Turned Red: The Battle of Antietam* (New York: Book of the Month Club, 1994), 25.

6. The date for this entry is incorrect. The first battle of Bull Run took place on July 21, 1861, not the twentieth.

7. Gen. Pierre Gustave Toutant Beauregard, commander of the Confederate forces at First Bull Run. For a biography, see Current, *Encyclopedia of the Confederacy,* vol. 1, 146–50.

8. Born in Martinsburg in June 1814, Dr. Boyd was the pastor of the Loudoun Street Presbyterian Church in Winchester, a position he held from 1842 until his death in December 1865. He was arrested and imprisoned several times by the Federals during the war because of his secessionist views, and many attributed his death to the harsh conditions he had to endure while imprisoned. See J. E. Norris, ed., *History of the Lower Shenandoah Valley* (Berryville, VA: A. Warner & Co., Publishers, 1890), 583.

9. This was Confederate cavalry under the command of Angus W. McDonald, who was the husband of Cornelia McDonald, a resident of Winchester, and who lived on the outskirts of town. Upon entering the service, he was commissioned a captain in the Virginia Cavalry and recruited Company D of the 17th battalion. In September 1862, the battalion consisted of six companies. On October 10, 1862, it was assigned to the 2nd Brigade under the command of Brig. Gen. William E. Jones and became known as the 11th Virginia Cavalry. See Cornelia McDonald, *A Diary with Reminiscences of the War and Refugee Life in the Shenandoah Valley, 1860–1865* (Nashville: Cullom & Ghertner Co., 1934), 33, n. 55.

10. Samuel Pancoast was a Quaker who resided in Hampshire County and spent much of his time in the Valley. At the start of the war, he

obtained permission from both the Federal and Confederate authorities to trade salt. As his neighbors noticed, he never had any trouble in crossing the Potomac River, which they found odd. He also never delivered a pound of salt south of the border, and in November 1861, the Confederates arrested him. He spent the next two years in prison. See Mahon, *The Shenandoah Valley,* 46–47.

11. Confederate cavalry commander Turner Ashby. Prior to the war, Ashby had organized a company of cavalry, and when hostilities broke out, his troops assisted in the capture of Harpers Ferry in April 1861. In July he was appointed second in command of the 7th Virginia Cavalry and ordered to protect the counties of the Lower Valley. Extremely popular with his men, he soon gained a reputation as an undisciplined yet effective cavalry commander. He was killed in a skirmish with Federal cavalry on June 6, 1862. See James I. Robertson, Jr., *Stonewall Jackson: The Man, the Soldier, the Legend* (New York: Simon & Schuster, 1997), 235–36; Current, *The Encyclopedia of the Confederacy,* vol. 1, 103–5.

12. This was the Confederate infantry brigade, consisting of the 2nd, 4th, 5th, 27th, and 33rd Virginia Infantry Regiments. At the start of the war, it was led by Gen. Thomas J. "Stonewall" Jackson, who in the aftermath of the Confederate victory at First Bull Run, was the most famous army commander in the Confederacy. See Robert G. Tanner, *Stonewall in the Valley: Thomas J. "Stonewall" Jackson's Shenandoah Valley Campaign, Spring 1862* (New York: Doubleday & Company, 1976).

13. General Scott was the Federal commander-in-chief of the Union armies at the start of the Civil War. In his seventies when the war started, he resigned his position on November 1, 1861. See Shelby Foote, *The Civil War* (New York: Random House, 1958), vol. 1, 109–11.

14. In September 1861, Col. James Mason of Virginia and Mr. John Slidell of Louisiana had been appointed ministers to England and France by Confederate president Jefferson Davis. They left for Europe in mid-October, and on November 8, the USS *San Jacinto* intercepted the British steamer *Trent* and removed the two Confederate ambassadors. Their removal from a British ship caused a major international incident between the United States and Great Britain. See James M. McPherson, *Battle Cry of Freedom* (New York: Oxford University Press, 1988), 387–91.

15. Fort Donelson was a Confederate fort situated on the Cumberland River in northwest Tennessee. By capturing the fort, the Federals were able to advance deep into the southern portion of the state. See Bruce

Catton, *Terrible Swift Sword* (New York: Doubleday & Company, 1963), 154–60.

CHAPTER 2: MARCH 1862–SEPTEMBER 1862

1. Dr. Hugh McGuire (1801–1875).
2. Mr. Philip Williams (1802–1868) was another of the town's leading residents. A councilman from the fourth ward during the war, Williams was arrested in the spring of 1864 and held hostage by the Federal authorities. See Norris, *Lower Shenandoah Valley,* 602–7; McDonald, *Reminiscences,* 87, n. 54; Garland R. Quarles, *Occupied Winchester, 1861–1865* (Stephens City, VA: Commercial Press, 1991), 11.
3. Robert Burwell, the eighteen-year-old son of Susan Lee Burwell, Laura's sister and the deceased sister of Hugh Holmes Lee, who had died in 1856. In April 1861, Robert joined the 2nd Virginia Infantry Regiment, which later became part of the famous Stonewall Brigade, commanded by Gen. Thomas J. "Stonewall" Jackson. He saw action at First Bull Run and was taken prisoner at the battle of Kernstown in March 1862. After being exchanged in August 1862, he continued to serve in the infantry and was wounded at the third battle of Winchester in September 1864. He later served in the Ordnance Department in Richmond. Compiled Service Records, M-324, roll 373, National Archives, Washington, DC; Garland R. Quarles, *Some Worthy Lives* (Winchester, VA: Farmer's and Merchants Banks, 1988), 142–43.
4. Dr. Robert Baldwin was one of Winchester's leading physicians, at the time of the Civil War. See McDonald, *Reminiscences,* 46, n. 11.
5. Brig. Gen. John Shields was one of the Federal division commanders under Maj. Gen. Banks when the Federals took possession of Winchester in March 1862. See Tanner, *Stonewall in the Valley,* 110–11.
6. Hugh was one of the Lee family slaves.
7. Evan was another of the Lee family slaves.
8. On March 23, 1862, the Federals under Brig. Gen. James Shields defeated Jackson at the battle of Kernstown. In the aftermath, Winchester was flooded with wounded from both sides. See Catton, *Terrible Swift Sword,* 265–68.
9. U.S. secretary of state William H. Seward.
10. Maj. Gen. Nathaniel P. Banks, Federal commander of the Union forces that occupied Winchester on March 12, 1862. He was defeated by Jackson in the 1862 Valley campaign and driven out of Winchester in

May, with the loss of large numbers of both men and supplies. See Ezra J. Warner, *Generals in Blue* (Baton Rouge: Louisiana State University Press, 1964), 17–18.

11. Dorothea Dix, who had helped establish the female nurses' corps. By the end of the war, over 3,000 Northern women had served as army nurses. See McPherson, *Battle Cry of Freedom,* 483.

12. The *Merrimac* was the Confederate ironclad warship, renamed the CSS *Virginia,* that had defeated the Union fleet outside Hampton Roads on March 8, 1862, sinking two warships and forcing a third to run aground. The next day the USS *Monitor* arrived, and the two ironclad ships engaged in a four-hour gun battle, with neither side gaining a decided advantage. See Current, *Encyclopedia of the Confederacy,* vol. 4, 1669–771.

13. At this time, the Confederate forces on the Virginia Peninsula, under the command of Maj. Gen. John B. Magruder, were holding the Federals, under Maj. Gen. George B. McClellan, at bay at defensive positions they had established just outside Yorktown. Rather than attack the enemy's fortifications, McClellan chose instead to implement siege operations against the Confederate positions. The two forces held their positions until early May, when the Confederates withdrew from the city. See Douglas Southall Freeman, *Lee's Lieutenants* (New York: Charles Scribner's Sons, 1942), vol. 1, 148–57.

14. Pittsburgh Landing, in southwest Tennessee, was the scene of a two-day battle between Federal major general Ulysses S. Grant and Confederate general Albert Sidney Johnston, also known as the battle of Shiloh. The Confederates were successful on the first day of the battle, driving the Federals from their positions, but the next day the Federals counterattacked and drove the Confederates back to their original positions. After the battle, the Confederates retreated south to Corinth, Mississippi. For particulars of the fighting, see James Lee McDonough, *Shiloh: In Hell before Night* (Knoxville: University of Tennessee Press, 1977).

15. David Strother was a native of Martinsburg, Virginia, who, when the war broke out, elected to side with the United States rather than the Confederacy. As a result, he was reviled by all his former associates and considered a traitor to the South. After entering the army, he saw service under Banks in the 1862 Valley campaign, with Maj. Gen. John Pope at Cedar Mountain and Second Bull Run and with Maj. Gen. Franz Sigel in the Valley campaign of 1864. An accomplished writer,

Strother kept a journal of his experiences during the war. When the war ended, he returned to his home in Berkeley Springs, where he wrote and published his journal, *Personal Recollections of the War.* For further details of his life and military experiences, see Cecil D. Eby, Jr., *A Virginia Yankee in the Civil War: The Diaries of David Hunter Strother* (Chapel Hill: University of North Carolina Press, 1962).

16. Harry McDonald was one of the children of Angus and Cornelia McDonald, who lived on the outskirts of Winchester.

17. Forts Jackson and St. Philip, eighty miles south of New Orleans, were the two forts that guarded the Mississippi and defended the city from the Federal Fleet. Between April 18 and 24, the Federal Fleet, under the command of Adm. David G. Farragut, attacked the two forts, and on the twenty-fourth, it steamed past the fortifications. With the fall of the two forts, New Orleans was defenseless, and on April 25, the Confederates evacuated the city. See Catton, *Terrible Swift Sword,* 248–63; McPherson, *Battle Cry of Freedom,* 418–22.

18. Corinth, Mississippi, was an important railway center in the Mississippi Valley, with both north-south and east-west railroads. At this time it was a supply base for the Confederate armies operating in the region.

19. Baton Rouge, the capital of Louisiana, is about eighty miles north of New Orleans. Following the fall of New Orleans, the Federal Fleet appeared before Baton Rouge on the morning of May 9, 1862 and the city surrendered without firing a shot. It was evacuated for a short time by the Federals, but they reoccupied the city in December 1862, and it remained in Federal control for the rest of the war. See *Encyclopedia of the Confederacy,* vol. 1, 140–41.

20. By this time of the war, numerous local citizens were reporting that vast numbers of slaves had left their homes. Those that did not go off on their own were often taken away by the Federals, who went throughout the region confiscating slaves from their owners. See Mahon, *Shenandoah Valley,* 59.

21. The Confederates were forced to abandon Norfolk on May 10, 1862, after the Federals occupied Yorktown. Not wanting the *Merrimac* to fall into enemy hands and unable to take her out to sea, the Confederates blew the ship up the next day. See Catton, *Terrible Swift Sword,* 279–80.

22. Emily was one of the Lee family slaves.

23. Mrs. Francis Barton was a close friend of the Lees and an equally avid supporter of the Confederate cause. She lost her son Marshall at the

first battle of Winchester and another son at the battle of Fredericks-burg in December 1862. See McDonald, *Reminiscences,* 68, 115.

24. Maj. Gen. Franz Sigel, born in Germany in 1824, came to America in 1852, after the German Revolution. Because of his influence with the immigrant population, Lincoln appointed him a brigadier general in August 1861. He rose to the rank of major general in March of the fol-lowing year. A division commander under Banks during the Valley campaign of 1862, he later commanded the Federal forces at the start of the 1864 Valley campaign. He was defeated at the Battle of New Market in May and subsequently was removed from field duty. See Warner, *Generals in Blue,* 447–48.

25. The Battles of Cross Keys, fought on June 8, 1862, and Port Republic, June 9. On June 8, Jackson's forces, although outnumbered almost two to one, defeated the Federal troops under the command of Maj. Gen. John Frémont at Cross Keys, a small village a few miles south of Har-risonburg. The next day, Jackson turned his attention to the Federal force at Port Republic, a few miles south. After holding their own for several hours, the Federals, under the command of Gen. James Shields, finally gave way, and Jackson's troops carried the field. See McPherson, *Battle Cry of Freedom,* 458–60; Freeman, *Lee's Lieutenants,* vol. 1, 438–69.

26. The fighting Julia refers to was the Seven Days' Battles before Rich-mond. In several different battles, between June 25 and July 1, 1862, Confederate general Robert E. Lee defeated the Federal army under the command of Gen. George McClellan, the outcome of which saved Richmond, the Confederate capital, from capture. For details of the campaign see Freeman, *Lee's Lieutenants,* vol. 1; Catton, *Terrible Swift Sword;* Foote, *Civil War,* vol. 1; and McPherson, *Battle Cry of Freedom.*

27. Maj. Gen. Richard S. Ewell was a division commander under Jackson during the Valley campaign of 1862. He lost a leg at the battle of Grover-ton in August 1862, but returned to active duty in June 1863, taking command of the II Corps following the death of Jackson. He saw action at Gettysburg, the Wilderness, and Spotsylvania, where he lost over half of his corps in the brutal fighting of May 12, 1864. He then was assigned to manage the defenses of Richmond, a position he held for the rest of the war. See Current, *Encyclopedia of the Confederacy,* vol. 2, 549–50.

28. John Hunt Morgan was a Confederate brigadier general and guerrilla raider who operated throughout Kentucky and Tennessee. During the first two years of the war, his raids made the Federals look like fools in

trying to defeat him. Though his command was never very large, fewer than 4,000 men, his actions caused considerable problems for the Federals, as they were forced to tie up large numbers of troops to guard supply lines from attack. Morgan was captured in the fall of 1863 but escaped in November. He was finally killed in September 1864 while attempting to escape Federal cavalry in Greenville, Tennessee. See Current, *Encyclopedia of the Confederacy,* vol. 3, 1086–87.

29. In July 1862, Maj. Gen. John Pope took command of the newly organized Army of Virginia, which was composed of the forces of Generals Banks's, Fremont's and McDowell's commands. He was totally defeated by Lee and Jackson at Second Bull Run in August 1862. He also raised the ire of the local civilian population when, on July 23, 1862, he issued orders that all civilians would be required to take an oath of allegiance to the United States; those who refused would be expelled beyond the Federal lines. As a result, he was one of the most despised Federal commanders in all of Virginia. See McPherson, *Battle Cry of Freedom,* 501, 527–33.

30. Brig. Gen. Abram S. Piatt was a brigade commander under General Pope and was the post commander at Winchester for a time during the summer of 1862. He later participated in the battle of Fredericksburg, where he was injured when his horse fell. This subsequently led him to resign from the army in February 1863. See Warner, *Generals in Blue,* 369–70.

31. Brig. Gen. Julius White was another post commander of Winchester for a time in August 1862. The following month, he surrendered the Federal garrison at Harpers Ferry at the start of the Confederate invasion of Maryland. He was then arrested and put on trial for surrendering the position but was later cleared by a board of inquiry. He subsequently served under Gen. Ambrose Burnside in Tennessee in 1863 and in Virginia the following summer. After participating in the beginning stages of the Petersburg Campaign, he resigned from the army in November 1864. See Warner, *Generals in Blue,* 556–57.

32. Robert Y. Conrad was fifty-six years old in 1861 and one of the leading citizens of Winchester. He had earlier resigned from West Point to study law and later served in the Virginia Senate from 1840 to 1844. During the secession crisis he was elected a delegate to the convention from Frederick County. He voted against the Ordinance of Secession in May 1861, but stated that if the people ratified it, he would abide by it. During the war, he was arrested several times by the Federal

authorities. See David F. Riggs, "Robert Y. Conrad and the Ordeal of Secession," *Virginia Magazine of History and Biography* 86 (1978): 261–74.

33. This was the battle of Antietam, where Confederate general Robert E. Lee fought Gen. George B. McClellan on September 17, 1862. The battle was the bloodiest one-day battle of the war, with total casualties on both sides exceeding 23,000 men. The battle itself ended in a stalemate, but because Lee was forced to retreat back into Virginia, it is looked upon as a Union victory. For details on the battle, see, McPherson, *Battle Cry of Freedom;* Catton, *Terrible Swift Sword,* Robertson, *Stonewall Jackson;* and Foote, *The Civil War,* vol. 1.

CHAPTER 3: OCTOBER 1862–MARCH 1863

1. J. E. B. Stuart was the Confederate cavalry commander of the Army of Northern Virginia. He entered Confederate service in April 1861 as a colonel, commanding the 1st Virginia Cavalry at Harpers Ferry under Gen. Thomas J. Jackson. A master horseman, Stuart taught his troopers cavalry tactics, and during the early stages of the war, the Federals were no match for their Southern counterparts. In October 1862, he took 1,800 of his cavalry and advanced into Pennsylvania, reaching Chambersburg on the night of October 10. After seizing arms, ammunition, military stores, and 1,200 horses, he returned to Virginia two days later without losing a single soldier. His exploits electrified the South and caused great consternation for the Federal commanders. For more details of this raid and Stuart's career, see Emory M. Thomas, *Bold Dragoon: The Life of J. E. B. Stuart* (New York: Harper Row, Publishers, 1986), 173–81.

2. At the time the city was under the control of the Federal army, commanded by Maj. Gen. William S. Rosecrans. On October 3, 1862, the Confederates, led by Maj. Gen. Earl Van Dorn, attacked from the north and drove the Union forces back to their inner line of defense. Van Dorn continued the attack the next day, but his forces were unable to break the Federal line, and rather than see his army destroyed in trying to take the city, he chose instead to withdraw, leaving the field to the Federals. See Current, *Encyclopedia of the Confederacy,* vol. 1, 413–15.

3. This was the Emancipation Proclamation, which stated that after January 1, 1863, all slaves in the territories under the control of the Confederacy were legally and forever free. In actual effect, the proclamation

did little, because it freed slaves where the Federals had no control, and it did not grant freedom to those slaves in the border states, Kentucky and Maryland. But politically it had a major impact, changing the meaning and course of the war. Now the United States was not only fighting to preserve the Union, but also to ensure the equal rights of all its citizens. The proclamation also eliminated any chance, slight as it was, that Great Britain or France would enter the war on the side of the Confederacy. See Catton, *Terrible Swift Sword,* 365–71; McPherson, *Battle Cry of Freedom,* 502–4, 557–58, 563, 706, 841–42.

4. Gen. James Longstreet was commander of the I Corps of the Army of Northern Virginia. Longstreet had entered the Confederate army in May 1861 as a colonel of infantry, and by October 1861 he had been promoted to major general. As commander of the I Corps, he saw action at the Seven Days' Battles, Second Bull Run, Antietam, Fredericksburg, and Gettysburg. He was severely wounded at the battle of the Wilderness in May 1864 but returned to duty in October 1864 and was with Lee when the Confederates surrendered to Grant at Appomattox Court House on April 9, 1865. For more on his career, see Jeffry D. Wert, *General James Longstreet: The Confederacy's Most Controversial Soldier* (New York: Simon & Schuster, 1993).

5. Aaron Griffith was a resident of Winchester and the owner of Brookland Woolen Mills, located a few miles east of town. A Quaker and a strong Unionist, he was arrested during the war and had lost most of the machinery from his factory and most of his fortune by the time the war ended. See the introduction to the Harriet H. Griffith Diary, 1861–1865, from the Hollingsworth Griffith Collection, Winchester-Frederick County Historical Archives, Handley Library, Winchester, Virginia.

6. Gen. Ambrose Burnside was a graduate of West Point and a veteran of the Mexican War. After resigning from the army, he became a successful businessman in Rhode Island prior to the war. In August 1861, he was appointed brigadier general, in large part because of his political influence. In January 1862, he led the Federal expedition against Roanoke Island on the North Carolina coast that ended in failure. Later promoted to major general, he assumed command of the Army of the Potomac after McClellan was dismissed in November 1862. In December 1862, he led the Union forces in the Battle of Fredericksburg, where the Federals were totally defeated. Removed from

command, Burnside served in the West in 1863. In 1864, he returned east to command a division in the Army of the Potomac and saw action up through the early stages of the Petersburg campaign. See Bruce Catton, *Mr. Lincoln's Army* (New York: Doubleday & Company, 1951), 254–57, 327–28; Foote, *The Civil War,* 227–30, 695–700.

7. This was the battle of Fredericksburg, where the Confederate Army of Northern Virginia defeated the Army of the Potomac on December 13, 1862. The Federals attacked the Confederates, a portion of whom were protected behind a stone wall, repeatedly for most of the day where they incurred terrible casualties. When the fighting had ended, the Federals had over 13,000 casualties; the Confederates had less than half that number. See Bruce Catton, *Never Call Retreat* (New York: Doubleday and Company, 1965), 12–24.

8. Gen. Robert H. Milroy was born on a farm near Salem, Indiana, in June 1816. At the start of the Civil War, he was appointed colonel of the 9th Indiana Infantry. In 1861, he served under McClellan in West Virginia and in September was promoted to brigadier general. The following March he was promoted to major general, and in June, he was assigned command of the forces at Winchester. In command for only six months, Milroy soon gained the enmity of the civilian population and was the most hated of all the Federal commanders who served there. Immediately upon assuming command, he had issued an order requiring all citizens to take an oath of allegiance; if they refused, they would not be permitted to purchase supplies in town. Soon after, he issued a number of other directives that outraged the local residents, the most odious being one that prohibited farm produce from being brought into town from the neighboring countryside. In June 1863, Milroy's command was totally defeated in the second battle of Winchester, losing over 3,400 men, all of his artillery, and vast quantities of military stores. Milroy, his staff, and only a few hundred cavalrymen were the only ones who made good their escape. After his defeat, Milroy never led forces in the field again. See Mahon, *Shenandoah Valley,* 77–80; Warner, *Generals in Blue,* 326.

9. The battle of Murfreesboro, also known as Stone's River, took place on December 31, 1862, and January 2, 1863. Maj. Gen. William S. Rosecrans commanded the Federal Army of the Cumberland; his opponent was Maj. Gen. Braxton Bragg, commanding the Confederate Army of Tennessee. On the last day of December, Bragg attacked and gave the

Federals a sound beating. The Federals lost one-fourth of their force and twenty-eight pieces of artillery, and a considerable number of stragglers had been drifting back from the front lines all day. On January 2, the Confederates renewed the attack but were driven back with severe loss. Outnumbered, his army battered from two hard days of fighting, having lost one-third of its men, Bragg had no other option but to retreat, which he did starting on January 3. See Catton, *Never Call Retreat,* 35–46; James Lee McDonough, *Stone's River: Bloody Winter in Tennessee* (Knoxville: University of Tennessee Press, 1980).

Rosecrans had seen duty in West Virginia in 1861. After being transferred to the West, he commanded Federal forces at the battle of Shiloh. He later commanded the Army of Mississippi at the battle of Corinth and the Army of the Cumberland at the battles of Stone's River and Chickamauga. See Foote, *The Civil War,* vol. 1, 181, 272, 545, 744; vol. 2, 85–103, 711–36.

Bragg had been promoted to major general in October 1861. He was directed to join the Confederate forces in Mississippi under the command of Gen. Albert Sidney Johnston, where he was given the dual assignment of being chief of staff of the army and commander of the II Corps. After the battle of Shiloh, he was made full general and given permanent command of the Army of Tennessee. He then led the Confederate army during the Perryville campaign in October 1862, the battle of Stone's River in January 1863, and the battle of Chickamauga in September 1863. After the Confederate defeat, he was relieved of command and given a position with the War Department in Richmond. See Current, *Encyclopedia of the Confederacy,* vol. 1, 203–6.

10. Maj. Gen. Joseph Hooker was commander of the Army of the Potomac during the Chancellorsville campaign. Prior to this time, Hooker had commanded Federal forces at the battles of Second Bull Run, Antietam, and Fredericksburg. After the Chancellorsville campaign, he later served in the West during the Chattanooga campaign under Grant. See Freeman Cleaves, *Meade of Gettysburg* (Norman: University of Oklahoma Press, 1960), 73–76, 78–80, 90, 103, 122, 208.

CHAPTER 4: APRIL 1863–SEPTEMBER 1863

1. Mrs. Ann G. Logan (1810–1873) was a friend of the Lees and an avid supporter of the Confederate cause. By this time, Milroy had become fed up with the insolent behavior of many of the town's residents. As

punishment, he chose to banish those who complained too loudly or defied Federal authority, and over the next several months, a number of other citizens were sent beyond Federal lines. See, Mahon, *Shenandoah Valley*, 86.

2. Mary T. Magill (1830–1899) was a close friend of the Lees, and a most avid and vocal supporter of the Confederate cause, who never wavered in chastising the Federals when given the opportunity. An example of her acidic tongue can be seen a few days after the Federals occupied Winchester in March 1862. After listening to how they had just whipped Gen. Turner Ashby in a skirmish, she told the Federals that "if they killed all the men of the South, the women would fight, and that when they were destroyed, the dogs would bark at them." She never ate in the Federals' presence, and when asked what she lived on, she replied, "On the hope of soon seeing our army back." She was expelled from Winchester a week after Mrs. Logan, when Milroy intercepted a letter she had written giving details of Mrs. Logan's exile the week before. See the Mrs. Hugh Lee Diary, entry for March 16, 1862, Winchester-Frederick County Historical Archives, Handley Library, Winchester, Virginia; Quarles, *Some Worthy Lives*, 170–71; Mahon, *The Shenandoah Valley*, 86.

3. This engagement was the battle of Chancellorsville, where between May 2 and 4, Lee defeated Hooker in the dense woods ten miles east of Fredericksburg. The victory was one of the most spectacular of the entire war. Outnumbered two to one, Lee nevertheless divided his forces, and in the late afternoon of May 2, Jackson and the entire II Corps swept down on the unsuspecting Federal right flank and drove them back several miles. Lee continued the offensive over the next two days, finally forcing Hooker to pull his beaten and battered army back across the Rappahannock River, ending the battle and the campaign. See Freeman, *Lee's Lieutenants*, vol. 2, 524–63; Foote, *Civil War*, vol. 2, 278–316.

4. Maj. Gen. A. P. Hill was the commander of the famous Light Division of the II Corps of the Army of Northern Virginia. He participated in all the major campaigns of the war, and following the death of Jackson, he was appointed commander of the newly formed III Corps of the army. He remained in this position for the rest of the war, leading his command in the battle of Gettysburg in July 1863 and the summer campaigns of 1864. He was killed on April 2, 1865 during the Confederate evacuation of Richmond. See James I. Robertson, Jr., *A. P.*

Hill: The Story of a Confederate Warrior (New York: Random House, 1987).

5. Jackson died on May 10, 1863. Shot by his own men during the night of May 2 while scouting the position of the Federal army after his assault of the late afternoon, he passed away quietly at Guiney Station from complications of pneumonia. For details of Jackson's final days, see Robertson, *Stonewall Jackson,* 739–53.

6. The Confederate fortress at Vicksburg, Mississippi, which lay astride the Mississippi River, was a vital position, because as long as the fort held out, the Federals would be denied complete access and use of the river. The Federals had been attempting to capture the fortress since December 1862. By May 1863, Maj. Gen. U. S. Grant had surrounded the fort and had implemented siege operations to force its surrender, which eventually proved successful. The fort was finally surrendered on July 4, 1863. See Bruce Catton, *Grant Moves South* (Boston: Little, Brown & Company, 1960), 376–82, 453–70, 483.

7. This was the second battle of Winchester. When the Confederate Army of Northern Virginia advanced into Pennsylvania in the summer of 1863, they marched by way of the Shenandoah Valley. The advance elements of the army reached Winchester on June 13, and the next day, the Confederates led by Gen. Jubal Early attacked the Federal forces under Milroy, routing his command and driving them from the town in short order. The Federals lost over 3,400 prisoners, all of their artillery, and vast quantities of military stores. See Freeman, *Lee's Lieutenants,* vol. 2, 20–27.

8. Maj. Gen. Jubal Early was at this time a division commander in the II Corps of the Army of Northern Virginia. Prior to this time, he had participated in most of the major campaigns of the army. He later saw action in the Wilderness and Spotsylvania campaigns and after being promoted to lieutenant general, he was placed in command of the Confederate forces in the Shenandoah Valley. In July 1864, he led his command on a raid against Washington, D.C., and in the fall opposed Gen. Philip Sheridan in the Valley campaign of 1864, where he was soundly defeated. See Current, *Encyclopedia of the Confederacy,* vol. 2, 501–3.

9. Col. Arthur James Lyon Fremantle was a member of the Coldstream Guards, an elite fighting unit of the British Army. He was traveling with the Confederate Army of Northern Virginia during the Gettysburg campaign and had attached himself to General James Longstreet's command. See Wert, *General James Longstreet,* 253–54.

10. Maj. Gen. George G. Meade was appointed commander of the Army of the Potomac on June 28, 1863. He led the Union army at the battle of Gettysburg and remained in that position for the rest of the war. Prior to his appointment, he had served as a brigade and division commander in the Army of the Potomac, seeing action in most of the campaigns during 1861 and 1862. For more on his career, see Cleaves, *Meade of Gettysburg.*

11. This was the battle of Gettysburg. The three-day fight between the Union and Confederate forces started on July 1 and ended on July 3. The battle was the bloodiest of the war, with each side sustaining casualties well over 20,000 men. The first two days of the battle were inconclusive; the Confederates had attacked the Federals several times, gaining small successes, but were unable to drive them from their defensive positions. On July 3, Lee attacked the Federal center with 15,000 men, in what has become known as "Pickett's Charge," but the Confederates were beaten back with fearful loss. Defeated, Lee had no other choice but to retreat back into Virginia. See Freeman, *Lee's Lieutenants,* vol. 2, 90–168; McPherson, *Battle Cry of Freedom,* 653–63; Foote, *The Civil War,* vol. 2, 467–581.

12. Port Hudson, Louisiana, was located about 100 miles north of Vicksburg on the Mississippi River. It was the second fortress on the Mississippi that had continued to hold out against the Federals up until this point. Following the fall of Vicksburg, the garrison defending the post held out until July 9, 1863, when, after a short siege, it surrendered. This was a major blow to the Confederates, as it split the Confederacy in two and gave the Federals free access of the Mississippi River. See Current, *Encyclopedia of the Confederacy,* vol. 3, 1238–39.

13. William C. Quantrill was a pro-Confederate guerrilla who operated in Kansas and Missouri. In retaliation for the death of five young women related to his family, he led his band of about 450 men to Lawrence, Kansas, where on August 21, 1863, they burned the town, killing about 150 unarmed men and boys. This act earned Quantrill universal hatred throughout the nation. Among those who traveled with Quantrill were Frank and Jesse James, who later became notorious outlaws in their own right. On May 10, 1865, Quantrill was shot and captured by Federal troops. He died from his wounds on June 6, 1865. See Current, *Encyclopedia of the Confederacy,* vol. 3, 1289.

14. This was the battle of Chickamauga. The two-day battle on September 19 and 20, 1863, was one of the bloodiest of the war. The Confederate

army, led by Gen. Braxton Bragg, attacked the Union army, led by Maj. Gen. William S. Rosecrans, in the wooded countryside in northwest Georgia, a short distance from Chattanooga, Tennessee. After two days of intense fighting, the Confederates split the Federal army in half and routed the Federals from the field, forcing them to retreat to Chattanooga. As a result of the defeat, Rosecrans was shortly after relieved of his command. For details of the battle, see Glenn Tucker, *Chickamauga: Bloody Battle in the West* (New York: Bobbs-Merrill Company, 1961).

CHAPTER 5: OCTOBER 1863–APRIL 1864

1. This is a reference to the Federal attempt to capture Fort Sumter in the fall of 1863. Battery Wagner was a Confederate fort on Morris Island that prevented the Federals from taking control of the island and then being able to pound Fort Sumter with heavy siege guns. Until Battery Wagner and Morris Island were captured, the Federals would be unable to capture Fort Sumter or the city of Charleston. See Catton, *Never Call Retreat,* 217–26.
2. Maj. Gen. Quincy Gilmore was the commander of the Federal forces attempting to capture Fort Sumter and Charleston.
3. After the battle of Chickamauga, General Longstreet's I Corps of the Army of Northern Virginia, along with other units from the Army of Tennessee, was sent on an expedition to East Tennessee to capture Knoxville. The short campaign ended in failure, with Longstreet finally returning to Virginia, and the other Confederate forces returning to the Army of Tennessee. See Wert, *General James Longstreet,* 340–58.
4. Brig. Gen. John D. Imboden was a native of Staunton, Virginia, and a staunch advocate of secession. Upon entering the Confederate army, he served under Jackson at Harpers Ferry in 1861. He later was appointed commander of a cavalry regiment that saw extended duty in the Valley, and in 1864, he was in charge of the cavalry under Early. See Current, *Encyclopedia of the Confederacy,* vol 2, 807.
5. Alexander H. Stephens was the vice president of the Confederacy. He did not go to France, as Julia asserted.
6. Clement L. Vallandigham was a former Ohio congressman who, by this time of the war, had become the leader of the Democratic peace movement. He advocated that the North withdraw its troops from the South, declare an armistice, and enter into negotiations to unite the nation. He was soon after arrested for disloyalty and exiled to the

Confederacy. He later returned to the North, was defeated when he ran for governor of Ohio in the fall of 1863, and was reported to have had dealings with Confederate agents in 1864. He was reviled as a traitor by most throughout the North. See McPherson, *Battle Cry of Freedom*, 591–97, 684–88, 765, 782–83.

7. Maj. Gen. George H. Thomas, though he was a Virginia native, remained loyal to the United States and served in the Federal army for the four years of the Civil War. He saw extended duty in the Army of the Cumberland, and acceded to command of that army shortly after Rosecrans's defeat at the battle of Chickamauga. He remained in command until the end of the war and gained victories over the Confederates at Franklin and Nashville in the winter of 1864. See Foote, *Civil War*, vol. 2, 81–85, 691–728, 785.

8. Maj. Gen. Ulysses S. Grant was, by this time of the war, the most successful general in the Union army. He had gained victories at Forts Henry and Donelson in February 1862, and the battle of Shiloh in April 1862; engineered the capture of Vicksburg in the summer of 1863; and had now been sent to Chattanooga to assume command of the Federal forces there. In the spring of 1864, he would be appointed commander-in-chief of all the Federal armies and would lead the Army of the Potomac against Lee and the Army of Northern Virginia in the East, finally forcing Lee to surrender in April 1865. For details of his life and military career, see, Catton, *Grant Moves South*, and Bruce Catton, *Grant Takes Command* (Little, Brown & Company, 1968).

9. Libby Prison was the infamous Confederate prison in Richmond that housed Federal soldiers during the war. Throughout the course of the war, approximately 125,000 Union prisoners were incarcerated there, about a third of whom were held for an extended period of time. See Current, *Encyclopedia of the Confederacy*, vol. 2, 930–32.

10. This was the battle of Missionary Ridge. On November 23, 1863, the Federal army charged up Missionary Ridge and drove the Confederates back from their positions in disarray and confusion. The victory raised the siege of Chattanooga and opened the way for the Federals to advance into Georgia. See Catton, *Grant Takes Command*, 63–83.

11. This was the Mine Run campaign, which took place November 26 to December 2, 1863, in Virginia between Lee and Meade. The Federals advanced against the Confederates, but because of harsh weather conditions and the strong defenses of the enemy, Meade called off the

attack, and the army went into winter quarters. See Freeman, *Lee's Lieutenants,* vol. 3, 271–80; John Hennessy, "I Dread the Spring: The Army of the Potomac Prepares for the Overland Campaign," in *The Wilderness Campaign,* ed. Gary W. Gallagher (Chapel Hill: University of North Carolina Press, 1997), 66–68.

12. Col. John S. Mosby was a Confederate raider who, with a small band of several hundred followers, operated in portions of northern Virginia and the Shenandoah Valley. By this time of the war, he had become almost a legend among the Confederate populace. He had also become quite a problem to the Federal armies operating in the region, terrorizing their communications and supply trains and forcing them to expend large numbers of troops to protect their lines of supply. See Jeffry D. Wert, *From Winchester to Cedar Creek: The Shenandoah Valley Campaign of 1864* (Carlisle, PA: South Mountain Press, 1987), 147–56.

13. Gen. William C. Averell was a Federal cavalry commander who had commanded a cavalry division in the Army of the Potomac under Hooker during the Chancellorsville campaign. He now commanded an independent brigade of cavalry that, in early December, launched a raid on the Virginia and Tennessee Railroad and several supply depots at Salem in Southwest Virginia. See Foote, *Civil War,* vol. 2, 888.

14. Maj. Gen. Fitzhugh Lee was a cavalry commander who served under J. E. B. Stuart. His uncle was Confederate general Robert E. Lee. He saw action in most of the campaigns of the Army of Northern Virginia throughout the war and later served in the Shenandoah Valley during the 1864 campaign. See Current, *Encyclopedia of the Confederacy,* vol. 2, 914–15.

15. William N. Dooley was a prominent Union sympathizer who was arrested by the Confederates. As seen in a number of the following entries, his arrest caused quite a commotion at the time. He was sent to Libby Prison, where he later died. See McDonald, *Reminiscences,* 152.

16. Maj. Gen. William T. Sherman was the commander of the Federal army in the West, having been appointed by Grant following his coming east in the spring of 1864. Like Grant, he had served the Federal army in the west since the start of the war and had gained an excellent reputation as an army commander. He led the Federal army in the advance and eventual capture of Atlanta, and afterward gained even more renown leading his army in his famous March to the Sea in the fall of 1864. For details of his life and military career, see John F. Marszalek, *Sherman: A Soldier's Passion for Order* (New York: The Free Press, 1993).

17. Brig. Gen. Judson Kilpatrick was a cavalry commander who led a raid against Richmond in March 1864 that ended in disaster. The Federals were defeated and forced to retreat in complete disarray. See Bruce Catton, *A Stillness at Appomattox* (New York: Doubleday & Company, Inc, 1953), 3–18.

18. Col. Ulric Dahlgren served under Kilpatrick on the raid against Richmond and was killed during the raid. But what caused a tremendous stir was that papers were found on his body saying that the Federals had orders that once they reached Richmond, they were to murder President Davis and all the members of the Confederate cabinet and then set the city ablaze. See Catton, *Stillness at Appomattox,* 5–17.

19. Sixteen-year-old Lewis Burwell was the younger son of Susan Lee Burwell, the sister of Mary Lee's deceased husband, Hugh. He entered the service in October 1861 as part of Company 4 of the 31st Virginia Militia. He saw action in the Shenandoah Valley throughout the war, and in 1864, he served on the staff of Gen. Jubal Early, a position he held until the end of the war. Compiled Service Records, M-324, roll 778, National Archives, Washington, DC; *Winchester Evening Star,* June 1, 1909.

20. In Northern states in the summer of 1862, free blacks had begun to organize into formal units. In January 1863, the state of Massachusetts received permission to train a black regiment and before long had enlisted enough men to form the 54th and 55th Massachusetts Infantry Regiments. The raising of African-American soldiers caused quite a bit of controversy in both the North and South, but before the war ended, more than 175,000 blacks had served in the army and close to 20,000 in the navy, and their contribution was vital to the North winning the war. See James M. McPherson, *Ordeal by Fire: The Civil War and Reconstruction* (New York: Alfred A. Knopf, 1982), 349–55.

21. Fort Pillow was located on the Mississippi River forty miles above Memphis. In April 1864, the Confederates attacked the fortress. After taking control of the post, they murdered many of the Federals, among them a considerable number of black soldiers. See Foote, *Civil War,* vol. 3, 108–12.

CHAPTER 6: MAY 1864–SEPTEMBER 1864

1. This fighting was the battle of the Wilderness, where on May 5 and 6, 1864, Grant and Lee fought each other in the dense woods east of Fredericksburg. The two-day battle was for the most part a draw, with neither side able to gain a decided advantage. When the fighting had

ceased, however, Grant, unlike all his predecessors, did not retreat back across the Rapidan. Instead, he continued to move south and engage the Confederate army. For a comprehensive study of the battle, see Gordon C. Rhea, *The Battle of the Wilderness: May 5–6, 1864* (Baton Rouge: Louisiana State University Press, 1994).

2. This was the battle of Spotsylvania Court House, where Grant, in several different engagements between May 7 and 12, 1864, continued to press the attack against Lee. The bloodiest of the fighting occurred on the twelfth, when Grant attacked and captured the Southern position known as the salient, in which the Confederates lost several thousand men killed, wounded, or captured. For a detailed study of the campaign, see Gordon C. Rhea, *The Battles for Spotsylvania Court House and the Road to Yellow Tavern: May 7–12, 1864* (Baton Rouge: Louisiana State University Press, 1997).

3. This was the battle of New Market, where on May 15, 1864, Confederate forces under the command of Maj. Gen. John C. Breckenridge defeated the Federal forces commanded by Maj. Gen. Franz Sigel. The outnumbered Confederates were so desperate to put men into the field that they even prevailed upon the 247-man corps of cadets from the Virginia Military Institute in Lexington. After driving back the Federals' advance guard, the Confederates shelled their infantry units with artillery, and then the entire command charged forward and swept the Yankees from the field. The defeat forced the Federals to retire back down the Valley and ended, at least for the time being, their attempt to gain control of the region. See Catton, *Never Call Retreat,* 352–53.

4. Maj. Gen. J. E. B. Stuart was mortally wounded in the fighting at the battle of Yellow Tavern on May 11, 1864. After being transported to Richmond, he died the next day. For details of his death, see Thomas, *Bold Dragoon,* 290–95.

5. Mrs. Gordon was the wife of Maj. Gen. John B. Gordon (see note 7).

6. After defeating Hunter at Lynchburg on June 18, 1864, Gen. Jubal Early led his command down the Valley, crossed over into Maryland, and reached the outskirts of Washington, D.C., on July 11. But after studying its defenses, Early realized that he did not have the strength to capture the Federal capital and soon after returned to Virginia. See Freeman, *Lee's Lieutenants,* vol. 3, 565–76.

7. Maj. Gen. John B. Gordon was a division commander in the II Corps of the Army of Northern Virginia. He had served in the army since the

start of the war and had seen action in most of the major engagements in the Eastern Theater. He was readily acknowledged for his bravery and leadership under fire and was one of the most respected officers in the army. He later rose to the rank of lieutenant general and command of the II Corps. See Freeman, *Lee's Lieutenants,* vol. 3, 33, 87–88, 325, 448, 553–56, 579–80, 582–83.

8. The Confederates burned most of the town of Chambersburg, Pennsylvania on July 30, 1864. This raid was led by cavalry commander John McCausland and was in retaliation for the Yankees' having burned the homes of several prominent Virginians a short time earlier. After arriving at the town, McCausland demanded $100,000 in gold or a half million dollars in greenbacks as retribution; if the townspeople refused, he would burn the town. The local citizens refused outright and after evacuating the residents, McCausland and his two brigades of cavalry set fire to the business district of the town. See Foote, *Civil War,* vol. 3, 539.

9. Maj. Gen. Philip H. Sheridan assumed command of the Federal forces in the Shenandoah Valley on August 5, 1864. Sheridan was a tough, pugnacious individual who loved combat and never backed away from a fight. For the first three years of the war, he had served in the Western Theater, eventually becoming an infantry division commander. Grant, who loved his hard nature, took Sheridan with him when he went east in the spring of 1864 and appointed him chief of cavalry in the Army of the Potomac. After the failures of Sigel and Hunter, he placed Sheridan in command with instructions to defeat the Confederate army and destroy all the agricultural resources of the Valley. See Mahon, *The Shenandoah Valley,* 114.

10. The Federal Army under Sherman captured Atlanta on September 2, 1864. This was a major blow to the Confederates, as the city had been a major manufacturing center throughout the war. In addition, the Federal victory helped bolster Lincoln's popularity in the 1864 election campaign in the North.

11. Maj. Gen. Lunsford L. Lomax was a Confederate officer who served as a staff officer under generals Van Dorn and Johnston in the West for the first two years of the war. He transferred to the East in the spring of 1863. He saw action at Brandy Station and Gettysburg as colonel of the 11th Virginia Cavalry in the summer of that year and for the remainder of the war, he was stationed in the Shenandoah Valley, commanding the

Confederate cavalry under Early during the 1864 Valley campaign. See Current, *Encyclopedia of the Confederacy,* vol 2, 943.

12. This fighting was the third battle of Winchester. The Federal forces under Sheridan attacked the Confederates under Early in the morning, and after several hours of hard fighting, the Yankees flanked the Confederate left. Their line broke and the Confederates fell back in complete disarray through the town to Fisher's Hill, about twenty miles south. The Confederates had lost over 3,600 men, almost 40 percent of their total force. For details of the battle, see Gary W. Gallagher, *Stephen Dodson Ramseur: Lee's Gallant General* (Chapel Hill: University of North Carolina Press, 1985), 140–46.

13. Maj. Gen. Stephen D. Ramseur was a division commander under Early during the 1864 Valley campaign. He had entered Confederate service in 1861, and had seen combat in almost all the major campaigns of the Army of Northern Virginia during the first three years of the war. Twice wounded, he had been appointed major general in June 1864. For details of his military career, see Gallagher, *Stephen Dodson Ramseur,* 30, 35–37, 40–44, 52–75, 118, 121–31, 137–65.

14. After the battle of Winchester, Sheridan followed Early up the Valley and on September 23, 1864, he attacked and defeated the Confederates again, this time even more decisively. Early lost another 1,000 men, most of them prisoners, and the remainder of his command did not stop running until they reached Waynesboro, seventy miles south at the base of the Blue Ridge Mountains. See Gallagher, *Stephen Dodson Ramseur,* 140–44.

CHAPTER 7: OCTOBER 1864–APRIL 1865

1. Laura Lee is referring to Sheridan's Valley campaign, in which he marched down and then up the Valley between September 21 and October 8, 1864, destroying what remained of the Valley's agricultural resources. For details of the campaign, see Mahon, *Shenandoah Valley,* 114–27.

2. This engagement was the battle of Cedar Creek. On the morning of October 19, 1864, General Early attacked the Federal army in its camp, driving the Union forces from their position. Later in the afternoon Sheridan counterattacked, recaptured all that the Federals had lost in the morning, and routed the Confederate army from the field. In the aftermath of the defeat, the Confederate army no longer was an

effective military force. For details of the battle, see Freeman, *Lee's Lieu-*
tenants, vol. 3, 597–610.

3. A brave and gallant officer, General Ramseur was mortally wounded
during the battle and died in Federal hands the next day. His wife had
just given birth to their daughter, Mary, three weeks earlier, whom he
never saw. See Gallagher, *Stephen Dodson Ramseur,* 162–65.

4. Lincoln was reelected president on November 8, 1864. He received 55
percent of the popular vote, and in the electoral college he won 212 to
21. Lincoln's reelection meant that the war would be fought to the bitter end, with no hope of a peace settlement agreeing to Southern independence. See McPherson, *Ordeal by Fire,* 456–57.

5. In late January 1865, following the fall of Fort Fisher, the last remain-
ing Confederate seaport fell, Francis Preston Blair, a longtime political
power in Washington, persuaded Lincoln to let him travel to Rich-
mond to see if he could start negotiations to reunite the North and
South. A meeting was finally arranged between Lincoln, Secretary of
State William Seward, and several Confederate peace commissioners:
Confederate Vice President Alexander Stephens, Senate President Pro
Tem Robert M. T. Hunter, and Assistant Secretary of War John A.
Campbell. Nothing came of the meeting, since neither side would
acknowledge the position of the other. See McPherson, *Battle Cry of*
Freedom, 821–23.

6. Located at the mouth of the Cape Fear River in Wilmington, North
Carolina, Fort Fisher by this time in the war was the last Confederate
seaport. In December 1864 and early January 1865, Union forces
launched two attacks against the fort that combined both sea and land
artillery bombardments. Unable to withstand this overpowering assault,
the fort was surrendered on January 15, 1865, thus cutting off all Confederate communication with the outside world. See Current, *Ency-*
clopedia of the Confederacy, vol. 2, 611–12.

7. Upon a directive from Grant, Sheridan marched south on February 28,
1865 with orders to destroy the Confederate supply base at Lynchburg
and the adjacent railroad lines, to ensure that they would be of no use
to the enemy in the upcoming campaign. Sheridan reached Staunton
on March 1 and then headed east towards Charlottesville. There he and
his men encountered what was left of Early's command, about 2,000
men, at Waynesboro. After a short fight, the Federals routed the Confederates from their position, scattering them in every direction. Over

1,500 troops and all the Confederate artillery were captured. Early and his staff managed to evade capture, but they were about the only ones so fortunate. See Catton, *Grant Takes Command,* 425–27.

8. The Confederates evacuated Richmond during the night of April 2, 1865. In the days following, Lee attempted to outdistance the Federal army and make his way south to join forces with Gen. Joseph E. Johnston in North Carolina, but with his army surrounded, Lee surrendered the Army of Northern Virginia to General Grant on April 9, 1865, at Appomattox Court House. See Freeman, *Lee's Lieutenants,* vol. 3, 685–86, 726–52.

BIBLIOGRAPHY

MANUSCRIPTS

The Wartime Diary of Julia Chase, 1861–1864, Handley Library, Winchester, Virginia

Harriet H. Griffith Diary, 1861–1865, Hollingsworth Griffith Collection, Winchester-Frederick County Historical Archives, Handley Library, Winchester, Virginia

Mrs. Hugh Lee Diary, Winchester-Frederick County Historical Archives, Handley Library, Winchester, Virginia

Diary of Laura Lee, Swem Library, College of William and Mary, Williamsburg, Virginia

GOVERNMENT RECORDS

Lewis Burwell, Compiled Service Records, National Archives, Washington, D.C.

Robert Burwell, Compiled Service Records, National Archives, Washington, D.C.

NEWSPAPERS

Winchester Evening Star

BOOKS AND ARTICLES

Catton, Bruce. *Grant Moves South*. Boston: Little Brown & Company, 1960.

————. *Grant Takes Command*. Boston: Little Brown & Company, 1968.

————. *Mr. Lincoln's Army*. New York: Doubleday & Company, 1951.

————. *Never Call Retreat*. New York: Doubleday & Company, 1965.

————. *A Stillness at Appomattox*. New York: Doubleday & Company, 1953.

—————. *Terrible Swift Sword*. New York: Doubleday & Comapny, 1963.

Cleaves, Freeman. *Meade of Gettysburg*. Norman: University of Oklahoma Press, 1960.

Current, Richard N., ed. *The Encyclopedia of the Confederacy*. 4 vols. New York: Simon & Schuster, 1993.

Eby, Cecil D., Jr. *A Virginia Yankee in the Civil War: The Diaries of David Hunter Strother*. Chapel Hill: University of North Carolina Press, 1962.

Foote, Shelby. *The Civil War*. 3 vols. New York: Random House, 1958–74.

Freeman, Douglas S. *Lee's Lieutenants*. 3 vols. New York: Charles Scribner's Sons, 1942–44.

Gallagher, Gary W. *Stephen Dodson Ramseur: Lee's Gallant General*. Chapel Hill: University of North Carolina Press, 1985.

—————, ed. *The Wilderness Campaign*. Chapel Hill: University of North Carolina Press, 1997.

Hennessy, John. "I Dread the Spring: The Army of the Potomac Prepares for the Overland Campaign." In *The Wilderness Campaign,* edited by Gary W. Gallagher. Chapel Hill: University of North Carolina Press, 1997.

Mahon, Michael G. *The Shenandoah Valley, 1861–1865: The Destruction of the Granary of the Confederacy*. Mechanicsburg, PA: Stackpole Books, 1999.

Marszalek, John F. *Sherman: A Soldier's Passion for Order*. New York: Free Press, 1993.

McDonald, Cornelia. *A Diary with Reminiscences of the War and Refugee Life in the Shenandoah Valley, 1860–1865*. Nashville: Cullom & Ghertner Co., 1934.

McDonough, James Lee. *Shiloh: In Hell before Night*. Knoxville: University of Tennessee Press, 1977.

—————. *Stones River: Bloody Winter in Tennessee*. Knoxville: University of Tennessee Press, 1980.

McPherson, James M. *Battle Cry of Freedom*. New York: Oxford Univesity Press, 1988.

—————. *Ordeal by Fire: The Civil War and Reconstruction*. New York: Alfred A. Knopf, 1982.

Norris, J. E. ed. *History of the Lower Shenandoah Valley*. Berryville, VA: A. Warner & Co., Publishers, 1890.

Quarles, Garland R. *Occupied Winchester, 1861–1865*. Reprint. Stephens City, VA: Commercial Press, 1991.

—————. *Some Worthy Lives.* Winchester, VA: Farmers and Merchants Banks, 1988.

Rhea, Gordon C. *The Battle of the Wilderness: May 5–6, 1864.* Baton Rouge: Louisiana State University Press, 1994.

—————. *The Battles for Spotsylvania Court House and the Road to Yellow Tavern: May 7–12, 1864.* Baton Rouge: Louisiana State University Press, 1997.

Riggs, David F. "Robert Y. Conrad and the Ordeal of Secession." *Virginia Magazine of History and Biography* 86 (1978): 259–74.

Robertson, James I., Jr. *A.P. Hill: The Story of a Confederate Warrior.* New York: Random House, 1987.

—————. *Stonewall Jackson: The Man, the Soldier, the Legend.* New York: Simon & Schuster, 1997.

Sears, Stephen W. *Landscape Turned Red: The Battle of Antietam.* Reprint. New York: Book of the Month Club, 1994.

Tanner, Robert G. *Stonewall in the Valley: Thomas J. "Stonewall" Jackson's Shenandoah Valley Campaign, Spring 1862.* New York: Doubleday & Company, 1976.

Thomas, Emory M. *Bold Dragoon: The Life of J. E. B. Stuart.* New York: Harper Row, Publishers, 1986.

Tucker, Glenn. *Chickamauga: Bloody Battle in the West.* New York: Bobbs-Merrill Company, 1961.

Warner, Ezra J. *Generals in Blue.* Baton Rouge: Louisiana State University Press, 1964.

Wert, Jeffry D. *From Winchester to Cedar Creek: The Shenandoah Valley Campaign of 1864.* Carlisle, PA: South Mountain Press, 1987.

—————. *General James Longstreet: The Confederacy's Most Controversial Soldier.* New York: Simon & Schuster, 1993.

INDEX

Jackson, Thomas J. "Stonewall,"
11, 15, 17, 18, 19, 20, 26, 33,
39, 41, 42, 45, 46, 64, 88,
89–90, 193n12, 197n25, 204–
n5
Jeff Davis bonnets, 35
Johnson, Bradley, 167
Johnson, Ed, 145, 162
Johnson, Mr. (broker), 10
Johnston, Albert Sydney, 90, 91,
195n14
Johnston, Joseph E., 33, 147, 154,
191n2
Jones, Anna, 70, 90
Jones, Gen., 68, 69, 144, 148
Jones, Marshall, 21
Jones, Mr., 135
Jones, Mr. and Mrs., 183
Jones, Susan, 45
Jordan's hospital, 103
Jordon Springs Hotel, 15
Jouls, Susan, 179

K
Kelley, Benjamin Franklin, 50
Kelly, Gen., 131
Kelly, Mr., 132
Kemp, Mr., 132
Kernstown, 12, 83, 159, 164
Kernstown, battle of, 26, 194n8
Kershaw, Gen., 165, 167
Kilpatrick, Judson, 135, 136, 209–
n17
Kingston, 106
Kinzel, Mr., 104
Kinzel, Mrs., 16
Klipstein, Mr., 52
Kneaster, Mr., 7
Kohlhousen, Mr., 93
Kyle, Maj., 165

L
Lal, 129, 132, 134, 135, 137, 183,
186
Latimer, Dr., 134
Lawley, Mr., 96
Lawson, Dr., 176, 177
Lee, Fitzhugh, 127, 136, 145, 164,
165, 208n14
Lee, Hugh Holmes, 194n3
Lee, Jennie, 186
Lee, Laura
soldiers attempt to confiscate
secession flag from house,
23–25, 43, 44–45
purchases clothing and supplies
from sutlers for Confederates, 81, 82
Col. Staunton takes rooms in
house, 82–83
house searched for contraband,
86
family rumored to be banished
from town, 87
food stolen from house, 119
told she would be sent beyond
lines, 181
ordered by Sheridan to be sent
beyond lines to Newtown,
182–84
travels after being sent South,
184–86
after war, 189
Lee, Lizzie, 183, 186
Lee, Mary, 22, 24, 82, 86, 87, 134,
178, 182–84, 186–87, 189
Lee, Ned, 154
Lee, Robert E., 97, 98, 101, 122,
138, 144, 145, 180, 187, 197–
n26, 203n3, 205n11, 207–
n11, 209n1, 210n2